Enhancing Thinking through Problem-based Learning Approaches

Other Educational books from
Thomson Learning

Problem-based Learning Innovation:
Using problems to power learning in the 21st century
by Oon-Seng Tan

Educational Psychology:
A Practitioner-Researcher Approach (An Asian Edition)
*by TAN Oon Seng, Richard D. PARSONS,
Stephanie Lewis HINSON and Deborah SARDO-BROWN*

www.thomsonlearningasia.com

Enhancing Thinking through Problem-based Learning Approaches

International Perspectives

Edited by

OON-SENG TAN

THOMSON

Australia • Canada • Mexico • Singapore • Spain • United Kingdom • United States

Enhancing Thinking Through Problem-Based Learning Approaches:
International Perspectives
Edited by Oon-Seng Tan

For more information, please contact:
Thomson Learning
(a division of Thomson Asia Pte Ltd)
5 Shenton Way
#01-01 UIC Building
Singapore 068808

Or visit our Internet site at *http://www.thomsonlearningasia.com*

Thomson Learning offices in Asia: Bangkok, Beijing, Hong Kong, Kuala Lumpur, Manila, Mumbai, Seoul, Singapore, Taipei, Tokyo.

Printed in Singapore
1 2 3 4 5 SLP 06 05 04 03

ISBN 981-243-718-5

CONTENTS

FOREWORD

For an educational innovation to have sustainable impact, it must be both grounded in theory and prolifically practiced. This appears to be the case for problem-based learning (PBL), which has gained significant momentum over the past decade in its use across different levels of education and disciplines. While much has been written and shared about the rationale for PBL and the practical aspects of its implementation, a need remains for literature and research to inform educators and PBL practitioners further about the psychological basis of PBL and strategies for enhancement of this active and interactive mode of learning. *Enhancing Thinking through Problem-based Learning Approaches: International Perspectives* is a timely contribution as many institutions worldwide have embarked on using PBL for educational reform and curricular innovation.

I first met the editor, Dr. Oon-Seng Tan, when we invited him to deliver a keynote address for the conference PBL2002: A Pathway to Better Learning hosted by the University of Delaware. Oon-Seng has been instrumental in many major PBL developments in Singapore and the Asia-Pacific region. When he was Director of the Temasek Centre for Problem-Based Learning, he won national recognition for his PBL initiatives. He also chaired the Second Asia-Pacific Conference in PBL in 2000, which was hosted in Singapore. At the university, he encouraged staff development in PBL and helped revamp the educational psychology curriculum with the use of PBL. At the recent Asia-Pacific Conference on Education 2003, Oon-Seng was program chair and made it a point to feature PBL as a major theme, in which I had the privilege to give a keynote address. I was deeply impressed by the interest in PBL expressed by many participants in the region, many of them already using PBL in a wide variety of settings.

In this book, Oon-Seng cleverly captures the art and science of PBL from the perspectives of pedagogy, psychology, and technology. His experience, enthusiasm, and expertise in psychology aptly position him as editor of this publication. The contributions come from an international pool of highly experienced and qualified PBL practitioners who are themselves champions and pioneers of PBL projects in their own institutions.

The international perspectives provide an excellent affirmation of key ideas and principles of PBL across a spectrum of contexts. Many of the contributors are familiar names in PBL networks internationally. Readers should be able to benefit tremendously from the rich and practical ideas presented.

I congratulate Dr. Oon-Seng Tan and the international team of contributors for their ideas, insights, and contributions in this volume and highly recommend it to educators worldwide in their quest to enhance thinking through PBL innovations.

George Watson
Associate Dean, College of Arts and Science
Unidel Professor of Physics and Astronomy
University of Delaware

PREFACE

Knowledge in this new millennium is increasingly characterized by the creative integration of information and learning from diverse disciplines. Biotechnology, the life sciences, telecommunications, material science, nanotechnology, and supercomputers are examples of multidisciplinary pursuits and learning. More than two millennia ago, the Greek thinker Aristotle believed that knowledge begins with experience and that the "intuitive leap" from uncertainty to knowledge is made possible by the mind. The word *knowledge*, which is *epistemê* in Greek, is translated as *scientia* in Latin. While information is growing at an ever-increasing speed, useful knowledge is fragmenting just as fast. To cope, we need to learn to integrate learning from different disciplines and develop strategies for the deep learning of things new and important to humanity. We need a new science of dealing with knowledge and information, and a new art of learning.

Problem-based learning (PBL) approaches are a step in that direction. They involve confronting ill-structured situations—situations where we are uncertain about information and solutions—and mastering the art of intuitive leap in the process of resolving the situations. That is why in PBL processes the mind of the learner—in other words, enhancing thinking—is our focus from the perspectives of pedagogy, psychology, and technology. The collection in this book attempts to provide international perspectives on how PBL practices can enhance thinking. The discussions are structured along three themes. The first is the psychology of cognition, metacognition, and self-regulated learning. The second is the idea of making thinking and mind visible through dialogue and inquiry. The use of dialogue in collaborative learning is an important aspect of developing higher-order thinking. The third theme is the use of technology, which is not only a tool but an important catalyst to enhance problem-based thinking. The possibilities and impact of technology are important considerations for any educational innovation.

Chapter 1 provides an overview of developments in the psychology of cognition and learning and explains why PBL can be a powerful vehicle for realizing the kinds of thinking competencies needed to address the challenges of the world today. In Chapter 2, Cindy Hmelo-Silver and her colleagues from Rutgers University reveal how the cognitive outcomes of PBL, such as constructing a solid knowledge base and becoming better at reasoning and self-directed learning, are underpinned by the development of psychological tools in the learning process. Peggy Weissinger of Indiana University–Purdue University elucidates in Chapter 3, from perspectives of both theory and practice, how critical thinking and inquiry are embedded in PBL. William Wu and Victor Forrester from Hong Kong Baptist University share their exploration of PBL incorporating the multiple intelligences model and focusing on PBL for talent development, in Chapter 4.

Good pedagogy begins with teachers themselves practicing what they advocate. Mary Sue Baldwin and Valerie McCombs have done superb work at their Center for Problem-Based Learning at Samford University in encouraging the use of PBL peer-reviewed course portfolios. In Chapter 5, Mary and Valerie demonstrate how reflective practice is enhanced through teaching portfolios. In Chapter 6, Boon-Tiong Ho from the National Institute of Education, Singapore, provides teachers with models of cognitive coaching for bringing about effective cognitive developments in PBL classrooms. PBL is used most prolifically in medical education. With his rich experience of using PBL in the Faculty of Medicine at the National University of Singapore, Matthew Gwee provides in Chapter 7 valuable insights on curriculum reform through the congruence of mission, development, and practice, and the alignment and strategic connection of key aspects of pedagogy.

In Chapter 8, Moira Lee and Oon-Seng Tan examine the paradigms and philosophical bases for collaborative learning and dialogue to provide a better understanding of critical openness. Ruth Beltran and Shane Merritt illustrate in Chapter 9 the practice of collaborative inquiry through a case introduced at the University of Sydney. In Chapter 10, Barbara Grabowski and her collaborators provide examples, through two major projects sponsored by the National Aeronautics Space Administration, of how PBL can enhance learning and thinking through the use of web-based resources and tools. George Watson reveals in Chapter 11 the potential for integrating PBL and technology in education and demonstrates the possibilities through excellent work done at the University of Delaware.

The book concludes by summarizing and reflecting on key ideas on PBL, looking ahead and pointing to possibilities of improving PBL practices in the light of developments in pedagogy, psychology, and technology. Some promises and implications for educational practices and further research are discussed.

It is my hope that this book will act as a catalyst for further discussions pertaining to the synergy of pedagogy, psychology, and technology in PBL practices.

Oon-Seng Tan PhD
Head of Psychological Studies,
National Institute of Education, Nanyang Technological University
President,
Educational Research Association of Singapore

CONTRIBUTORS

Oon-Seng Tan, PhD, is Associate Professor and Head of Psychological Studies at the National Institute of Education, Nanyang Technological University, Singapore. He is also Director of the Singapore Centre for Teaching Thinking and the current elected President of the Educational Research Association, Singapore. He was Director of the Temasek Centre for Problem-Based Learning when he won the Enterprise Challenge Innovator Award from the Prime Minister's Office for co-pioneering a project on educational innovation. Dr. Tan is a frequent keynote speaker at international conferences on problem-based learning (PBL) and publishes extensively on cognition and learning. He is the author of *Problem-based Learning Innovation: Using Problems to Power Learning in the 21st Century*, as well as the main co-author of *Educational Psychology: A Practitioner– Researcher Approach (An Asian Edition)*.

Mary Sue Baldwin, MSN, EdS, is Director of the Teaching, Learning and Scholarship Center (formerly Center for Problem-Based Learning) at Samford University. She is also Co-Director of the Problem-Based Learning: Peer Review grant sponsored by Samford and the Pew Charitable Trusts. Drawing upon her experiences in nursing and her involvement as one of the PBL pioneers at Samford, she has co-authored articles, portfolios, and a monograph on the use of PBL in nursing education as well as made numerous presentations on the use and documentation of PBL.

Ruth O. Beltran, MA, OTRP, AccOT, studied occupational therapy and sociology at the University of the Philippines. She is teaching in the undergraduate and graduate programs in occupational therapy at the School of Occupation and Leisure Sciences, Faculty of Health Sciences, University of Sydney. She has practiced as an occupational therapist in mental health in the Philippines and Australia and taught at the University of the Philippines before joining Sydney University. At Sydney, Ruth has conducted educational projects in the Philippines, Thailand, and Singapore. Her publications and research interests are in the areas of refugee and migrant mental health, occupational therapy and mental health, and occupational therapy theory.

Ellina Chernobilsky holds a Master's degree in Teaching from the University of Memphis, Tennessee. She is pursuing a doctoral degree at the Department of Educational Psychology, Rutgers University. A language teacher for a number of years, Ellina's area of interest is language development and language learning. She is also interested in innovative teaching strategies and methods and how they can be applied in language teaching.

Maria Carolina DaCosta is a PhD student in Educational Psychology at Rutgers University. Her research interests include how people reason when dealing with complex problems and the role of critical thinking in complex decision making. She has taught educational psychology at Rutgers. Maria has a joint MBA degree from Fundacao Getulio Vargas in Brazil and the University of Texas at Austin and was director of business development for Latin America at Intellifact International (a business research and information portal based in Austin, Texas).

Victor Forrester, EdD, is Assistant Professor at the Department of Education Studies, Hong Kong Baptist University. He has published extensively on cognition and learning and is a reviewer for several international journals. Dr. Forrester has been a speaker at numerous international conferences on PBL. His research interests include gender studies, change management, and curriculum development.

Barbara Grabowski, PhD, is Associate Professor of Education in the Instructional Systems Program at the Pennsylvania State University and Principal Investigator of two major research grants from the National Aeronautics and Space Administration (NASA). Her prior experience with a distance delivery program and as a designer of multimedia materials drives her research on learning with technology. She has written extensively, including some 40 technical reports on technology use, and has made numerous presentations and addresses worldwide. She has been recognized by the International University Continuing Education Association for the programs she has developed, and she received an outstanding book award for *Individual Differences: Learning and Instruction* (with Jonassen).

Matthew C. E. Gwee is Professor of Pharmacology in the Faculty of Medicine, National University of Singapore. He is also Interim Director of the Medical Education Unit and Chairman of the Problem-Based Learning Committee in the faculty, as well as Associate Director of the Centre for Development of Teaching and Learning of the university. Professor Gwee also serves as a member of the University Committee on Educational Policy.

Cindy E. Hmelo-Silver, PhD, is Assistant Professor of Educational Psychology at Rutgers University. She received her PhD in Cognitive Studies from Vanderbilt University and served postdoctoral fellowships at the Georgia Institute of Technology and the University of Pittsburgh's Learning Research and Development Center. Her research focuses on complex learning, scaffolding collaborative knowledge construction, and complex systems. She was awarded the Best Paper by a New Investigator from the American Educational Research Association's Division I for her research on PBL. She edited a special issue of the *Journal of the Learning Sciences* on learning through problem solving and co-edited *Problem-based Learning: A Research Perspective on Learning Interactions*.

Boon-Tiong Ho, MEd, is a lecturer at the Science and Technology Education Academic Group, National Institute of Education, Nanyang Technological University, Singapore. His introduction to PBL began with the training he received from the Illinois Mathematics and Science Academy in 1995. Since then, he has conducted numerous PBL workshops and studies. His other research interests include teacher education, science education, curriculum development, teaching of thinking, school effectiveness and improvement, and organizational management. He is completing his doctoral study in the field of science teacher education with a focus on pedagogical content knowledge.

Younghoon Kim has participated as a research assistant in the KaAMS (Kids as Airborne Mission Scientists) research project funded by a NASA grant. His research interests include problem- and inquiry-based learning; technology tools to promote learners' critical, reflective, and metacognitive thinking; and distributed cognition in technology-enhanced learning environments. He is a PhD candidate in Instructional Systems at the Pennsylvania State University studying the cultivation of students' reflective thinking in an online learning context.

Tiffany A. Koszalka, PhD, is Associate Professor in the Instructional Design, Development and Evaluation Program at Syracuse University in Syracuse, New York. She has worked in the fields of instructional and educational technologies for over 20 years and has managed large-scale projects integrating leading-edge technology into case-based and PBL environments. Most recently, she has collaborated on research projects funded by NASA and the National Science Foundation that focus on the use of Internet technologies to enhance multiple teaching and learning methods, including PBL. She has written on learning environment design factors that influence reflective thinking in PBL environments and the design of PBL lesson plans.

Moira G. C. Lee, PhD, is manager of the Staff and Educational Development Division, Human Resource and Staff Development Department at Temasek Polytechnic in Singapore. Her abiding interest is in adult learning and her doctoral research at the University of Nottingham focused on collaborative learning. She has published in both these areas. Dr. Lee has conducted doctoral seminars on models of adult learning in the Asian setting. Her areas of educational specialization include professional development workshops on qualitative educational research, professional staff development, teacher mentoring, and adult learning.

Valerie McCombs, MEd, is an instructional design specialist in the Instructional Technology Department at the University of Alabama at Birmingham. She was the Electronic Portfolio Coordinator and Research Associate for the Center for Problem-Based Learning at Samford University when the portfolios were written. During her tenure at Samford, she was responsible for designing and managing the center's web site, conducting research, and assisting in the publication of the newsletter *PBL Insight*. Her latest publication is *Assessing and Researching Problem-based Learning*.

Shane Merritt, MA in Psychology, is from the Indigenous Kamilaroi people of Northern New South Wales. He lectures and develops subjects in mental health at the University of Sydney. Before joining the university in 1997, Shane had worked as a graduate drugs and alcohol counselor, in mental health, and with charity organizations in London. During that period, he worked with AIDS patients, single parents, and people with obsessive compulsive disorders. Shane is also a psychologist registered with the New South Wales Psychologists Registration Board and is a full member of the Australian Psychological Society.

George Watson, PhD, is Associate Dean in the College of Arts and Science and Unidel Professor of Physics and Astronomy at the University of Delaware. He joined the faculty in 1987 after a postdoctoral position at AT&T Bell Laboratories and receiving a PhD in physics from Delaware. He was the principal investigator on a grant from the National Science Foundation program on institution-wide reform of undergraduate education, which led to the creation of the Institute for Transforming Undergraduate Education at Delaware, a faculty development enterprise for PBL and instructional technology. He is the principal investigator on projects to develop PBL curricula for physics and to reform science and mathematics education in Peru.

Peggy A. Weissinger, EdD, is Director of Instructional Design and Development in the Office for Professional Development at Indiana University–Purdue University, Indianapolis, and an adjunct faculty in the School of Education. In her on-campus research, she has looked at critical thinking foundation skills of graduate students enrolled in a PBL curriculum. She is also a co-facilitator of a faculty learning community focusing on PBL. She was state president for the National Association for Developmental Education and is a national core committee member of the Professional and Organizational Development Network in Higher Education.

William Y. Wu, PhD, a counseling and educational psychologist by training from the University of California Los Angeles, is with the Department of Education Studies, Hong Kong Baptist University, teaching educational psychology. He is one of three directors of the Thinking Qualities Initiative Project, Centre for Educational Development, at the same university. He has been experimenting with the direct teaching of higher-order thinking skills, PBL, and the infusion of thinking skills into the school curriculum in Hong Kong.

CHAPTER 1

Cognition, Metacognition, and Problem-based Learning

Oon-Seng Tan

Cognition and Pedagogy

Once upon a time, good pedagogy was about making content knowledge "visible" to students. Teaching involved providing clear explanations to students in disseminating knowledge and solving problems. In the industrial age, this sufficed for the classroom. Toward the last decade of the 20th century, good pedagogy was about making teachers' thinking visible. In other words, effective teaching was characterized by modeling the process of learning so that students could observe and learn process skills, problem-solving skills, and thinking skills while acquiring content knowledge.

In the 21st century, the knowledge-based economy—fueled by information explosion and accessibility, rapid proliferation of technology, globalization, and demands for new competencies—calls for a different paradigm in pedagogy. Educators have to unlearn the old ways and confront new ways of looking at knowledge and at participation in the learning process. Pedagogy in the 21st century has to go beyond making content visible and making teachers' thinking visible. Good pedagogy today is about making students' thinking visible. The challenge of education is to design learning environments and processes where students' ways of thinking and knowing are manifested in active, collaborative, self-regulated, and self-directed learning. The role of the teacher is to enable students to recognize the state, repertoire, and depth of various dimensions of their thinking and to sharpen their abilities to deal with real-world problems. The "visibility" of students' cognition is a prerequisite for effective mediation and facilitation.

The progressive challenges of pedagogy can be summed up as follows:

- Making content knowledge visible to learners
- Making teachers' thinking visible to learners
- Making learners' thinking visible to themselves, their peers, and the teacher

Developments in Psychology

Behavioristic psychology, as the science of learning, provided the basis for effective teaching and learning in the first half of the last century. The behavioristic establishment led by Skinner continued its influence and contributions through the 1960s and 1970s (Skinner, 1953, 1987, 1989a, b). Making content knowledge visible to the learner was probably underpinned by behavioral science where specific behavioral objectives followed by the management and reinforcement of learning led to the attainment of the desired knowledge and skills.

In the 1960s, recognition of Piaget's work gained momentum (although Piaget began his work in the 1920s). Piaget addressed the internal world of the individual in relation to intelligence and questions pertaining to the structure of the mind (Piaget, 1956, 1959; Piaget & Inhelder, 1969). His work was based on three interrelated conceptions: (1) the relation between action and thought, (2) the construction of the cognitive structure, and (3) the role of self-regulation. According to Piaget, logical thinking and reasoning about complex situations represents the highest form of cognitive development.

Sternberg (1990) noted that Piaget dealt primarily with the relationship of intelligence to the internal world of the individual and that Piaget believed intelligence essentially matures from the inside and directs itself outward. In the 1970s, cognitive psychology gained new ground as interest in "mentalism" grew (Bourne, Dominowski, & Loftus, 1979). Vygotsky (1978), in contrast to Piaget, believed that intelligence begins in the social environment and directs itself inward and that all psychological processes are in genesis essentially social processes, initially shared among people. Vygotsky (1978, 1962) posited that higher mental processes are functions of mediated activity. He contributed significantly to the understanding of intelligence in the theory of internalization, the theory of the convergence of speech and practical activity, and the zone of proximal development (Vygotsky, 1978). In the classroom, an expert teacher may model many approaches of a problem-solving process for the students. The students will need to internalize these processes as their own problem-solving activities if they are to develop effective self-regulation and metacognitive abilities. Within the context of the gradual internalization of cognitive activities through interaction, Vygotsky (1978) defined the zone of proximal development as "the distance between the actual developmental level as determined by individual problem solving and the level of potential development as determined through problem solving under adult guidance or in collaboration with more capable peers" (p. 86). In his view, logical memory, voluntary attention, categorical perception, and self-regulation of behavior represent the highest forms of psychological functioning.

The cognitive revolution rooted in major works such as those of Piaget and Vygotsky provided much impetus for the psychology of thinking. Although the general goal of thoughtfulness as a hallmark of liberal education has often been articulated, the 1980s saw emphasis on the "teaching of thinking" as a relatively new concept (Resnick, 1987; Costa & Lowery, 1989). Staff development in teaching thinking was stressed, and making teachers' thinking visible was in many ways the next wave of good pedagogy.

Feuerstein contributed to our further understanding of cognition and mediation. Feuerstein began his work in the 1950s, but his contributions gained recognition only in the 1990s. He had an interesting way of thinking beyond the traditions of his time. Instead of being concerned about what students failed to learn, he turned his focus to what they could learn. When assessment was static and summative, he made it dynamic and truly formative (i.e., developmental). When others were modifying teaching materials for children with learning disabilities, he chose to invest his energies in modifying these learners directly. When behaviorists were looking at stimuli and output behaviors, Feuerstein chose to focus on not only the organism but also the inner structure of cognition. While intervention programs were often concerned with content, he was more concerned with cognitive processes pertaining to learning to learn and thinking about thinking. While psychoanalysts were concerned with emotions and antecedent, he preferred to search for a more proximal and optimistic determinant of cognitive development. Helping learners discover their learning potentials and gain awareness of their thinking and thinking about thinking calls for an important factor: the presence of a competent mediator. Building on the insights of cognitive psychologists Piaget and Rey from the Genevan school, Feuerstein developed a theory of mediated learning experience, which provides the psychological basis for pedagogy that helps make students' thinking visible.

Mediated Learning Experience, Metacognition, and Self-Regulation

According to Feuerstein, Rand, Hoffman, and Miller (1980, 385), "cognitive factors can be considered key elements to the individual's successful adaptation, particularly in a technological and rapidly changing society." In other words, sufficient attention must be given not only to learners' ability to think but also to what is going on in their mind in terms of their cognitive processes. At the heart of Feuerstein's Theory of Structural Cognitive Modifiability (SCM) is the modifiability of cognition. Feuerstein (1990) argued that a person's capacity to learn is not solely determined by one's genetic endowment; on the contrary, cognitive capacity can be enhanced through mediation. He highlighted the importance of understanding specific cognitive functions (e.g., planning behavior, systematic thinking, inferential thinking, and analogical thinking) and creating learning environments for mediating these cognitive functions. Cognitive enhancement in SCM refers not merely to the development of specific behaviors but also to changes of a "structural nature" (i.e., internal changes in cognition rather than external changes in behavior). Such cognitive changes should be durable and substantial and should impact on the individual holistically (i.e., affecting dispositional traits, thinking ability, and the general level of competence).

How do we bring about such a structural modification of cognition? The question relates to the basis for effective intervention or interaction. Embedded in the SCM theory is the Theory of Mediated Learning Experience (MLE). Simply put, this theory states that the quality of interaction between the individual and the environment via an intentional human being (the mediator) plays a pivotal role in the cognitive development of the individual. Feuerstein and Feuerstein (1991) identified several parameters that characterize MLE. Three of these parameters are indispensable to a mediated interaction: (1) intentionality and reciprocity, (2) mediation of meaning, and (3) transcendence. Tan, Parsons, Hinson, and Sardo-Brown (2003) represent the parameters as a repertoire for educators as shown in Figure 1.

SCM is consistent with modern theories of intelligences, which include ideas about intelligence being learnable (Perkins & Grotzer, 1997), about the diversification and multiplicity of intelligence (Gardner, 1983), and about developing components of intelligence to enhance cognition (Sternberg, 1985).

MLE principles are consistent with two major areas of research in cognition: metacognition and self-regulation (Borkowski, 1992; Pintrich, 2000; Zimmerman, 2001). Metacognition involves the interaction between

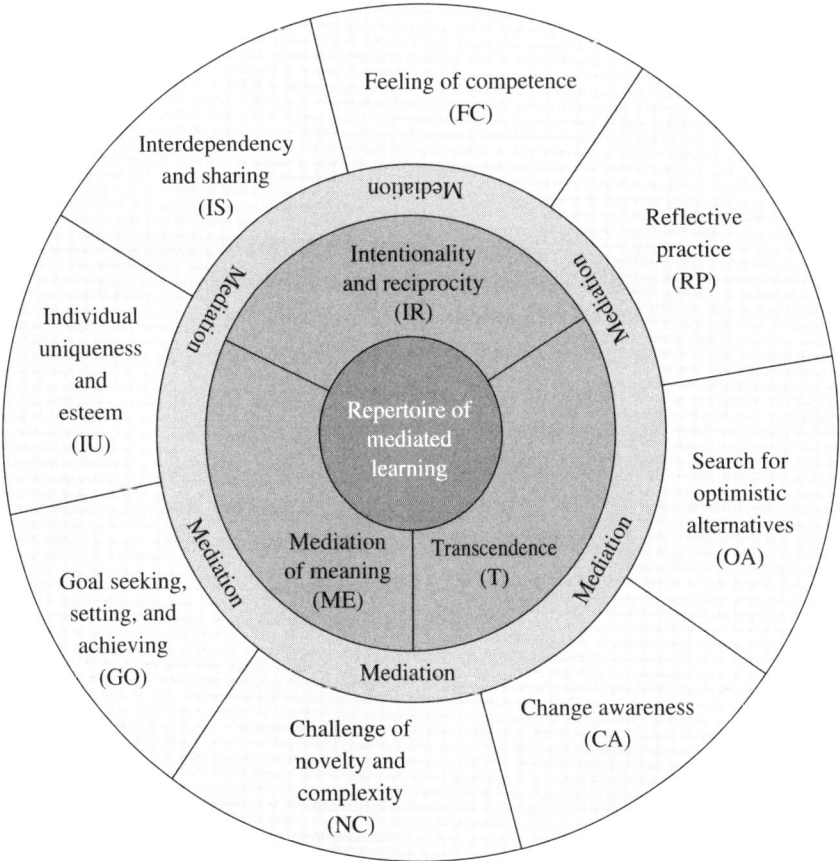

FIGURE 1 Repertoire of mediated learning

Source: Tan, Parsons, Hinson, & Sardo-Brown (2003, 61).

an individual, a task, and the strategies used to accomplish the task (Flavell, 1979). Strategies are crucial for effective learning and problem solving, and strategy use is an integral part of effective thinking and dealing with novelty. MLE parameters (see Figure 1) such as esteem and change awareness pertain to positive attributional beliefs and self-efficacy, which can be explicitly developed (Bandura, 1997; Borkowski, Chan, & Muthukrishna, 2000). It is recognized that problem solving in a socially relevant learning atmosphere can promote effective strategy use. According to Borkowski (1992), motivation drives and energizes self-regulation, and such processes shape strategy selection, implementation, and monitoring, especially when a learner faces a challenging task such as solving a novel problem. When solving a problem, learners have to put in effort to plan, evaluate, and regulate their use of strategies. They also have to commit to the task as well as feel competent in handling the task and expect some success. The use of challenging learning environments, as in problem-based learning activities, encourages questioning and overcomes the fear of making mistakes. Borkowski, Chan, and Muthukrishna (2000) argued that students should be given opportunities to take initiative in solving tasks, independently and collaboratively.

Pintrich (2000) described self-regulated learning as a process by which students engage in different strategies to regulate their cognition, motivation, and behavior, as well as the context. Problem-based learning processes call for strategies that are goal-directed and self-directed, although they are influenced by the context of the problem. Facilitating the acquisition of self-regulated learning strategies is an important aspect of metacognition.

Metacognition, self-regulated learning, control, and regulation are generally related to metacognitive monitoring activities. In most models of regulation, it is assumed that attempts to control, regulate, and change cognition should be related to cognitive monitoring activities that provide information about the relative discrepancy between a goal and the current progress toward that goal (Pintrich & Schunk, 2002). One of the central aspects of the control and regulation of cognition is the actual selection and use of various cognitive strategies for learning. Pintrich (2000) observed that the selection of appropriate cognitive strategies can have a positive influence on learning and performance. He noted three general types of cognitive strategies: (1) rehearsal, (2) elaboration, and (3) organization and general metacognitive self-regulation. Rehearsal strategies include attempts to memorize material by repeating it over and over or using other types of more "shallow" processing. In contrast, elaboration strategies reflect a "deeper" approach to learning, by attempting to summarize and paraphrase the material. Organizational strategies involve deeper processing through the use of various tactics, such as developing schemas or concept maps to organize the material. Metacognitive self-regulation includes various planning, monitoring, and regulating strategies for learning.

Contextual control strategies involve attempts by the learner to control the context of learning. In the traditional classroom, teachers usually have more control over the context than students have, but in today's knowledge-based era we need to train students to exert control over their learning environment. In problem-based learning, students learn to seek help in getting information and learning new things in order to solve a problem. Karabenick (1998) maintained that help-seeking is a self-regulated learning strategy that involves both behavioral as well as contextual control. Students can actively seek help from teachers, other adults, or peers to increase their learning so as to solve problems. They also need to seek instrumental help, where they focus on learning and understanding and not just on getting the answer (Karabenick, 1998).

Problem-based Learning

Problem-based learning (PBL) focuses on the challenge of making students' thinking visible. Like most pedagogical innovations, PBL was not developed on the basis of learning or psychological theories, although the PBL process embraces the use of metacognition and self-regulation. PBL is recognized as a progressive active-learning and learner-centered approach where unstructured problems (real-world or simulated complex problems) are used as the starting point and anchor for the learning process.

In recent years, PBL has gained new momentum as a result of several developments. The first is the increasing demand for bridging the gap between theory and practice. This demand is particularly evident in medical education (Balla, 1990a, b). Norman and Schmidt (1992) found that PBL enhances the transfer of concepts to new problems, the integration of concepts, the intrinsic interest in learning, and learning skills. Albanese and Mitchell (1993) revealed that, compared with traditional teaching approaches, PBL helps students in knowledge construction and reasoning skills.

The second factor is information accessibility and knowledge explosion. Educators have always appreciated the value of using problems to stimulate learning and thinking, but when to pose a problem as well as the nature and scope of the problem were limited by the learner's lack of knowledge and of accessibility to information. Thus, problems were usually given only after the dissemination of knowledge and were often delimited by what was already taught. However, the advent of Internet technologies has ushered in new possibilities with PBL.

Thirdly, the emphasis on real-world competencies, such as skills in independent learning, collaborative learning, problem solving, and decision making, provides a strong rationale for adopting PBL. Glasgow (1997) argued that the real world is filled with problems, projects, and challenges and thus creating a "curriculum that reflects this reality makes sense" (p. 14).

Fourthly, developments in learning, psychology, and pedagogy appear to support the use of PBL. For example, research on memory and knowledge points to the importance of memory not only as associations but, more importantly, as connections and meaningful coherent structures (National Research Council, 1999). We now know more about "novice" learners and "expert" learners. We can develop better learning in individuals by providing opportunities for acquisition of procedures and skills through dealing with information in a problem space and learning of general strategies of problem solving. From the pedagogical perspective, PBL is based on the constructivist theory of learning (Schmidt, 1993; Savery & Duffy, 1995; Hendry & Murphy, 1995). In PBL approaches, understanding is derived from interaction with the problem scenario and the learning environment. Engagement with the problem and the problem inquiry process create cognitive dissonance that stimulates learning, and knowledge evolves through collaborative processes of social negotiation and evaluation of the viability of one's point of view. Metacognitive strategies and self-regulation are therefore integral aspects of PBL processes.

PBL Processes

PBL approaches in a curriculum usually include the following characteristics (Tan, 2003):

- The *problem* is the starting point of learning.
- The problem is usually a *real-world* problem that appears unstructured. If it is a simulated problem, it should be as authentic as possible.

- The problem calls for *multiple perspectives*. The use of cross-disciplinary knowledge is a key feature in many PBL curricula. In any case, PBL encourages the solution of the problem by making use of knowledge from various subjects and topics.
- The problem challenges students' current knowledge, attitudes, and competencies, thus calling for identification of learning needs and *new areas of learning*.
- *Self-directed learning* is primary. Thus, students assume major responsibility for the acquisition of information and knowledge.
- *Harnessing of a variety of knowledge sources* and the use and evaluation of information resources are essential PBL processes.
- Learning is *collaborative, communicative, and cooperative*. Students work in small groups with a high level of interaction for peer learning, peer teaching, and group presentations.
- Development of *inquiry and problem-solving skills* is as important as content knowledge acquisition for the solution of the problem. The PBL tutor thus facilitates and coaches through questioning and cognitive coaching.
- Closure in the PBL process includes *synthesis and integration* of learning.
- PBL also concludes with an *evaluation and review* of the learner's experience and the learning process.

Figure 2 illustrates the key components in the PBL process.

The goals of PBL include content learning, acquisition of process skills and problem-solving skills, and lifewide learning. I introduce the term *lifewide learning* to emphasize skills such as self-directed learning, independent information mining, collaborative learning, and reflective thinking. Lifewide learning is acquisition of competencies that can be transferred across various life and work situations. The skills learned are applicable to learning in a new discipline or learning to do something new.

In many PBL approaches, the student confronts a situation where he or she needs to accomplish an objective, and the means (i.e., the information, process, and actions to be taken) is something new or unknown to the student. In many ways, the pedagogy of PBL helps make visible or explicit the thinking and the richness of the cognitive structuring and processes involved.

A problem triggers the context for engagement, curiosity, inquiry, and a quest to address real-world issues. Figure 3 illustrates what goes on in the mind of the learner (cognition) and the probable changes in behavior (learning) that are triggered by the problem.

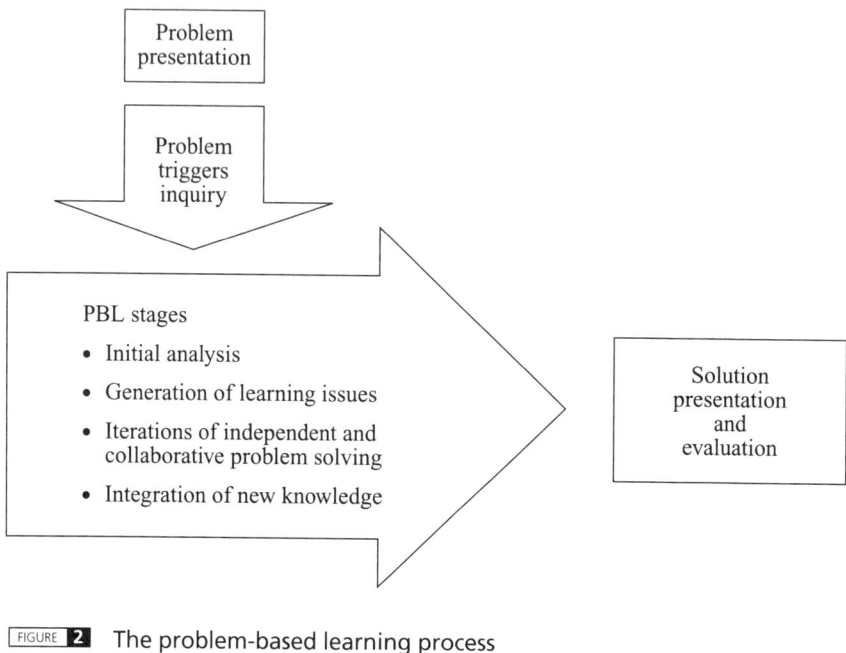

FIGURE **2**   The problem-based learning process

The challenge in diversifying educational methods is to design learning through the effective use of problems. Depending on the nature of the discipline, the goals of the curriculum, the flexibility of cross-disciplinary integration, and the availability of resources (e.g., time, infrastructure, information systems), problems can be used appropriately, strategically, and powerfully.

PBL and Cognitive Processes

The development of problem-solving acumen and of competencies for creative problem solving is an important goal of PBL. This requires the PBL tutor or coach to intervene in many cognitive, self-regulatory, and metacognitive processes as described in the MLE model and in research on metacognition. For example, the processes that follow engagement of the problem include: (1) problem clarification, (2) problem definition and reframing, (3) problem analysis, and (4) problem summary and synthesis. In order to clarify, define, and reframe the problem in their own words, students should realize the need to take time to think and plan.

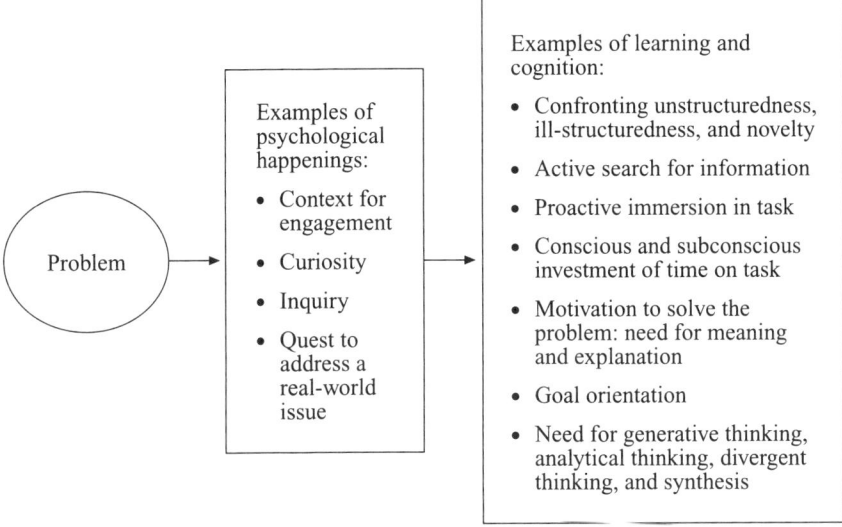

FIGURE **3** Problem-based learning and cognition

Cognitive coaching involves helping students to refrain from unplanned (impulsive) reactions and to overcome sweeping and unwarranted narrow perceptions. By repeatedly querying about the facts to obtain a clear mental picture, problem solvers also learn to develop systematic and more thorough information-gathering skills. PBL processes and coaching involve getting the mind to make connections through reflection, articulation, and learning to see different perspectives. In the PBL process, the problem scenario and scaffolding help learners develop cognitive connections. Having obtained more data and new information, learners need to apply analytical thinking skills, such as comparing, classifying, logical thinking, and inferential thinking. Good analytical thinking involves not only logic but also knowing when we have to interpolate and extrapolate.

Manktelow (1999) noted that a substantial amount of psychological research supports the observation that bias and error in human reasoning are widespread. Evans, Venn, and Feeney (2002) found in a study of undergraduates that there is a tendency for people to focus on a single hypothesis when solving a problem. People also tend to have what they termed "pseudo-diagnostic" response, rather than diagnostic response, based on their background and beliefs. The authors gave the following example: Suppose a patient has symptom S and it is known that symptom S is present in 95 percent of people suffering from disease X. Jumping to the conclusion that the patient is likely to suffer from X without further probing constitutes weak reasoning. To deduce if the patient is likely to be suffering from X, at least two further pieces of information are needed: (1) the prevalence of X relative to other diseases and (2) the likelihood of S being present in other diseases.

The PBL process and coaching help develop flexibility and helicopter views by enhancing connectivity. According to Chin and Brewer (2001), data evaluation should be the central goal of student learning. When solving problems, the ability to construct an accurate model and to elaborate on the model is often limited. Poor problem solving also occurs because of the tendency to accept or reject particular key linkages. In other words, a set of cognitive strategies (such as those pertaining to searching for alternative causes and so on) for dealing effectively with a given set of data is often lacking. Research indicates that multiple mechanisms are operating when people work on tasks and that fluency in performance can be developed through the exercise of general strategies and appropriate attention shifts (Lee & Anderson, 2001). PBL trains learners to develop and internalize problem-solving competencies by increasing their awareness of different ways of thinking needed in working on a problem.

Lapses in reasoning and in thinking can occur in any of the phases of information processing. In PBL, the practice of scanning the information field, paraphrasing, dialogue, peer critique, and articulation helps sharpen thinking by collecting, connecting, and communicating information.

Facilitating inquiry for deeper learning is a major challenge. The interactive style of dialogue can be a very effective form of learning, provided that the teacher exercises a good amount of scaffolding through good questions (Chi et al., 2001). Effective PBL tutoring employs a good range of scaffolding and questioning techniques. In real life, scientists, entrepreneurs, and decision makers who are effective know how to ask good questions to help arrive at solutions. The goal of inquiry in PBL is to help students internalize such dialogues.

Referring to the MLE model in Figure 1 earlier, PBL interactions should include the three indispensable parameters. In terms of the first parameter, intentionality and reciprocity (IR), the PBL tutor should have a clear intention of what inquiries to elicit and be alert to how the learner responds to the intention of the PBL process. The presence of this parameter implies that an explicit and purposeful outcome should result from the interaction. PBL tutors need to be clear about their intentions and the desired outcomes, such as content learning and the development of problem-solving skills and lifewide learning skills, as described earlier. The next major parameter is the mediation of meaning (ME). In any learning situation, the awareness of meaning constitutes a major component of the motivation system. The power of problem scenarios is in their real-world context and the meaningfulness they present. In the coaching and probing process, many "why" questions are raised. An effective mediator helps the learner discover the significance of working on such a problem as well as the value of the PBL process. The third parameter, transcendence (T), refers to the transfer of learning across contexts and situations. One main reason PBL is advocated in many curricula is its effectiveness in bringing about transfer of learning. Students learn to take a lifewide approach to learning so that they actually learn how to learn.

These three parameters (IR, ME, and T), represented in the inner ring of Figure 1, are necessary and sufficient conditions for MLE. The other parameters are often present whenever applicable in learning situations. Mediation of feelings of competence (FC) relates to the need to provide "successful experiences" in the tasks given to learners and to remove the unwarranted fear of failure. FC is important as the fear of making mistakes often deters learners from trying again. The purpose of scaffolding is to help develop the sense of competence in problem solving.

In PBL, dialogue and questions between tutor and learner and between learners are a cornerstone of learning. Questions such as these are posed: What comes to your mind as you approach the problem scenario? What are your hypotheses? What strategies might we use? What might you do differently if the criteria are now changed? This is the mediation of reflective practice (RP), which relates to self-regulatory and metacognitive behaviors. Metacognition is an essential competence in PBL, as pointed out by Gijselaers (1996).

Mediation of interdependence and sharing (IS) refers to instilling a "sense of belonging" and sharing behavior. One of the roles of the PBL tutor is to broaden students' perspectives on learning. When it comes to understanding a real-world situation and getting a full perspective, "none of us is as smart as all of us." Furthermore, the ability to harness information from others and build a pool of people resources is a life skill. The tutor in PBL encourages students to get out of their comfort zones and learn to seek information from various sources and from people. Teamwork, interdependence, and knowledge sharing are attributes emphasized in today's world.

The challenge of solving a real-world problem, the formulation of learning issues in PBL, and the requirement of peer teaching provide strong goal-directed behaviors (GO). The tutor's role is to guide and ensure that individuals and groups are constantly engaged in such goal-seeking and goal-attaining behaviors. PBL programs must also be designed to offer sufficient challenge and novelty, hence the NC parameter. After all, PBL aims to enhance intelligence to confront ill-structured and novel problems.

To summarize, PBL is about making students' thinking visible and stimulating multiple ways of thinking to confront problems that are ill-structured and novel. PBL coaching involves active mediation of purpose, meaning, transfer of learning, optimistic seeking of alternatives, goal-directedness, challenge, collaboration, and self-reflection. These metacognitive and self-regulatory processes are key to enhancing thinking in the 21st century.

References

Albanese, M. A., & Mitchell, S. (1993). Problem-based learning: A review of literature on its outcomes and implementation issues. *Academic Medicine, 68*, 52–81.

Balla, J. I. (1990a). Insight into some aspects of clinical education, I: Clinical practice. *Postgraduate Medical Journal, 66*, 212–17.

Balla, J. I. (1990b). Insights into some aspects of clinical education, II: A theory for clinical education. *Postgraduate Medical Journal, 66*, 297–301.

Bandura, A. (1997). *Self-efficacy: The exercise of control.* New York: Freeman.

Borkowski, J. G. (1992). Metacognitive theory: A framework for teaching literacy, writing, and math skills. *Journal of Learning Disabilities, 25*, 253–57.

Borkowski, J. G., Chan, L. K. S., & Muthukrishna, N. (2000). A process-oriented model of metacognition: Links between motivation and executive functioning. In J. C. Impara & L. L. Murphy (Eds.), *Buros-Nebraska series on measurement and testing: Issues in the measurement of metacognition* (pp. 1–41). Lincoln, NE: Buros Institute of Mental Measurement.

Bourne, L. E. Jr., Dominowski, R. L., & Loftus, E. F. (1979). *Cognitive processes.* Englewood Cliffs, NJ: Prentice Hall.

Chi, M. T. H., Siler, S. A., Jeong, H., Yamauchi, T., & Hausmann, R. (2001). Learning from human tutoring. *Cognitive Science, 25*, 471–533.

Chin, C. A., & Brewer, W. F. (2001). Models of data: A theory of how people evaluate data. *Cognition and Instruction, 19*, 323–51.

Costa, A. L., & Lowery, L. F. (1989). *Techniques for teaching thinking.* Pacific Grove, CA: Midwest.

Evans, J. B. T., Venn, S., & Feeney, A. (2002). Implicit and explicit processes in a hypothesis testing task. *British Journal of Psychology, 93*, 31–46.

Feuerstein, R. (1990). The theory of structural modifiability. In B. Presseisen (Ed.), *Learning and thinking styles: Classroom interaction*. Washington, DC: National Education Association.

Feuerstein, R., & Feuerstein, S. (1991). Mediated learning experience: A theoretical review. In R. Feuerstein, P. S. Klein, & A. J. Tannenbaum (Eds.), *Mediated learning experience (MLE): Theoretical, psychosocial and learning implications* (pp. 3–51). London: Freund.

Feuerstein, R., Rand, Y., Hoffman, M. B., & Miller, R. (1980). *Instrumental enrichment: An intervention program for cognitive modifiability*. Baltimore, MD: University Park Press.

Flavell, J. H. (1979). Metacognition and cognitive monitoring: A new area of cognitive-developmental inquiry. *American Psychologist, 34*, 906–11.

Gardner, H. (1983). *Frames of mind: The theory of multiple intelligences*. New York: Basic Books.

Gijselaers, W. H. (1996). Connecting problem-based practices with educational theory. In L. Wilkerson & W. H. Gijselaers (Eds.), *Bringing problem-based learning to higher education: Theory and practice* (pp. 13–21). New directions for teaching and learning, No. 68. San Francisco: Jossey-Bass.

Glasgow, N. A. (1997). *New curriculum for new times: A guide to student-centered, problem-based learning*. Thousand Oaks, CA: Corwin Press.

Hendry, G. D., & Murphy, L. B. (1995). Constructivism and problem-based learning. In P. Little, M. Ostwald, & G. Ryan (Eds.), *Research and development in problem-based learning*, Vol. 3: *Assessment and evaluation*. Newcastle: Australian Problem Based Learning Network.

Karabenick, S. A. (1998). *Strategic help-seeking: Implications for learning and teaching*. Mahwah, NJ: Erlbaum.

Lee, F. J., & Anderson, J. R. (2001). Does learning a complex task have to be complex? A study in learning decomposition. *Cognitive Psychology, 42*, 267–316.

Manktelow, K. I. (1999). *Reasoning and thinking*. Hove, East Sussex: Psychology Press.

National Research Council (1999). *How people learn: Bridging research and practice*. Washington, DC: National Academy Press.

Norman, G. R., & Schmidt, H. G. (1992). The psychological basis of problem-based learning: A review of the evidence. *Academic Medicine, 67*, 557–65.

Perkins, D. N., & Grotzer, T. A. (1997). Teaching intelligence. *American Psychologist, 52*, 1125–33.

Piaget, J. (1956). *The psychology of intelligence*. Totowa, NJ: Littlefield, Adams and Co.

Piaget, J. (1959). *The thought and language of the child*. London: Routledge and Kegan Paul.

Piaget, J., & Inhelder, B. (1969). *The psychology of the child*. New York: Basic Books.

Pintrich, P. R. (2000). The role of goal orientation in self-regulated learning. In M. Boekaerts, P. R. Pintrich, & M. Zeidner (Eds.), *Handbook of self-regulation* (pp. 451–502). San Diego, CA: Academic Press.

Pintrich, P. R., & Schunk, D. H. (2002). *Motivation in education: Theory, research, and applications*. Upper Saddle River, NJ: Merrill Prentice Hall.

Resnick, L. B. (1987). *Education and learning to think*. Washington, DC: National Academy Press.

Savery, J. R., & Duffy, T. M. (1995). Problem-based learning: An instructional model and its constructivist framework. *Educational Technology, 35*, 31–38.

Schmidt, H. G. (1993). Foundations of problem-based learning: Some explanatory notes. *Medical Education, 27*, 422–32.

Skinner, B. F. (1953). *The science of human behavior*. New York: Macmillan.

Skinner, B. F. (1987). *Upon further reflection*. Englewood Cliffs, NJ: Prentice Hall.

Skinner, B. F. (1989a). *Recent issues in the analysis of behavior*. Columbus, OH: Merrill.

Skinner, B. F. (1989b). The origins of cognitive thought. *American Psychologist, 44*, 13–18.

Sternberg, R. J. (1985). Approaches to intelligence. In S. F. Chipman, J. W. Segal, & R. Glaser (Eds.), *Thinking and learning skills*, Vol. 2: *Research and open questions*. Hillsdale, NJ: Erlbaum.

Sternberg, R. J. (1990). *Metaphors of mind: Conceptions of the nature of intelligence*. New York: Cambridge University Press.

Tan, O. S. (2003). *Problem-based learning innovation: Using problems to power learning in the 21st century*. Singapore: Thomson Learning.

Tan, O. S., Parsons, R. D., Hinson, S. L., & Sardo-Brown, D. (2003). *Educational psychology: A practitioner–researcher approach (An Asian edition)*. Singapore: Thomson Learning.

Vygotsky, L. S. (1962). *Thought and language* (E. Hanfmann & G. Vakar, Eds. & Trans.). Cambridge, MA: MIT Press.

Vygotsky, L. S. (1978). *Mind in society: The development of higher psychological processes* (M. Cole, V. John-Steiner, S. Scribner, & E. Souberman, Eds. & Trans.). Cambridge, MA: Harvard University Press (original works published 1930–33).

Zimmerman, B. J. (2001). Theories of self-regulated learning and academic achievement: An overview and analysis. In D. H. Schunk & B. J. Zimmerman (Eds.), *Self-regulated learning and academic achievement* (2nd ed., pp. 1–37). Mahwah, NJ: Erlbaum.

CHAPTER 2

Psychological Tools in Problem-based Learning

Cindy E. Hmelo-Silver
Ellina Chernobilsky
Maria Carolina DaCosta

Theoretical Framework

In this chapter, we will examine how cultural and psychological tools are integral parts of the problem-based learning (PBL) process. Using both medical school and pre-service teacher education as contexts, we have examined students' ways of knowing—both what they learn and the learning processes they engage in. Examination of cognitive outcomes addresses how well students meet the three goals of PBL: (1) constructing a solid knowledge base, (2) becoming better reasoners, and (3) becoming self-directed learners. Cognitive outcomes were examined through the lenses of two major theoretical positions: transfer-appropriate processing theory and psychological tools theory. This chapter's goal is to show how both of these theories have provided useful frameworks for understanding cognition and learning in PBL contexts. As we shall discuss, the transfer-appropriate processing theory is a useful tool for understanding learning outcomes, but the psychological tools perspective has been more fruitful in understanding learning processes *and* outcomes.

Our initial work was guided by the transfer-appropriate processing theory, which states that people who learn in a problem-solving context should be able to retrieve that information when they need to (Adams et al., 1988). Spontaneous transfer of knowledge and strategies is generally hard to achieve; but with increasing practice and expertise, the likelihood of transfer is improved (Novick, 1988; Novick & Holyoak, 1991). Transfer often fails because problem solvers fail to retrieve an appropriate analog. Since in PBL the knowledge is encoded in a problem-solving context, students are more likely to retrieve that knowledge when faced with future problems, which is especially important in professional education. Students of professional education are often learning foundational disciplines (e.g., basic sciences for medicine and psychology in teacher education), and the goal of learning is often not to learn these disciplines in isolation but to be able to apply this knowledge to problem solving. As PBL students learn domain knowledge (e.g., basic biomedical sciences in the case of medical students), hypothesis-driven reasoning strategies,[1] and self-directed learning strategies in the context of solving problems, it is reasonable to expect transfer-appropriate processing mechanisms to come into play. In ill-structured domains such as medicine and teaching, transfer is a particularly thorny issue because concepts apply irregularly across different problem situations (Spiro, Coulsen, Feltovich, & Anderson, 1988).

A more general cognitive analysis of PBL suggests that, as students are presented with problems, they access their prior knowledge, establish a problem space, search for new information to help reach their problem-solving goals, and in the process may construct new mental representations or restructure existing representations that include the conditions in which the knowledge might be used. This process involves developing metacognitive awareness of one's progress in both learning and problem solving (Hmelo & Lin, 2000).

In studies by Hmelo (1998) and Hmelo and Lin (2000), 75 first-year medical students (from both PBL and traditional medical curricula) were studied at three points over their first year of medical school and were given pathophysiological explanation problems to solve. Hmelo (1998) demonstrated that the PBL students were more likely to transfer their knowledge, reasoning, and learning strategies to new problems than the

---

[1] Hypothesis-driven strategies involve reasoning based on one's theoretical framework and assumptions, such as a hypothesized disease process or psychological theory, versus a focus on situational features such as signs and symptoms or characteristics of the problem setting.

students in traditional medical education. This study also showed that the PBL students became more accurate in their diagnostic hypotheses on the new problems than their traditional counterparts. They also learned to produce more coherent explanations. Moreover, the study provided evidence that the PBL students were more likely to use science concepts in their problem solving—supporting a transfer-appropriate processing interpretation of the efficacy of PBL. Another finding that supported this interpretation is that the PBL students were more likely to transfer the reasoning strategies that were modeled to new problems. Hmelo and Lin (2000) compared these same students on their self-directed learning strategies. After each problem that the students solved, they were asked what else they would need to know in order to better solve the problem and how they would go about getting that information. This analysis found that the PBL students used their hypothesis-driven reasoning strategies to guide their self-directed learning. They were more likely to identify holes in their knowledge that were related to their hypotheses, whereas the "traditional" students were more likely to focus on clinical signs and symptoms. Moreover, the PBL students had better-defined plans for how to proceed with their learning than students from the traditional curriculum. At the end of the last problem-solving session, all the students were asked to read several paragraphs relevant to the case they were working on and then to generate a new explanation. The analysis of these explanations indicated that the PBL students integrated more of the new knowledge into their explanations than the traditional students, providing additional support that they had learned how to learn. Thus, this study demonstrated that the PBL students were able to apply their reasoning strategies to their self-directed learning— in other words, they approached their learning with their hypotheses in mind. They were able to transfer the metacognitive strategies of planning their learning to novel problems.

By applying a transfer-appropriate processing framework to these findings, we can conclude:

- Students who learn knowledge in a problem-solving context such as PBL are likely to retrieve and transfer their knowledge to new problems.
- Similarly, students who learn reasoning and self-directed learning strategies in a problem-solving context and have extensive practice in applying them are likely to retrieve and apply these strategies to new problems.

Both of these findings suggest that students are achieving the goals of constructing a solid knowledge base and becoming good reasoners and effective self-directed learners. This work provided a great deal of information about what students learn but not about how they learn, and it provided only limited information about how they use knowledge as a psychological tool to solve problems. Because of these limitations, we turned to another framework: that of psychological tools for learning. This allowed us to focus on the processes of learning as well as the outcomes. This has paralleled our theoretical evolution from a transfer-appropriate processing view (e.g., Adams et al., 1988; Perfetto, Bransford, & Franks, 1983) to more sociocultural theories that emphasize the role of tools in mediating activity (Engström, 1993; Lave & Wenger, 1991). The notion of mediated activity is a critical concept in sociocultural theories of learning (Engström, 1999; Kozulin, 1998). A key aspect of mediation is that people control their behavior by using and creating artifacts and other tools. Thus, studying the role of such tools is central to understanding learning. This evolution in thinking led us to reinterpret our earlier results by considering that the PBL students were more successful in their problem solving because they were able to use their science knowledge and the strategies that they developed as tools for their thinking. Kozulin (1998) defines psychological tools as "those symbolic artifacts—signs, symbols, tests, formulae, graphic–symbolic devices—that help individuals master their own 'natural' psychological functions of perception, memory, attention, and so on. Psychological tools serve as a bridge between individual acts of cognition and the symbolic sociocultural prerequisites of these acts" (p. 1). These tools mediate both individual and collective activities. It is important to note that tools are involved in a dialectic in which learners both transform and are transformed by the tools they use in their activities (John-Steiner & Mahn, 1996). In our studies of learning processes, we examined the role of several kinds of psychological tools, which are classified as conceptual tools (e.g., knowledge, strategies, language) or representational tools that students construct (and that may be used to scaffold and guide their learning). By scaffolding, we mean providing support that learners could not do without in order to accomplish tasks (Hmelo & Guzdial, 1996; Vygotsky, 1978). Such support might help model and communicate a process, elicit articulation and reflection, or provide other forms of coaching.

Conceptual Tools in PBL

Knowledge, strategies, and language help mediate goal-directed activity by helping one make inferences and reason about one's activities. Students use language as a tool to help them construct meaning. Among the various psychological tools, language plays a critical role in the development of cognition (Vygotsky, 1978). The use of language allows its further development and subsequent mastery. As Lave and Wenger (1991) pointed out, this mastery allows students to progress in becoming participants in the sociocultural practices of communities.

PBL provides many opportunities for students to engage with conceptual tools such as language and domain knowledge. Adequate language practice is essential for being a part of a community of practitioners—a group of people who share goals, ideas, and interests in order to solve similar problems. Through participation and discussion, practitioners have a chance to appropriate and manipulate newly acquired vocabulary, negotiate word meanings, and interact with other members of the community (Brown et al., 1993). PBL allows for such talk to take place. As students work in small comfortable settings, they have a chance to both share what they have learned and find out what they still need to learn. Such talk is an ideal environment for students to appropriate the conceptual language of a discipline as they practice it and have a chance to learn from their mistakes.

In addition to language, one's knowledge and strategies can serve as important tools for problem solving. In PBL, students appropriate new knowledge and strategies as they engage with problems. This is different from acquisition of content knowledge because implicit in the notion of tools is the instrumental value of this knowledge (Kozulin, 1998). Knowledge is only a tool if "it is appropriated as a generalized instrument capable of organizing individual cognitive and learning processes in different contexts and in applications to different tasks" (p. 86). A psychological tools perspective suggests that some reinterpretation of the Hmelo (1998) and Hmelo and Lin (2000) results is needed. From this perspective, the notion that students in the PBL curriculum are using their science concepts and hypothesis-driven reasoning strategies to produce good-quality explanations on a variety of problems suggests that these concepts and strategies are serving this instrumental purpose. In addition, the hypothesis-driven strategies that they use in their reasoning also serve to mediate their self-directed learning. This occurs because learners can use their hypotheses as a way to make principled judgments about the relevance of new information for the problem at hand. In other words, this approach helps by constraining the set of possible concepts that might be explored as well as allowing learners to evaluate the value of the information with respect to the hypotheses that they are considering (Hmelo & Lin, 2000). For example, a learning issue related to a disease leads students to consider abnormal laboratory values in the context rather than as an isolated feature, as in this example: "the physiology of the adrenal gland: what are the compounds which it synthesizes, and what are the systemic effects of their release into blood in abnormally elevated levels?" (p. 237). This example refers to a patient with an adrenal tumor. We can also see the effect of using hypothesis-driven reasoning as a tool in another example:

> If Ms. Dupree does indeed have MG (and she did improve with anticholinesterase, which is used to determine a diagnosis of MG), most of her symptoms are characteristic of this disease, including ptosis, difficulty swallowing, and respiratory distress. The pathophysiological process that accounts for her symptoms is that insufficient amounts of Ach are binding to neural receptors (Hmelo & Lin, 2000, 244).

This student was basically testing her hypothesis of MG (myasthenia gravis, a neuromuscular disorder) using textual information and then inferring that the causal mechanism accounted for this patient's problems. At the same time, she was engaging in knowledge construction that connected what she already knew to new information. Thus, she had used her reasoning and learning strategies as tools for knowledge construction.

Representational Tools in PBL

In addition to conceptual psychological tools, representations can serve as tools for students' thinking. Constructing representations is an important social practice for learning. Different representations afford and constrain social knowledge construction in several ways (Pea, 1993; Roth, 1998). First, representations serve as a shared concrete referent for all the members of a group and provide common ground for negotiation. Second, the structure of the representation can guide student discussions (Suthers & Hundhausen, 2001). In PBL, several representational artifacts may be constructed. One representation is the formal structured PBL whiteboard with its facts, ideas or hypotheses, learning issues, and action plan. This helps guide the discourse to consider certain issues and not others. The whiteboard serves as an external memory for the students—it reminds them of their ideas, both solidified and tentative, as well as hypotheses that they need to test. One ritualized aspect of the PBL tutorial is "cleaning up the boards" (Hmelo-Silver, 2002a). This occurs several times, but in particular after students have discussed the resources they used for their self-directed learning. Here students evaluate each of their hypotheses, look at the fit to data, and determine how that maps onto what they have gleaned from their self-directed learning. The discussion of what hypotheses are viable, which ones are more or less likely, leads to substantive discussions that are centered around what needs to be filled in on the whiteboard (see example in Figure 1). Students often discuss how hypotheses should be ranked or when they should be added or deleted. Similar discussions revolve around learning

Hypotheses	Facts*	Learning issues
Diabetic neuropathy	Ann George	Guidelines for
Multiple sclerosis	72 Y F	hypertension
Alcoholic neuropathy	CC: Numbness on bottoms	Diabetic neuropathy
Malnutrition	of feet	Multiple sclerosis
Afferent neuropathy	HPI	Peripheral neuritis
Peripheral neuritis	Numbness in feet for 4-5	Innervation of foot and
Guillain-Barré syndrome	weeks	blood supply
Spinal cord lesion	Weak tingling in fingers	Pathophysiology of
Spinal cord tumor	EXAM	numbness
Compression fracture	HR 72	Guillain Barré
Herniated disc	T 98.6	Paresthesia
Hypothyroidism	RESP 16	Paralysis
Toxicity	HT 5' 6"	Afferent tracts
Arsenic	Broad-based gait	Arcus senilis
Lead	PMH	Broad-based gait
Anemia	Tonsillectomy age 10	Romberg
Pernicious	Hysterectomy age 60	Cerebellar function
Scleroderma	No meds	Muscle tone resistance
Electrolyte problem		Olivopontocerebellar
Psychiatric disorder	ROS	atrophy
CNS tumor	O HA, migraines	CSF studies
CNS infection	Chest: O dyspnea	
	Gait and station	
	Romberg	
	Coordination	
	ROM	
	Tone	
	etc.	

*The Facts column has been abridged for illustrative purposes.

FIGURE 1 Example of whiteboard

Source: Hmelo-Silver & Barrows (2003).

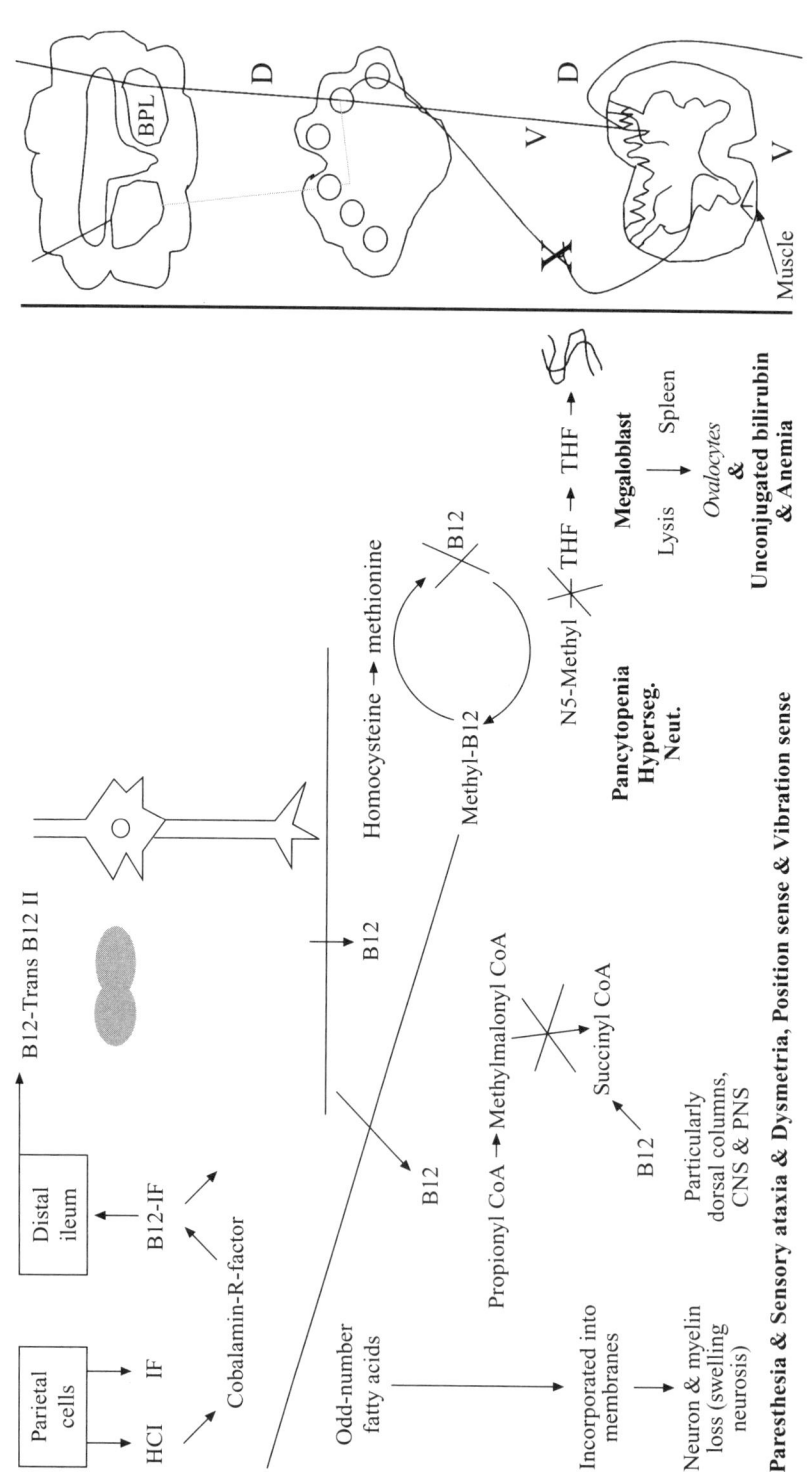

Student-generated representation

issues (Hmelo-Silver & Barrows, 2003). The formal whiteboards serve as a focus for students to negotiate their ideas and identify those that need to be held in abeyance. When students mark something as needing to be entered onto the whiteboard, it also signifies agreement by the group that the item is worth attending to. The use of the whiteboard is a fluid part of the tutorial that supports reasoning, knowledge construction, and self-directed learning as students use it to remind them of what they are considering, what they know, and what they still need to learn.

Other representational tools students may construct are less formal representations, such as flowcharts, concept maps, and diagrams. For example, students may draw a flowchart or anatomic diagram as shown in Figure 2. In the next section, we will demonstrate how these tools support reasoning and knowledge construction.

Illustrations of Psychological Tools in PBL

PBL in Medical Education

In medical education, we have conducted detailed analyses of students' representational activity and discourse as key components of social knowledge construction. In a fine-grained analysis of a second-year PBL tutorial group, we examined how the act of creating inscriptions served as a tool for both representing and transforming the group's understanding (Hmelo-Silver, 2002a, b). To examine this, we attempted to identify focal representational events in the five hours of video that we analyzed of medical students and an expert facilitator. We found that there were very few that stood out as independent events but rather they were clearly an integral part of the discussion, serving as a tool in their deliberations.

The major representational episode that we identified occurred late in the tutorial process. One strategy that a facilitator may use to help students integrate their knowledge is asking them to draw a diagram (Hmelo-Silver, 2002a). The students in the video decided on a particular epistemic form, a flowchart, that subsequently guided and helped consolidate their theory construction. An epistemic form is a structure that supports knowledge construction through the use of a general structure that guides inquiry (Collins & Ferguson, 1993). The particular form that the students chose helped guide their construction of a coherent causal explanation. In this 20-minute episode, the students drew both a flowchart of the causal processes involved in a patient's problem (pernicious anemia) and a diagram of the nervous system to help them locate the source of the patient's physical complaints (shown in Figure 2). As the students made connections between different levels of explanation (e.g., between biochemical and clinical phenomena), they engaged in a great deal of causal explanation and metacognitive thinking.

In the following excerpt, the group was moving back and forth in their drawing activity between representing anatomy and physiology and clinical signs and symptoms. At this point, they were considering how what is happening in the neuron could cause paralysis. The scribe (Jeff) was drawing the lower left part of the flowchart and beginning the anatomic diagram on the right. As he was doing this, Mary noted: "And you get neuronal also, um, various things that happen. I believe you get neuronal cell swelling within the membrane and then you can get neuronal death. And that's when you get the paralysis and once it progresses to that stage, as we know, neurons will regenerate." Thus, as Jeff was drawing those two parts of the representation, Mary was noting how what is happening at the anatomic level leads to an effect observed at the clinical level. The students continued to make these bridges between the causal mechanisms and the symptoms. The need to complete an aspect of the drawing often led to substantive discussions. It also served as a referent that the students gestured toward in their negotiations. For example, as the students were trying to locate the source of a problem at the cellular level, they frequently referred to and pointed at the diagram:

Jim:	But what are the nucleotides?
Mary:	The nu . . .
Jeff:	In fact, this is supposed to be more related to like the neurons and . . .
Mary:	No that at, this one is more related to the red blood cells. (circular gesture toward diagram)
Jim:	This part is, right? (gesturing at diagram)
Denise:	Yeah.
Mary:	That, this whole thing, right.
Jim:	The whole thing is. Okay.
Mary:	Right, because remember think about why this is happening. Because you need, you need the tetrahydrofolate for the purines or to incorporate those into the DNA.
Jeff:	Okay.

Mary: Where is the DNA in the cell? It's in the nucleus.
Channing: Uh hmm.
Mary: You can, if you cannot do nuclear synthesis, you can't reproduce new cells. There's no way you can get progeny.

So here Jim was trying to understand where the nucleotides were with respect to the flowchart and Jeff was trying to get a handle on how that was related to the neurons (nerve cells). There is some ambiguity about what was going on in the blood cells versus the nerve cells. Mary and Jim used their gestures and the flowchart to help disambiguate these two structures. The students continued to use their collaborative representational activity to make their understanding coherent and to fill in most of the blanks. As the students were drawing, they elaborated their understanding. When the scribe was switching levels in the drawing, for example between the biochemistry and the clinical signs, the students engaged in causal reasoning. In addition, the parts of the anatomic drawing (on the right side of Figure 2) became issues that the students realized they needed to learn more about. This demonstrates how the representational tools provided a concrete reference for negotiation that helped guide the students' thinking and provided an external memory to guide and support problem solving.

PBL in Teacher Education

Our discussion of tools in PBL switches context here from medical education to teacher education. Using PBL in teacher education provides special, additional challenges. Rather than having one facilitator for every group, there were one or two facilitators for six to seven groups. With the facilitator not available at all times, some of the facilitation function was offloaded onto the representations that students used—in particular, the whiteboards (or in this case, large 2.5 x 2 foot stick-on notes). Thus, in this context, the external tools served to scaffold the development of the internal tools. In preparing pre-service teachers, examination of the artifacts that they produced has provided a great deal of insight into their thinking and collaborative activity, as well as how the artifacts served as a mechanism for knowledge diffusion (Hmelo-Silver, 2000).

The context for this study was an undergraduate educational psychology class. Analysis of student artifacts (the group whiteboards and papers) provided evidence that the students crisscrossed the landscape of educational psychology as they deepened their understanding of the psychological concepts. The group whiteboards were divided into four columns, for facts (about the case), ideas (about the cause of the problem and potential solutions), learning issues, and action plan. The students initially used the whiteboards in small-group discussions; then the groups were brought together to share their work. The students used the whiteboard in their own group as a scaffold—a reminder of what they needed to attend to. It provided an external memory so that important ideas did not get lost. It also provided a mechanism for ideas to spread out among the groups as the whiteboards were always visible to every group. During the whole-class reporting, ideas were diffused among the groups. For example, during the fourth problem of the semester, only one group had "information processing" as a learning issue. After the large-group discussion, this idea spread to all the groups and appeared in their papers. Thus, the whiteboards and the ideas contained on them helped support social knowledge construction. This is an example of how representational tools support the development of conceptual tools.

Moreover, the students' knowledge became increasingly differentiated as they applied it to subsequent problems. The first time the students applied a concept, it was often used as a way to display their knowledge, as in this example:

> Basic knowledge is the main focus of another group's approach to teaching but it can only be accomplished through memory. By going back to basic concepts and incorporating new ideas memory is a necessary attribute in the success of knowledge based learning. Memory is the processes [*sic*] by which information is encoded, stored, and retrieved. Long term memory becomes the goal of the students in this teaching approach (Hmelo-Silver, 2000, 51).

They went on to provide more details about long-term memory, but all of this discussion was abstract—they were not putting the knowledge to work as a psychological tool to help them solve their problem (in this case, choosing among several theory-based approaches to instruction). In their final problem in the course, the students actually applied the information processing concepts to the problem:

> The first thing that Mr. Johnson should have done was to introduce a unit on static electricity by asking the students what they already knew about static electricity. We suggest that Mr. Johnson create a concept map using what the students already know about static electricity from their other classes or everyday lives. "Prior knowledge is stored in the form of schemas. Teachers can activate these schemas in a number of ways including: reviewing, questioning, or developing with the students a concept map of prior knowledge" (Knowledge Web, the Prior Knowledge

Use [*sic*]).[2] A concept map is extremely important because teachers use students' prior knowledge to explain and discuss increasingly more sophisticated concepts. "Prior knowledge becomes a platform upon which new understanding is constructed" (Knowledge Web, the Prior Knowledge Use [*sic*]). . . . When the students are done explaining to Mr. Johnson what they previously knew about static electricity, we suggested he give a brief lecture to fill in the gaps and add to the concept map what the students missed. The new knowledge that students learn from the lecture provides them with an integral tool that will allow them to make more meaningful connections when they see the experiment (Hmelo-Silver, 2000, 53).

Here the students were using the concepts as a tool for thinking about how they would redesign a lesson. They were applying information processing theory to describe the importance of prior knowledge in learning, indicating that they were thinking deeply about memory. These results suggest that for students to use knowledge as a tool for problem solving they need to engage with it.

In a subsequent study, we examined the artifacts for evidence that students' use of professional vocabulary became richer and more flexible as they engaged in a problem-based course in educational psychology (Chernobilsky & Hmelo-Silver, 2002). Language is an important conceptual tool because it helps shape thinking. Our approach was to examine language changes using written narratives that students constructed, both in groups and individually. The decision to focus on narrative artifacts was based on the ideas of Bakhtin (1981) and Vygotsky (1978), who viewed speech and writing as a coherent whole with a dynamic interaction between them. Examining language expressed in writing is one way to assess the level of knowledge that students constructed during learning activities (Bereiter & Scardamalia, 1987).

We examined how students developed professional language in an educational psychology course for pre-service teachers over the course of seven problems that the students worked on in a single semester. In order to examine language change over time, we concentrated on such constructs as professional jargon, definitions used, and identification of theories and theorists as indicators of professional language. We also examined students' use of sources because the skill of locating sources and critically evaluating

---

[2] The students were referring to the knowledge web at *www.wcer.wisc.edu/step*, which is a hypermedia web site on learning science instruction. See Steinkuehler, Derry, Hmelo-Silver, and DelMarcelle (2002) for further details.

their reliability is an indication of how students use professional sources as tools for thinking (Wineburg, 1991). For this analysis, we looked at a number of group and individual artifacts. Group artifacts included whiteboards, concept maps, and group-generated papers. Students' learning logs (reflective journals) and midterm and final examinations constituted individual artifacts. The quantitative analysis of the data showed an overall linear trend in the growth of vocabulary usage in the students' individual work. The use of professional language in the group artifacts showed a similar but nonsignificant trend. Group data also indicated that groups identified many more concepts and used more vocabulary than the students did individually. This supports the sociocultural notion that when students work in groups their work is more elaborated than when done individually (Hmelo-Silver, 2000).

To capture the dynamics of group learning in PBL and to better understand the quantitative results, we examined three representative groups for qualitative trends. This analysis indicated that strong, well-functioning groups that devoted time to scaffolding weaker students performed better in comparison to other groups. It also showed that weaker groups who spent a lot of time resolving issues that were not related to their learning task (e.g., conflicts among group members) and did not engage in peer scaffolding did not show the same increase in the sophistication of vocabulary and idea development as other groups. These analyses show that language learning is tied to group dynamics and to the situations students create while working in groups. PBL allows for maximizing of a positive environment for learning and at the same time allows students to internalize their thinking.

While looking at language learning and development during PBL activities is useful, one needs to keep in mind that language does not exist in isolation. Examining language development together with knowledge in PBL adds another dimension to our understanding of how students construct and apply psychological tools.

To examine how pre-service teachers' knowledge changed, we studied their individual and group artifacts generated during a single PBL problem (Hmelo-Silver, DaCosta, & Chernobilsky, 2002). In this problem, students observed a videocase of real-life instruction and suggested ideas for redesigning the instruction. Looking at student-generated artifacts during a PBL activity allowed us to examine how students used knowledge as a tool in their problem solving, as we did in Hmelo-Silver (2000). Because we had made some changes to the PBL model to include some initial and final individual phases in addition to the group work, we were able to examine how individual use of knowledge was related to the knowledge applied in the group phase of the activity. We had two goals for the analysis of the individual and group artifacts that students generated. The first was to analyze how concepts flowed from individual to group artifacts and vice versa. This was an attempt to understand the role of shared knowledge in developing ideas. The second goal was to examine how students dealt with relevant concepts and whether they achieved more sophisticated levels of knowledge development during the activity.

We coded individual and group artifacts for the educational psychology concepts represented in the case and for the level of knowledge development they engaged when applying such concepts. Knowledge development ranged from an undeveloped *telling* level to a more advanced *transforming* level, with *elaborated telling* being an intermediate level between the two (Bereiter & Scardamalia, 1989). Concepts coded at the *transforming* level were those that were properly elaborated and applied to the case. Knowledge transformation implies that students are using knowledge as a tool in their problem solving. Unelaborated concept naming with no connections to the case was coded as just *telling*. The intermediate level of *elaborated telling* occurred when students provided conceptual explanations but still no connection to the case. The results of our analysis demonstrated that groups differed in levels of shared knowledge and knowledge development while solving the problem. Greater proportions of shared knowledge (i.e., transfer of concepts across individual and group artifacts) seemed to have contributed to higher levels of knowledge development during the activity. For example, the group that engaged mostly in knowledge transforming was also the group with the highest proportion of shared knowledge. At the same time, groups without sufficient shared knowledge before solving the problem often engaged in knowledge telling, just listing or mentioning the concepts without applying them to the problem. More effective groups were those in which members were able to establish a common and rich knowledge base, which allowed them to go beyond telling to transforming. The sooner a common knowledge base was established in a learning community, the more opportunities students had to elaborate and deepen their understanding. The shared knowledge served as a tool by creating common ground that the students could build on and apply toward solving the problem.

To summarize, the structural representations in PBL pre-service teacher education take an even bigger role than in other PBL settings. As Pea (1993) pointed out, language (which is a conceptual tool in itself) and representational tools are the means through which intelligence gets distributed and discussed. By making ideas and thought visible to students, such tools help extend working memory capacity, which now can be occupied with higher-order thinking and more knowledge construction. As a result, knowledge, which is also a conceptual tool, is growing, and this allows students to build their professional base and to engage in active social participation in the community of practitioners.

Discussion and Implications

Psychological tools are a key component of PBL. They work for students as well as helping students accomplish their problem solving and understanding. Initially, students treat concepts as isolated entities that have names to be learned and defined. Our data from both medical students and pre-service teachers demonstrate that, as students participate in PBL, they learn to put their knowledge to work and the language they appropriate allows them to engage with that knowledge in productive ways. They learn to use professional language in their discourse to help them understand and solve meaningful problems. This helps them to see the big picture and to engage in constructing a solid knowledge base, and it provides opportunities for them to see how knowledge can be applied. The feedback they get in their PBL tutorials helps them refine their language and subsequently their ideas. In addition, using appropriate professional language supports their self-directed learning, as they are better able to find what they need from their learning resources. It is important for teachers using PBL to understand that part of their role is modeling professional language, at times revoicing students' ideas in the appropriate terminology. Although it is important not to be focused just on vocabulary, this more subtle demonstration of how language is used can support students' knowledge construction and enhance their effectiveness as self-directed learners.

As our research has demonstrated, these tools help students achieve the goals of PBL. In addition to conceptual and linguistic tools, student-generated artifacts serve as psychological tools to help remind students where they have been and where they are going. The whiteboard structure can help guide the discourse in productive ways that support social knowledge construction. The whiteboard reminds students of their hypotheses and serves as a focus for generating and testing ideas, a process that supports the development of reasoning skills. As students try to generate and evaluate ideas with each other, they are forced to justify their thinking and explain their reasoning. The "learning issues" column makes it salient that gaps in their knowledge are valued as opportunities to learn, thus supporting the development of self-directed learning skills. In addition, the structured whiteboards and other representations that students construct become tools for them to externalize their thinking and can become a focal point for them to negotiate meaning and revise their understanding, as we saw in the case of the medical students. Finally, because these representations are public and available to other groups, they promote social knowledge construction as ideas diffuse across a classroom. Other representations, such as concept maps and flowcharts, can also be used to help synthesize a coherent understanding.

This research has implications for practice. It is important to realize that merely posing a problem does not in and of itself guarantee learning. In the example of medical education, there was one facilitator for every five to seven students. In the case of the pre-service teachers, we used a combination of large-group and small-group discussions and the teacher served as a wandering facilitator. This model makes it harder to encourage students to think deeply and to model appropriate professional language. An important issue is to consider how the use of psychological tools can be modeled and scaffolded in such settings. Providing procedural facilitations is one approach that we have used (Hmelo-Silver, 2002a). In this approach, students rotate the facilitator role. The student-facilitators are given prompt cards, as shown in Figure 3, with questions that they might ask at different points in the PBL process, as well as explaining the reason for asking the question.

The whiteboards themselves have served as useful tools in the wandering facilitation model. Using large pieces of newsprint or whiteboards for each group serves to make students' thinking visible, quite literally. With a quick scan about the room, the facilitator can determine from the boards how groups are progressing in their problem solving and what their knowledge gaps are. This allows wandering facilitators to scaffold more effectively by allocating their effort as needed and adapting to the needs of different groups.

Varying the structure of the whiteboard is another approach that can help scaffold the development of psychological tools. In our current work, we have modified the whiteboard and structured the PBL process to specifically support analysis and redesign of classroom cases. Students are prompted to think about particular aspects of instruction in the way that a skilled facilitator might, if one were constantly available (Steinkuehler, Derry, Hmelo-Silver, & DelMarcelle, 2002). Approaches such as this offer

---

2) GENERATING MULTIPLE HYPOTHESES

Students should brainstorm their first instincts about:

IDEAS: how to solve the problem
FACTS: information we know about the problem and *from our own knowledge*
LEARNING ISSUES: information we need to know
ACTION: what we can do to start solving the problem

The scribe will begin to write down what the group says on the whiteboard/ big paper.

Ask for clarification of terms written down in the FACTS and IDEAS columns.

EXAMPLES:

- What does that term mean?
- What does "expert" mean in this case?

If students can't clarify or define their ideas, these become LEARNING ISSUES.

Goal: To help students understand what they don't know.

FIGURE **3**   Example procedural facilitation card

promise by using representations as psychological tools to help support the development of conceptual tools. Teachers might think about how the labels on whiteboard columns might model a problem-solving process or support the development of conceptual tools in specific subjects.

In summary, the various psychological tools discussed in this chapter have direct applications to practice in achieving the goals of PBL. The teacher has an important role in asking questions that help students understand how conceptual tools can support their problem solving. The whiteboards can be used to extend the facilitation—by providing a model of problem solving that can support the development of reasoning, knowledge construction, and self-directed learning. The generic whiteboard structure with its hypotheses, facts, and learning issues makes it applicable in a variety of contexts. On the other hand, when trying to facilitate many groups, the facilitator may wish to adapt the whiteboard for a particular domain. In other words, teachers may want to specialize the representational tools to help support the development of conceptual tools in particular subjects.

Psychological tools have many important roles in the PBL process, but these may need adaptation to one's unique context.

Acknowledgments

This research was partially funded by a National Academy of Education/Spencer Foundation Postdoctoral Fellowship to the first author and a National Science Foundation ROLE grant #107032 to Sharon J. Derry and Cindy E. Hmelo-Silver. Any opinions, findings, and conclusions or recommendations expressed in this chapter are those of the authors and do not necessarily reflect the views of the National Science Foundation.

References

Adams, L., Kasserman, J., Yearwood, A., Perfetto, G., Bransford, J., & Franks, J. (1988). The effect of fact versus problem oriented acquisition. *Memory and Cognition*, *16*, 167–75.

Bakhtin, M. (1981). Discourse in the novel (C. Emerson & M. Holquist, Trans.). In M. Holquist (Ed.), *The dialogic imagination: Four essays by M. M. Bakhtin* (pp. 252–422). Austin: University of Texas Press.

Bereiter, C., & Scardamalia, M. (1987). *The psychology of written composition*. Hillsdale, NJ: Erlbaum.

Bereiter, C., & Scardamalia, M. (1989). Intentional learning as a goal of instruction. In L. B. Resnick (Ed.), *Knowing, learning, and instruction: Essays in honor of Robert Glaser* (pp. 361–92). Hillsdale, NJ: Erlbaum.

Brown, A. L., Ash, D., Rutherford, M., Nakagawa, K., Gordon, A., & Campione, J. C. (1993). Distributed expertise in the classroom. In G. Salomon (Ed.), *Distributed cognitions: Psychological and educational considerations* (pp. 188–228). New York: Cambridge University Press.

Chernobilsky, E., & Hmelo-Silver, C. E. (2002). Learning to talk the educational psychology talk through a problem-based course in educational psychology. Paper presented at the PBL2002 conference. Baltimore, MD, June.

Collins, A., & Ferguson, W. (1993). Epistemic forms and epistemic games: Structures and strategies to guide inquiry. *Educational Psychologist*, *28*, 25–42.

Engström, Y. (1993). A developmental study of work as a test bench of activity theory: The case of primary care medical practice. In S. Chaiklin & J. Lave (Eds.), *Understanding practice: Perspectives on activity and context* (pp. 64–103). Cambridge: Cambridge University Press.

Engström, Y. (1999). Activity theory and individual and social transformation. In Y. Engström, R. Miettinen, & R. Punamaki (Eds.), *Perspectives on activity theory* (pp. 19–38). New York: Cambridge University Press.

Hmelo, C. E. (1998). Problem-based learning: Effects on the early acquisition of cognitive skill in medicine. *Journal of the Learning Sciences*, *7*, 173–208.

Hmelo, C. E., & Guzdial, M. (1996). Of black and glass boxes: Scaffolding for learning and doing. In D. C. Edelson & E. A. Domeshek (Eds.), *Proceedings of ICLS 96* (pp. 128–34). Charlottesville, VA: Association for the Advancement of Computing in Education.

Hmelo, C. E., & Lin, X. (2000). Becoming self-directed learners: Strategy development in problem-based learning. In D. H. Evensen & C. E. Hmelo (Eds.), *Problem-based learning: A research perspective on learning interactions* (pp. 227–50). Mahwah, NJ: Erlbaum.

Hmelo-Silver, C. E. (2000). Knowledge recycling: Crisscrossing the landscape of educational psychology in a problem-based learning course for preservice teachers. *Journal of Excellence in College Teaching, 11,* 41–56.

Hmelo-Silver, C. E. (2002a). Collaborative ways of knowing: Issues in facilitation. In G. Stahl (Ed.), *Proceedings of CSCL 2002* (pp. 199–208). Hillsdale, NJ: Erlbaum.

Hmelo-Silver, C. E. (2002b). Getting the big picture: Discourse, representation, and reflection in a tutorial group. Unpublished manuscript.

Hmelo-Silver, C. E., & Barrows, H. S. (2003). Facilitating collaborative ways of knowing. *Cognition and Instruction,* in press.

Hmelo-Silver, C. E., DaCosta, M. C., & Chernobilsky, E. (2002). Knowledge construction using online videocases. Paper presented at the Fifth International Conference on the Learning Sciences. Seattle, WA, October.

John-Steiner, V., & Mahn, H. (1996). Sociocultural approaches to learning and development: A Vygotskian framework. *Educational Psychologist, 31,* 191–206.

Kozulin, A. (1998). *Psychological tools.* Cambridge, MA: Harvard University Press.

Lave, J., & Wenger, E. (1991). *Situated learning: Legitimate peripheral participation.* New York: Cambridge University Press.

Novick, L. R. (1988). Analogical transfer, problem similarity, and expertise. *Journal of Experimental Psychology: Learning, Memory, and Cognition, 14,* 510–20.

Novick, L. R., & Holyoak, K. J. (1991). Mathematical problem solving by analogy. *Journal of Experimental Psychology: Learning, Memory, and Cognition, 17,* 398–415.

Pea, R. D. (1993). Practices of distributed intelligence and designs for education. In G. Salomon (Ed.), *Distributed cognitions: Psychological and educational considerations* (pp. 47–87). New York: Cambridge University Press.

Perfetto, G. A., Bransford, J. D., & Franks, J. J. (1983). Constraints on access in a problem-solving context. *Memory and Cognition, 11,* 24–31.

Roth, W.-M. (1998). Inscriptions: Toward a theory of representing as social practice. *Review of Educational Research, 68,* 35–60.

Spiro, R. J., Coulsen, R. L., Feltovich, P. J., & Anderson, D. K. (1988). Cognitive flexibility theory: Advanced knowledge acquisition in ill-structured domains. In *Proceedings of the Tenth Annual Conference of the Cognitive Science Society* (pp. 375–83). Hillsdale, NJ: Erlbaum.

Steinkuehler, C. A., Derry, S. J., Hmelo-Silver, C. E., & DelMarcelle, M. (2002). Cracking the resource nut with distributed problem-based learning in secondary teacher education. *Journal of Distance Education, 23,* 23–39.

Suthers, D., & Hundhausen, C. (2001). Learning by constructing collaborative representations: An empirical comparison of three alternatives. In P. Dillenbourg, A. Eurelings, & K. Hakkarainen (Eds.), *Proceedings of the First European Conference on Computer-supported Collaborative Learning* (pp. 577–84). Maastricht: Universiteit Maastricht.

Vygotsky, L. S. (1978). *Mind in society: The development of higher psychological processes.* Cambridge, MA: Harvard University Press.

Wineburg, S. S. (1991). Historical problem solving: A study of the cognitive processes used in the evaluation of documentary and pictorial evidence. *Journal of Educational Psychology, 83,* 73–87.

CHAPTER 3

Critical Thinking, Metacognition, and Problem-based Learning

Peggy A. Weissinger

Why Critical Thinking?

Accepting critical thinking as an educational ideal brings with it ramifications for *what* we teach and *how* we teach. A paradigm shift in our education system is required that facilitates development of the critical thinking skills that modern society demands.

Critical thinking, which involves knowledge of strategies as well as a propensity toward applying them, is a major component of higher education and a national priority for American colleges and universities (Brookfield, 1987; National Education Goals Panel, 1991; Nelson, 1994; U.S. Congress, 1994). The broadly defined benefits of higher education are often operationalized under the construct of critical thinking (Wood, 1997); in other words, the aim of higher education is to transfer abstract principles to concrete applications. University mission statements contain references to critical thinking, but have colleges and universities cultivated student awareness of difficult real-world problems and prepared their graduates to evaluate the merits and demerits of proposed solutions? While faculty in all disciplines want students to perform complex mental operations that will allow them to be successful in coursework, in future careers, and in their personal lives (Pellegrino, 1995; Siegel, 1980; Weiss, 1992/1993), is higher education doing its job? The answers to these questions have concrete implications for what happens in the classroom and how it is assessed.

Does Critical Thinking Just Happen?

Development of thinking skills is not a natural occurrence, an accidental outcome of experience, or an automatic byproduct of study in a subject area (de Sanchez, 1995; Taba, 1965, as cited in Beyer, 1987). It requires deliberate, continuing instruction and practice in order to develop it to its full potential (Arons, 1979; Kirby & Goodpaster, 1999; Perkins, 1985, as cited in Beyer, 1987; Thoms, 1998). Unfortunately, the traditional instruction paradigm, a 50-minute lecture intended to disseminate information, cannot fulfill critical thinking objectives (Barr & Tagg, 1995), and critical thinking will not take place if a student's goal is simply "an exit score from school necessary to enter a professional course, [which only] involves surface approaches to learning with (inappropriate) assessment-driven learning" (Aldred & Aldred, 1998, 654).

Pre-college Preparation

There is a misconception that anyone going to college already possesses critical thinking skills. With concepts presented didactically and with limited exposure to tasks that stimulate thinking, students do not develop critical thinking skills in high school (Arons, 1985; Neilson, 1989). Assignments and tests focus on the end result of subject matter acquisition rather than on reasoning (Arons, 1985); the majority of questions asked by K–12 teachers call only for a "yes" or "no" answer (Sirotnik, 1983) and "less than 1% of teacher talk requires that students think beyond the recall level" (Davidson & Worsham, 1992, xv). Taught in this manner, students receive information passively, lack the ability to question, are not encouraged to engage in lateral thought, and do not deal well with ambiguous situations (Aldred & Aldred, 1998; de Sanchez, 1995). Students enter college with a simple view of knowledge and are not ready for courses that use formal operations (Arons, 1990, as cited in Nelson, 1997; Perry, 1970). Incoming undergraduate students may even bring with them a culture that is antithetical to critical thinking, and the result of these influences does not disappear when they enter college classrooms (Kurfiss, 1988).

Traditional Undergraduate Education

Critical thinking is not a certain outcome of postsecondary education: while it is highly revered in the abstract by educators, it is often systematically ignored in practice (Browne & Keeley, 1994). Although research supports improvement between the thinking abilities of college freshmen and college seniors, the increase is modest (Angelo, 1995). Students learn in college, but whether they learn to *think* in college is debatable (McKeachie, 1999). "Most of the thinking skills deficiencies that college students demonstrate have their origin, at least in part, in academic settings that emphasize memorization of isolated knowledge components, which are devoid of meaning, lack transferability, and are easily forgotten" (de Sanchez, 1995, 73). Ideally, thinking activities should abound in coursework throughout the university; but when today's educators view curriculum as content and require students only to listen passively and recall information, opportunities for developing higher-order thinking skills are limited. What happens when the facts are forgotten? What happens when the "facts" change?

Students who begin college at the dualistic developmental position view the world as dichotomous—right/wrong, black/white, either/or. They regard the professor as the authority and the textbook as the final word (Perry, 1970). With lecture as the predominant teaching method, faculty perpetuate this belief with the teacher-directed, content-oriented approach, giving the impression that learning is simply a process-transfer operation (Cooper, 1995; Neilson, 1989; Nelson, 1999; Perry, 1970). Students blindly accept the accuracy and validity of information; they do not know how to evaluate resources (Blumberg, 2000) and may even be resistant to critical thinking (Nelson, 1999; Perry, 1970). Faculty cite limited time when questioned about alternative teaching strategies. They feel like they must "cover the material," but dissemination of information does not equal comprehension and reciting facts does not equal understanding of concepts. In other words, "the greatest enemy of understanding is [the notion of] coverage" (Gardner, as cited by Brandt, 1993, 7).

Students at the multiplicity level realize that uncertainties exist in the world but do not analyze or evaluate why. Students who do not master foundation skills in critical thinking rarely move past the multiplicity position, making this a crucial turning point for development of critical thinking (Kurfiss, 1988; Ryan, 1984). The potential stagnation carries serious implications for higher education. If critical thinking is the desired outcome, but students are only required to memorize facts, evidence is sufficient to speculate that the development of critical thinking skills is not taking place except as a possible result of increase in age or maturity (Chickering, 1981).

A major shortcoming of traditional college classrooms is that faculty present *products* of their skills, failing to model their own thinking processes for students (Arons, 1985; Davidson & Worsham, 1992; Nelson, 1997). The reality may be that, while faculty value students' upper-level thinking abilities, it is easier to teach and assess lower levels of learning—knowledge and understanding—than to teach and assess higher-order thinking, in particular critical thinking. If classroom activities lie at the bottom of Bloom's (1956) taxonomy of educational objectives, requiring students only to listen passively and recall information, then critical thinking is not consciously being developed, and colleges and universities do not produce the critical thinkers they think they do (Belenky, Clinchy, Goldberger, & Tarule, 1986; Browne & Keeley, 1994; Chickering, 1981; King & Kitchener, 1994).

If critical thinking remains an educational objective, then changes in curriculum design and teaching methods should be considered. Institutions of higher education and faculty in every classroom must provide students with a foundation of critical thinking skills, an environment that encourages the use of critical thinking, and opportunities "to manipulate information and ideas in ways that transform their meaning and implications, such as when students combine facts and ideas in order to synthesize, generalize, explain, hypothesize, or arrive at some conclusion or interpretation" (Newmann & Wehlage, 1993, 9; Facione, Facione, & Giancarlo, 1997).

Is Defining Critical Thinking Really Such a Problem?

While definitions of critical thinking vary and are sometimes vague, they generally contain verbs located within the upper levels of Bloom's taxonomy (Facione, n.d.). Four basic components surface across and are threaded through many definitions of critical thinking: foundation skills, knowledge base, a willingness to question, and self-reflection (Beyer, 1987; Facione, n.d.; Halpern, 1998; McPeck, 1981; Weissinger, 2003). For that reason, definitions of critical thinking should encompass all four of those components. Critics purport that critical thinking is not the identification of foundation skills but an attitude requiring knowledge in a designated domain (Siegel & Carey, 1989). These views need not be exclusive.

Foundation skills can and should be viewed within the framework of sister components. The components are not only equal in importance but are interrelated and should be integrated into any definition of critical thinking, as in the following:

> Critical thinking is defined as an awareness of one's own thinking (self-reflection) and the ability (foundation skills) and willingness (willingness to question) to clarify and improve understanding which aids in drawing appropriate conclusions and making the best decisions possible within a context (knowledge base) (Weissinger, 2003).

Figure 1 is a visual representation of a comprehensive definition of critical thinking. The upper circles of the Venn diagram in the figure—foundation skills and knowledge base—sit upon the attitudinal components of critical thinking—willingness to question and self-reflection. If a person has foundation skills and knowledge base but neither monitors the process nor is willing to use those foundation skills, then according to this comprehensive definition, critical thinking is not taking place. In other words, a critical thinker must not only be able to perform basic critical thinking skills but be willing to perform them within a context that he or she understands and can use as a basis for evaluation. Let's look at each of these components.

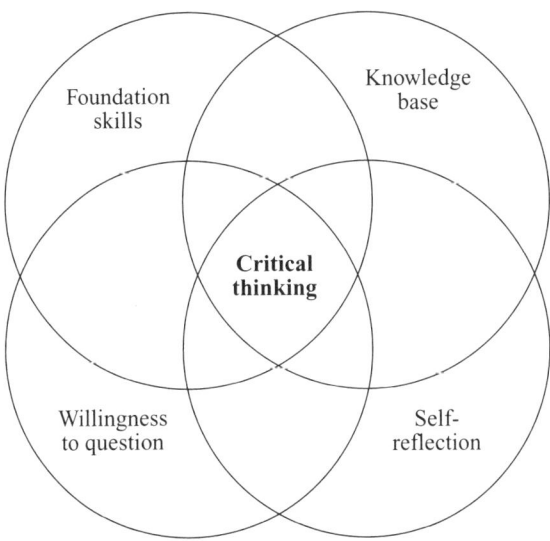

FIGURE **1**   The four basic and interrelated components identified in definitions of critical thinking

Foundation Skills

While critical thinking is an abstract concept, embedded within are core skills that are directly observable. Competencies include the ability to judge the credibility of sources; to identify issues, conclusions, reasons, and assumptions; to judge the quality of an argument including its reasons, assumptions, and evidence; to develop and defend a position on an issue; to ask appropriate clarifying questions; and to draw conclusions when warranted, with caution (Beyer, 1987; Brookfield, 1987; Dressel & Mayhew, 1954; Ennis, 1993).

Critical thinking foundation skills are necessary but probably not sufficient to progress to higher levels of thinking (Kurfiss, 1988). High performance across the entire set of critical thinking skills is an unrealistic expectation for most students (King & Kitchener, 1994; Wolcott, 1999). But once taught and if they can then recognize and apply foundation skills, "students will be more effective thinkers" (Halpern, 1996, 32).

Critics argue that focusing on foundation skills is narrow in scope and does not allow for transfer (McPeck, 1981; Siegel & Carey, 1989). I disagree. If opportunities to apply foundation skills were limited to worksheet "skill and drill" activities, perhaps these critics are correct; but it is the honing of these skills and their application in various contexts that allow learners to transfer. Students "must master less complex skills before they can master more complex skills" (Wolcott, 1999, 4). Foundation skills are tools, and without them students may never progress beyond Perry's (1970) multiplicity stage.

Knowledge Base

A knowledge base provides the context for foundation skills to be applied. Generally, the term *knowledge* implies academic knowledge (factual information) and ignores applied knowledge (Maudsley & Strivens, 2000). But even with an expanded view, true knowledge competence is not a substitute for thinking and vice versa (de Bono, 1978). Both components are necessary, and neither alone is sufficient for critical thinking to take place.

Knowledge mastery—understanding rather than memorization—is the ability to transfer knowledge to new situations (Bransford, Brown, & Cocking, 2000). It is a deep foundation of factual knowledge, understanding facts and ideas in the context of a conceptual framework, and the ability to organize that knowledge in ways that facilitate retrieval and application

(Garetto, 2001). This includes the ability to select pertinent information for the solution, to make relevant hypotheses, to draw valid conclusions, and to judge the validity of inferences (Dressel & Mayhew, 1954). Does the claim come from a credible source? Is there reason to suspect bias in the source? Without a knowledge base, people have no information upon which to make judgments.

Willingness to Question

Underlying the development of abilities are the attitudes and inclinations to use them (Ennis, 1996). Critical thinking necessitates learning in both the cognitive and affective domains (McPeck, 1981). Attitudinal components include the disposition to question, persistence at a task, monitoring one's thinking, maintaining an open mind, and working cooperatively with others (Halpern & Nummedal, 1995). Students' resistance to critical thinking frequently arises because they are stagnated in one of two fundamental epistemological belief systems—dualism or multiplicity (Kurfiss, 1988). Traditional, didactic pedagogy encourages this stagnation. After years of enrollment in a structured lecture format, students can be resistant to challenges aimed at moving them beyond being told what facts are important. Even if they see all points of view, they may not be able to discriminate between them, assuming all have equal value. Thinking involves operations, knowledge, and dispositions: "Each builds out of, and contributes to, the others" (Beyer, 1987, 20).

Self-Reflection (Metacognition)

Dewey (1910) first defined critical thinking as *suspended judgment*. Although vague, the definition carries an important implication: the willingness to think critically and to reflect on one's own thinking. Metacognition is thinking about one's own thinking process for functional purposes (Beyer, 1987; Flavell, 1979; Halpern, 1998; Hanley, 1995). It is the ability to monitor one's current level of understanding and determine when it is not adequate (Garetto, 2001). It is "stepping back from whatever one takes for granted (a fact, a decision, a problem) and examining the evidence or basis for its acceptance" (Siegel & Carey, 1989, 16).

Self-reflection drives and supports the development of thinking skills as well as the habits and disposition to use them. While the major operations of planning, monitoring, executing, and assessing a plan appear to be sequential, in reality they are recursive (Beyer, 1987). Ideally, students should assess their thinking before, during, and after a problem-solving or decision-making process; they should monitor the level of their understanding and be aware of their improvements, acknowledging where they need to develop cognitive skills or correct faulty thinking patterns (Bransford et al., 2000; Halpern, 1998; Hanley, 1995; Woolfolk, 2001). This is metacognition.

Is Problem-based Learning a Sound Instructional Strategy?

To create an ideal learning opportunity, instructional design theory recommends the alignment of learning objectives, classroom activities, and assessment strategies. If the objective is to improve critical thinking, then faculty should choose instructional strategies that are effective for achieving this objective. One of those strategies is problem-based learning (PBL). "Problem-based learning is an instructional strategy that encourages students to develop critical thinking and problem-solving skills that they can carry with them throughout their lifetimes" (Samford University, n.d.). PBL is an excellent environment within which to develop critical thinking skills because it provides opportunities to grow in all four components of critical thinking (see Figure 2): (1) PBL can provide a strong grasp of knowledge base—factual and applied; (2) it provides opportunities for the development of critical appraisal skills; (3) its environment encourages students to question; and (4) in PBL faculty step back and allow students to direct their own learning, which becomes the foundation for future professional behaviors.

In a group setting, students are presented open-ended, messy problems that they work together to form a better understanding through the listing of known facts, generation of possible solutions, identification of issues that need further research, and eventual proposal of a resolution with rationale. Students are encouraged to activate their prior knowledge; perform in a context that resembles the "real world" where the problem will be applied; and better understand, process, elaborate, and recall information (Bridges & Hallinger, 1998). PBL "mirrors [adult learning theorist Malcomb] Knowles' context for supporting lifelong learning, particularly address[ing] self-directed learning; accessing up-to-date information resources efficiently and habitually; and interaction between learners for critical reflection through multiple perspectives" (Maudsley & Strivens, 2000, 542).

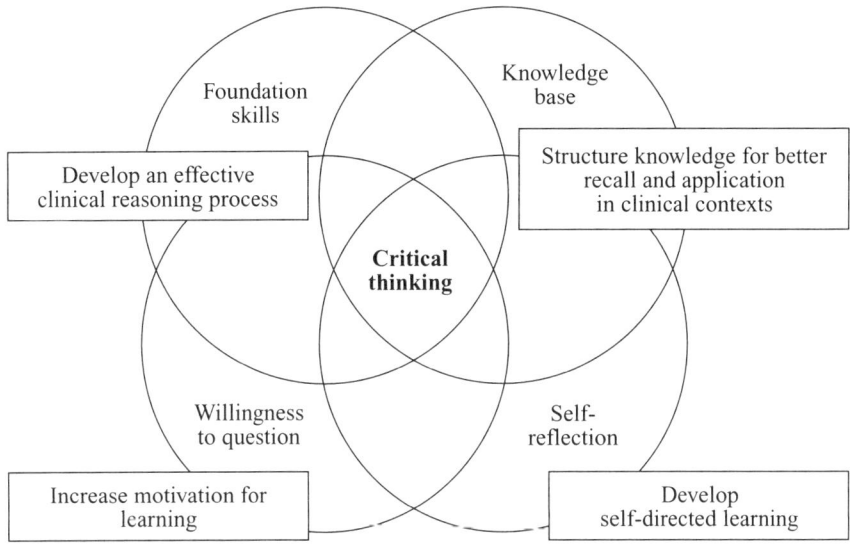

FIGURE 2   Alignment of the main objectives of problem-based learning with the four basic components identified in definitions of critical thinking

PBL, an Outgrowth of Behaviorist and Cognitive Models of Learning

The student-centered learning environment in PBL is an outgrowth of both behaviorist and cognitive models of learning. Behaviorist models focus on observable behaviors without identifying specific critical periods of development or the need for motivation (Schunk, 2000; Svinicki, 1999). Learning is a process of forming connections between stimuli and responses or stimuli with other stimuli. Pedagogical responses to this model were simple: "organize the learning environment to ensure that correct responses [are] likely to occur, and when they [do], reward them" (Svinicki, 1999, 6). Outgrowths of this movement, popular in the 1960s and 1970s, still exist today with some elements evident in PBL: self-paced instruction; incorporation of immediate, specific feedback; and criterion-referenced evaluation. Where PBL diverges from the behaviorist model is in *not* sequencing behaviors to achieve final mastery of learning. In PBL, "the problem always comes first; content is never presented prior to the engagement of the student/student group in the critical thinking required to analyze the problem" (Fincham & Schuler, 2001, 409). After that, the students themselves identify what they need to know and determine the direction of their learning.

Early cognitive theorists viewed learning as acquiring facts, so instruction was organized to direct a learner's attention to key points. Later cognitive theorists shifted the focus from memorization of information to processing it, describing learning as a restructuring of memory to make sense of the world (Schunk, 2000). The teacher determined how to link new material with old information and provided support in the form of examples, analogies, or mnemonics to assist learners. Background knowledge and existing schemata influenced the processing and storage of the new information (Ausubel, Novak, & Hanesian, 1978, as cited in Svinicki, 1991; Bransford et al., 2000). Problems arose when students' preconceived misconceptions hindered learning. PBL diverges from these learning models too. Rather than the teacher determining the value and sequence of material, the students ascertain what is needed to help solve the problem.

Later constructivist models required the learner's role to change from passive to more active, encouraging self-regulation and self-determination of learning. In other words, learners were encouraged to engage in metacognition. They conduct their own background knowledge probes and determine the next steps in the learning process, with the focus on *process* rather than only on the dissemination and receiving of facts. Factual information remains important, but the idea of *knowing* shifts from being able to repeat information to being able to find, organize, and *use* that information (Simon, 1996, as cited in Bransford et al., 2000). This is vital in a field of study where the amount of knowledge increases daily. The result is a higher quality of learning where students value understanding over rote learning (Coles, 1990; Newble & Clarke, 1986; Rhem, 1998), the opposite of learning in traditional programs of study (Vernon & Blake, 1993).

The Role of Faculty in PBL

Traditional, teacher-dominated pedagogy does not create conditions for higher-order learning nor emphasize student responsibility for learning (Fincham & Shuler, 2001). In contrast, an instructor who consistently models reflective behavior, verbalizes his or her own thinking process, and explains the reasons is a highly effective tool for expanding students' awareness of the critical thinking process (Brookfield, 1987). Student participation, encouragement, and peer interactions have statistically significant relationships with positive change in critical thinking. Not surprisingly, time spent memorizing facts is associated with negative changes (Smith, 1977). The goal is thus to create a safe, nurturing environment that cultivates, encourages, expects, and rewards reflective thinking over scripted problem solving.

While faculty cannot control everything in their students' lives (nor would they want to), what they can control is classroom environment. Faculty are an integral element in the learning process: they make the decisions about instructional activities, choose which types of questions to ask in class, and decide whether to allow time for discussion and reflection. Their decisions should be congruent with instructional objectives. Students' cognitive gains have been linked to their interaction with faculty. The PBL method recognizes this relationship; it values intellectual interaction with students. With the tutor questioning, encouraging, coaching, and modeling, cognitive apprenticeship—another strategy based on constructivist theory—develops in the PBL context (Kerka, 1997). "Interaction between teachers and learners is one of the most powerful factors in promoting learning; interaction among learners is another" (Angelo, 1993, 7). PBL provides opportunities for both.

Educators who value critical thinking must evaluate their own roles in the incremental development of critical thinking (Facione et al., 1997; Greeno, 1989). They must model the type of behavior they hope to develop in students (Savery & Duffy, 1995). When learners are responsible for their own learning—and the self-regulation of that learning via metacognition—the role of faculty shifts from expert to metacognitive coach (Stepien, Gallagher, & Workman, 1993).

Faculty Opposition and Student Resistance

No one thinks PBL is easier or takes less time than traditional educational approaches. Faculty opposition to the methodology may be equaled by student resistance to the method (Rhem, 1998). "In the beginning, the learning curve for PBL students schooled in traditional, positivist approaches is steep" (Banta, Black, & Kline, 2000, 6). Students find it difficult to make the transition from didactic lecture and assessment involving recall of memorized facts to a more ambiguous environment where they must pose their own questions and discover answers independently (Stinson & Milter, 1996; Weissinger, 2003). The recommendation is to persist.

One key to teaching critical thinking is helping students keep a balance between old and new modes of thinking while providing a framework for newly acquired methods (Brookfield, 1987). In PBL, the learning environment is deliberately organized to create cognitive dissonance or disequilibrium, which students must struggle to resolve (Finkel, 2000; Woods, 1994). It involves sensitive gauging—too much and students experience frustration and overload; too little and learning is limited. Helping students with the transition to this very different approach to learning involves orientation, replete with opportunities for student self-reflection and faculty acknowledgment of impending frustration after more than 12 years of success in a didactic format (Weissinger, 2003). With skillful mentoring, "all but the most regimented of students make the transition and eventually thrive in the new learning environment" (Stinson & Milter, 1996, 41).

Why Metacognition?

As noted earlier in this chapter, metacognition, or self-reflection, is an important part of learning. It is a major component in developing critical thinking skills. However, the concept of metacognition is almost as vague as that of critical thinking. What does "thinking about thinking" mean? Positioned in the affective domain, metacognition slows down the thinking process so that learners take deliberate control of it (Beyer, 1987). It is consciously making logical connections between what is known (a person's internal representation of reality) and what is new (information heard or read). It is the intentional structuring and storage of information for later retrieval (Flavell, 1981; Hacker, Dunlosky, & Graesser, 1998). It is eliminating unrelated distractions during the process. It is acknowledging one's personal filtered version of the world. In other words, it is the self-management of learning (Hacker et al., 1998).

How successful one is depends on how skillful one is with the process. Just as any skill, it improves with practice. The PBL process provides many opportunities to develop and practice metacognition. For example, when confronted with a new idea or problem, students engaging in metacognition propose a plan, monitor it during implementation, and, when completed, determine how it went. The internal dialogue continues as one reflects on how things could or should be adjusted if a similar situation arises in the future (Costa & O'Leary, 1992). This is where and when true learning occurs.

As a teacher, most likely you are engaging regularly in metacognition yourself. Your self-reflection enables you to establish a deliberate environment for learning. You monitor how a class session is going, determining what is and what is not working as well as making mental notes on how you might change things the next time the topic is presented (Davidson & Worsham, 1992). This is the same type of internal dialogue in which your students should engage.

Opportunities for metacognition woven into the curriculum have increased the degree to which students transfer learning to new settings and across domains (Bransford et al., 2000; Everson, Tobias, & Laitusis, 1997). Metacognition focuses on oneself using good judgment with respect to knowledge. Journaling, discussion, and self-evaluation all provide opportunities for metacognition.

Metacognition may be new for your students, but it can be eased into the process with a few simple steps. Modeling the process is imperative. First, think aloud. Share with students how you have arrived at certain conclusions. Then, designate classroom time for this important step in learning. Pause and have the students think about what has occurred thus far in the class session. Have them restate what new information they have been presented and how that links to what they already know. Does knowing this new information change previous perceptions? Does the information affect how behaviors or approaches might change in the future? Suggest to students that they do the same when completing homework assignments or research.

In a PBL environment, students regularly engage in metacognition. When discussing a PBL problem, students think aloud, sharing their thoughts via description and/or visual representation. Other students in the group question for clarification or check for accuracy (Davidson & Worsham, 1992; Weissinger, 2003). At the same time, those listening should be thinking, "What am I hearing that supports what I thought before?" These exchanges begin the process of metacognition.

The goal is to enable students to become reflective critical thinkers who demonstrate a consistent intrinsic motivation to be aware, inquisitive, organized, analytical, confident, tolerant, judicious when weighing alternatives, and intellectually honest when judging whether to accept others' ideas and philosophies as truth or when challenged by circumstances (Facione et al., 1997; Hunkins, 1989; McCombs & Whisler, 1997). Their attitudes also should shift toward openness and a tolerance for diversity (Pascarella & Terenzini, 1991). Ultimately, transformative change occurs when people are willing to examine and challenge their own thinking (Senge, 1990).

What Is Holistic Assessment of Critical Thinking?

Critical thinking assessment looks to see whether anything is happening in the mind besides a huge acquisition and storage of information (White, 1970). Because thinking processes cannot be seen, it is difficult to determine when critical thinking has occurred. It is made easier when observable behaviors of critical thinking are identified. The purposes of critical thinking assessment include diagnosing the level of students' critical thinking; giving students feedback about their critical thinking prowess; motivating students to be better at critical thinking; informing faculty about the success of their efforts; conducting research on the topic; and holding schools accountable for the critical thinking competence of their students (Ennis, 1993). But assessing higher-order thinking skills, and critical thinking in particular, is difficult to accomplish because the thinking process cannot easily be "seen."

As the terms *critical thinking* and *problem solving* are sometimes used interchangeably, extracting critical thinking from the related concept, problem solving, is suggested. Critical thinking is the evaluative process that assists one in selecting the best solution. Problem solving is choosing a solution. Hunkins (1989) separates the concepts further, stating "problem solving . . . is not a thinking strategy but rather a heuristic organizer that allows us to contemplate ways in which we can and perhaps should organize and reorganize knowledge in order to solve perceived difficulty" (p. 9).

This model (Weissinger, 2003) advocates looking at all four components of critical thinking development, acknowledging that learning does not take place in a vacuum and may be influenced by outside factors. The key is using a mixture of multiple and varied measures to include normed instruments, locally prepared assessments, and other measures readily available through student records (Halpern, 1987). Instruments should be chosen because they complement the objectives of the PBL curriculum and target the basic components of critical thinking, which we shall discuss next (see also Figure 3).

Knowledge Base

A natural place to begin a tradition of longitudinal student assessment is in cognitive development (Astin, 1987). This implies drawing on assessment

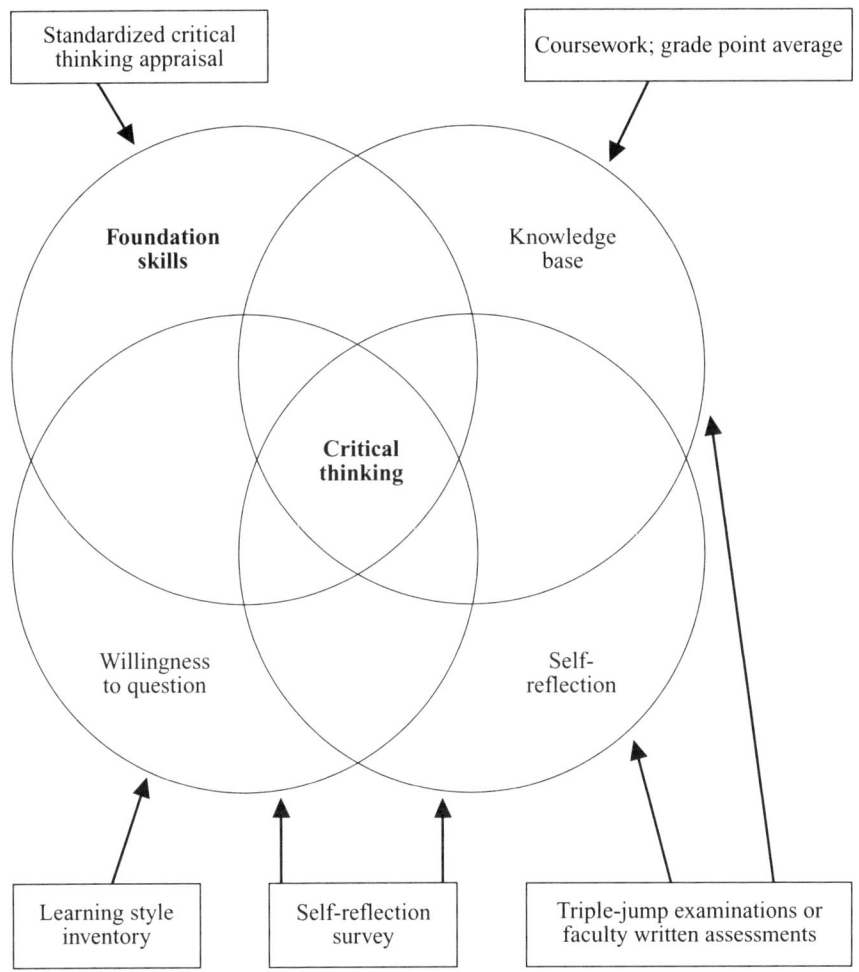

Standardized critical thinking appraisal

Coursework; grade point average

Foundation skills

Knowledge base

Critical thinking

Willingness to question

Self-reflection

Learning style inventory

Self-reflection survey

Triple-jump examinations or faculty written assessments

FIGURE **3**   Proposed instrumentation to assess the impact of the basic components of critical thinking on the change in critical thinking foundation skills

strategies currently in use in coursework. With an emphasis on outcomes, traditional evaluation methods such as objective, fact-based tests remain the most used method of assessment. Change in the knowledge base can be represented by course grade, semester GPA (grade point average), or other forms of faculty assessment. Assessment could also include monitoring the long-term retention and recall of information. The problem is that, while this can provide information about the knowledge base, it is often too narrow in scope to assess all that PBL claims to do.

Foundation Skills

Using a nationally standardized test lends credibility to a study and provides a basis for comparison with accepted normed measures. "Normed referenced tests are often broader in focus than criterion-references tests" (Mehrens & Lehmann, 1987, 19). There is no perfect test; each instrument has strengths and limitations as well as its critics and supporters.

Standardized tests have their fair share of critics (McPeck, 1981; Pike, 2001). First, conventional closed-response formats are criticized for being narrow in focus, providing only a snapshot of learning at one moment in time. However, that is precisely why they are a good option for assessing critical thinking foundation skills when used as both pretest and posttest. Second, most nationally standardized critical thinking tests use neutral content based on general information. A discipline-neutral content is actually appropriate when assessing critical thinking foundation skills and not knowledge base. At present, it is the best alternative, especially when based on the assumption that critical thinking skills are transferable across domains (Halpern, 1999). "To be proficient in a thinking skill or strategy means to be able to use that operation effectively and efficiently on one's own in a variety of appropriate contexts" (Beyer, 1987, 163). Therefore, you should locate a nationally standardized test that assesses skills similar to those identified as goals in PBL.

Willingness to Question

Surveys allow us a glimpse of student perceptions of their learning process. Student self-report surveys are a modest way to begin assessment (Astin, 1987). While self-report surveys have been scrutinized as legitimate forms of assessment (Hansen, 1998; Mehrens & Lehmann, 1987), in recent years student self-report surveys have "received serious consideration as valid means of assessment . . . as there is no reason why students cannot assess themselves on all content and lifelong learning standards" (Marzano, Pickering, & McTighe, 1993, 35). In an environment where self-assessment is a regular part of the process and since thinking takes place in one's mind, it seems natural to ask students to share their thoughts.

Choosing an established self-report survey is not always an option for two reasons. First, alternatives are limited; second, if you are interested in students' reflections about specific elements in the PBL process, then the survey items need to address those elements. Consider developing your own exit survey to assess students' perception of factors that may have an impact on the growth of critical thinking. Using a five-point Likert-type scale ranging from 5 (strongly agree) to 1 (strongly disagree), students can select responses corresponding to their level of agreement with statements. Some items can ask about students' perceptions of PBL as a methodology (e.g., PBL provides a safe environment for learning); some can reflect PBL's foundation in constructivist theory (e.g., I am able to tie new information to previous knowledge as a result of the PBL format). Items should be designed to inform faculty and to provide insight into student metacognition. Survey results, in combination with the ongoing self-reflection via written assessments, provide a realistic picture of the students.

Self-Reflection

Critical thinking is a dynamic process and must be coupled with opportunities for ongoing self-reflection (Arons, 1985; Brookfield, 1987; Halpern, 1999; McKeachie, 1999). Self-reflection is transformative; it provides a means for self-correcting actions (Moore & Hunter, 1993). As students reflect, they open their minds, learn new skills, and become confident about the application of their reasoning skills in academe and in life. Traditional, densely packed curricula often do not allow sufficient time for reflection (Fincham & Shuler, 2001). Students who assess their performance as critical thinkers are encouraged to improve continuously (Wolcott, 1999); assessment plays a major role in the transferability of skills to new situations (Doherty et al., 1996).

Self-report survey items can assess the self-reflection process too. Questions can search for insights on their personal experiences with PBL (e.g., The critical thinking strategies learned in this curriculum stimulate my thinking). Other items may ask students to assess their own level of critical thinking skills (e.g., I am confident in analyzing and evaluating what I read and/or hear). Other evaluation options include written assignments and projects, clinical evaluations and proficiencies, faculty and peer evaluations, and journaling. However, no consensus about the best method has been reached (Lim & Chen, 1999).

Conclusion

Change involves risk. The most difficult instructional development moment for a student is at the transition from knowledge as a discrete entity to a conception of knowledge specific to contextual relationships (Perry, 1970). Critical thinking is a pedagogical tool that creates discord but then helps students resolve the resulting cognitive conflict (Finkel, 2000; Woods, 1994). Students are pressed to identify and challenge assumptions; to explore alternative ways of thinking so that *artificial* resolutions do not occur; and to be flexible risk-takers (Brookfield, 1987). "Risk-taking is central to critical thinkers, for a hypothesis that is never generated can never be tested" (Siegel & Carey, 1989, 2).

Developmental journeys are not straight paths and cannot be fully explained by theory (Love & Guthrie, 1999). "Offering students the opportunity for self-determination, for soaring and crashing, is essential if they are to function in complex ways when they leave college" (Baxter Magolda, 1992, 362). As critical thinkers, students are asked to set aside familiar modes they have used for years that connect them to prior teachings (Nelson, 1999). A safe environment with opportunities for students to engage in metacognition involves them in their learning and hopefully will develop them into lifelong learners.

References

Aldred, M. J., & Aldred, S. E. (1998). Problem-based learning: The good, the bad, and the ugly. *Journal of Dental Education, 62,* 650–55.

Angelo, T. A. (1993). A teacher's dozen: Fourteen general, research-based principles for improving higher learning in our classrooms. *AAHE Bulletin, 45,* 3–13.

Angelo, T. A. (1995). Beginning the dialogue: Thoughts on promoting critical thinking. *Teaching of Psychology, 22,* 6–7.

Arons, A. B. (1979). Some thoughts on reasoning capacities implicitly expected of college students. In J. Lockhead & J. Clement (Eds.), *Cognitive process instruction: Research on teaching thinking skills* (pp. 209–15). Philadelphia: Franklin Institute Press.

Arons, A. B. (1985). Critical thinking and the baccalaureate curriculum. *Liberal Education, 71,* 141–57.

Arons, A. B. (1990). *A guide to introductory physics teaching.* New York: Wiley.

Astin, A. W. (1987). Assessment, value-added, and educational excellence. In D. F. Halpern (Ed.), *Student outcomes assessment: What institutions stand to gain* (pp. 89–107). New directions for higher education, No. 59. San Francisco: Jossey-Bass.

Ausubel, D. P., Novak, J. D., & Hanesian, H. (1978). *Educational psychology: A cognitive view* (2nd ed.). New York: Holt, Rinehart and Winston.

Banta, T. W., Black, K. E., & Kline, K. A. (2000). PBL 2000 plenary address offers evidence for and against problem-based learning. *PBL Insight, 3*, 1–11.

Barr, R. B., & Tagg, J. (1995). From teaching to learning: A new paradigm for undergraduate education. *Change, 27*, 13–25.

Baxter Magolda, M. (1992). *Knowing and reasoning in college: Gender-related patterns in students' intellectual development.* San Francisco: Jossey-Bass.

Belenky, M. F., Clinchy, B. M., Goldberger, N. R., & Tarule, J. M. (1986). *Women's ways of knowing: The development of self, voice, and mind.* New York: Basic Books.

Beyer, B. K. (1987). *Practical strategies for the teaching of thinking.* Boston: Allyn and Bacon.

Bloom, B. S. (Ed.) (1956). *Taxonomy of educational objectives: The classification of educational goals by a committee of college and university examiners.* New York: Longman.

Blumberg, P. (2000). Evaluating the evidence that problem-based learners are self-directed learners: A review of the literature. In D. H. Evensen & C. E. Hmelo (Eds.), *Problem-based learning: A research perspective on learning interactions* (pp. 199–226). Mahwah, NJ: Erlbaum.

Brandt, R. (1993). On teaching for understanding: A conversation with Howard Gardner. *Educational Leadership, 50*, 4–7.

Bransford, J. D., Brown, A. L., & Cocking, R. R. (Eds.) (2000). *How people learn: Brain, mind, experience, and school.* Washington, DC: National Academy Press.

Bridges, E. M., & Hallinger, P. (1998). Problem-based learning in medical and managerial education. In R. Fogarty (Ed.), *Problem-based learning: A collection of articles* (pp. 3–19). Arlington Heights, IL: Skylight.

Brookfield, S. D. (1987). *Developing critical thinkers: Challenging adults to explore alternative ways of thinking and acting.* San Francisco: Jossey-Bass.

Browne, M. N., & Keeley, S. N. (1994). *Asking the right questions: A guide to critical thinking.* Englewood Cliffs, NJ: Prentice Hall.

Chickering, A. W. (1981). *The modern American college.* San Francisco: Jossey-Bass.

Coles, C. R. (1990). Evaluating the effects curricula have on student learning: Toward a more competent theory for medical education. In Z. M. Nooman, H. G. Schmidt, & E. S. Ezzat (Eds.), *Innovation in medical education: An evaluation of its present status* (pp. 76–93). New York: Springer.

Cooper, J. L. (1995). Cooperative learning and critical thinking. *Teaching of Psychology, 22*, 7–9.

Costa, A. L., & O'Leary, P. W. (1992). The cooperative development of the intellect. In N. Davidson & T. Worsham (Eds.), *Enhancing thinking through cooperative learning* (pp. 41–65). New York: Teachers College Press.

Davidson, N., & Worsham, T. (Eds.) (1992). *Enhancing thinking through cooperative learning.* New York: Teachers College Press.

de Bono, E. (1978). *Teaching thinking.* Harmondsworth: Pelican.

de Sanchez, M. A. (1995). Using critical-thinking principles as a guide to college-level instruction. *Teaching of Psychology, 22*, 72–74.

Dewey, J. (1910). *How we think.* Boston: D. C. Heath.

Doherty, A., Chenevert, J., Miller, R. R., Roth, J. L., & Truchan, L. C. (1996). Developing intellectual skills. In J. G. Gaff, J. L. Ratcliff, & Associates (Eds.), *Handbook of the undergraduate curriculum: A comprehensive guide to purposes, structures, practices, and change* (pp. 170–89). San Francisco: Jossey-Bass.

Dressel, P. L., & Mayhew, L. B. (1954). *General education: Exploration in evaluation.* Final report of the Cooperative Study of Evaluation in General Education. Washington, DC: American Council on Education.

Ennis, R. H. (1993). Critical thinking assessment. *Theory into Practice, 32,* 179–86.

Ennis, R. H. (1996). *Critical thinking.* Upper Saddle River, NJ: Prentice Hall.

Everson, H. T., Tobias, S., & Laitusis, V. (1997). Do metacognitive skills and learning strategies transfer across domains? Paper presented at the Annual Convention of the American Educational Research Association. Chicago, IL (ERIC Document Reproduction Service No. ED 410 262).

Facione, P. A. (n.d.). *Critical thinking: What it is and why it counts.* http://www.calpress.com/critical.html.

Facione, P. A., Facione, N. C., & Giancarlo, C. A. F. (1996). The motivation to think in working and learning. In E. A. Jones (Ed.), *Preparing competent college graduates: Setting new and higher expectations for student learning* (pp. 67–79). New directions for higher education, No. 96. San Francisco: Jossey-Bass.

Fincham, A. G., & Shuler, C. F. (2001). The changing face of dental education: The impact of PBL. *Journal of Dental Education, 65,* 406–21.

Finkel, D. L. (2000). *Teaching with your mouth shut.* Portsmouth, NH: Boynton/Cook.

Flavell, J. H. (1979). Metacognition and cognitive monitoring: A new area of cognitive-developmental inquiry. *American Psychologist, 34,* 906–11.

Flavell, J. H. (1981). Cognitive monitoring. In W. P. Dickson (Ed.), *Children's oral communication skills* (pp. 906–11). New York: Academic Press.

Garetto, L. (2001). Tutor training workshop. Presentation for the Indiana University School of Dentistry, Indianapolis. September 13.

Greeno, J. G. (1989). A perspective on thinking. *American Psychologist, 44,* 134–41.

Hacker, D. J., Dunlosky, J., & Graesser, A. C. (1998) (Eds.), *Metacognition in educational theory and practice.* Mahwah, NJ: Erlbaum.

Halpern, D. F. (Ed.) (1987). *Student outcomes assessment: What institutions stand to gain.* New directions for higher education, No. 59. San Francisco: Jossey-Bass.

Halpern, D. F. (1996). *Thought and knowledge* (3rd ed.). Mahwah, NJ: Erlbaum.

Halpern, D. F. (1998). Teaching critical thinking for transfer across domains: Dispositions, skills, structure training, and metacognitive monitoring. *American Psychologist, 53,* 449–55.

Halpern, D. F. (1999). Teaching for critical thinking: Helping college students develop the skills and dispositions of a critical thinker. In M. D. Svinicki (Ed.), *Teaching and learning on the edge of the millennium: Building on what we have learned* (pp. 69–74). New directions for teaching and learning, No. 80. San Francisco: Jossey-Bass.

Halpern, D. F., & Nummedal, S. G. (1995). Closing thoughts about helping students improve how they think. *Teaching of Psychology, 22,* 82–83.

Hanley, G. L. (1995). Teaching critical thinking: Focusing on metacognitive skills and problem solving. *Teaching of Psychology, 22*, 68–72.

Hansen, E. J. (1998). Essential demographics of today's college students. *AAHE Bulletin, 51*, 3–5.

Hunkins, F. P. (1989). *Teaching thinking through effective questioning.* Boston: Christopher-Gordon.

Kerka, S. (1997). *Constructivism, workplace learning, and vocational education.* EDRS document link, http://orders.edrs.com/members/sp.cfm?AN=ED407573.

King, P. M., & Kitchener, K. S. (1994). *Developing reflective judgment: Understanding and promoting intellectual growth and critical thinking in adolescents and adults.* San Francisco: Jossey-Bass.

Kirby, G. R., & Goodpaster, J. (1999). *Instructor's manual for Thinking* (2nd ed.). Upper Saddle River, NJ: Prentice Hall.

Kurfiss, J. G. (1988). *Critical thinking: Theory, research, practice, and possibilities.* ASHE–ERIC higher education report No. 2. Washington, DC: Association for the Study of Higher Education.

Lim, L. P., & Chen, A. Y. (1999). Challenges and relevance of problem-based learning in dental education. *European Journal of Dental Education, 3*, 20–26.

Love, P. G., & Guthrie, V. L. (1999). *Understanding and applying cognitive development theory.* New directions for student services, No. 88. San Francisco: Jossey-Bass.

Marzano, R. J., Pickering, D., & McTighe, J. (1993). *Assessing student outcomes.* Alexandria, VA: Association for Supervision and Curriculum Development.

Maudsley, G., & Strivens, J. (2000). Promoting professional knowledge, experiential learning and critical thinking for medical students. *Medical Education, 34*, 535–44.

McCombs, B. L., & Whisler, J. S. (1997). *The learner-centered classroom and school.* San Francisco: Jossey-Bass.

McKeachie, W. J. (1999). *Teaching tips: Strategies, research, and theory for college and university teachers* (10th ed.). Boston: Houghton Mifflin.

McPeck, J. E. (1981). *Critical thinking and education.* Oxford: Martin Robertson.

Mehrens, W. A., & Lehmann, I. J. (1987). *Using standardized tests in education.* White Plains, NY: Longman.

Moore, W. S., & Hunter, S. (1993). Beyond "mildly interesting facts": Student self-evaluations and outcomes assessment. In J. MacGregor (Ed.), *Student self-evaluation: Fostering reflective learning* (pp. 65–82). New directions for teaching and learning, No. 56. San Francisco: Jossey-Bass.

National Education Goals Panel (1991). *The national education goals report.* Washington, DC.

Neilson, A. R. (1989). *Critical thinking and reading: Empowering learners to think and act.* Urbana, IL: National Council of Teachers of English.

Nelson, C. E. (1994). Critical thinking and collaborative learning. In K. Bosworth & S. J. Hamilton (Eds.), *Collaborative learning: Underlying processes and effective techniques* (pp. 45–58). New directions for teaching and learning, No. 59. San Francisco: Jossey-Bass.

Nelson, C. E. (1997). Tools for tampering with teaching's taboos. In W. E. Campbell & K. A. Smith (Eds.), *New paradigms for college teaching* (pp. 51–77). Edina, MN: Interaction Book Co.

Nelson, C. E. (1999). On the persistence of unicorns: The trade-off between content and critical thinking revisited. In B. A. Pescosolido & R. Aminzade (Eds.), *The social worlds of higher education: Handbook for teaching in a new century* (pp. 168–84). Thousand Oaks, CA: Pine Forge Press.

Newble, D. I., & Clarke, R. M. (1986). The approaches to learning of students in a traditional and in an innovative problem-based medical school. *Medical Education, 19,* 267–73.

Newmann, F. M., & Wehlage, G. G. (1993). Five standards of authentic instruction. *Educational Leadership, 50,* 8–12.

Pascarella, E. T., & Terenzini, P. T. (1991). *How college affects students: Findings and insights from twenty years of research.* San Francisco: Jossey-Bass.

Pellegrino, J. W. (1995). Technology in support of critical thinking. *Teaching of Psychology, 22,* 11–12.

Perkins, D. N. (1985). Thinking frames: An integrative perspective on teaching cognitive skills. Paper presented at the ASCD Conference on Approaches to Teaching Thinking. Alexandria, VA, August.

Perry, W. G. (1970). *Forms of intellectual and ethical development in the college years.* New York: Holt, Rinehart and Winston.

Pike, G. R. (2001). Assessment measures: The CRESST problem solving measures. *Assessment Update, 13,* 14–15.

Rhem, J. (1998). Problem-based learning: An introduction. *National Teaching and Learning Forum, 8,* 1–4.

Ryan, M. P. (1984). Monitoring text comprehension: Individual differences in epistemological standards. *Journal of Educational Psychology, 76,* 248–58.

Samford University (n.d.). *Problem-based learning.* http://www.samford.edu/pbl.what.html.

Savery, J. R., & Duffy, T. M. (1995). Problem-based learning: An instructional model and its constructivist framework. *Educational Technology, 35,* 31–38.

Schunk, D. H. (2000). *Learning theories: An educational perspective* (3rd ed.). Upper Saddle River, NJ: Merrill.

Senge, P. M. (1990). *The fifth discipline: The art and practice of the learning organization.* New York: Doubleday.

Siegel, H. (1980). Critical thinking as an educational ideal. *Educational Forum, 45,* 7–23.

Siegel, M., & Carey, R. F. (1989). *Critical thinking: A semiotic perspective.* Bloomington, IN: ERIC Clearinghouse on Reading and Communication Skills.

Simon, H. A. (1996). Observations on the sciences of science learning. Paper prepared for the Committee on Developments in the Science of Learning for the Sciences of Science Learning: An Interdisciplinary Discussion. Department of Psychology, Carnegie Mellon University.

Sirotnik, K. (1983). What you see is what you get: Consistency, persistency, and mediocrity in classrooms. *Harvard Education Review, 53,* 16–31.

Smith, D. G. (1977). College classroom interactions and critical thinking. *Journal of Educational Psychology*, *69*, 180–90.

Stepien, W. J., Gallagher, S. A., & Workman, D. (1993). Problem-based learning for traditional and interdisciplinary classrooms. *Journal for the Education of the Gifted*, *16*, 338–57.

Stinson, J. E., & Milter, R. G. (1996). Problem-based learning in business education: Curriculum design and implementation issues. In L. Wilkerson & W. H. Gijselaers (Eds.), *Bringing problem-based learning to higher education: Theory and practice* (pp. 33–42). New directions for teaching and learning, No. 68. San Francisco: Jossey-Bass.

Svinicki, M. D. (1991). Practical implications of cognitive theories. In R. J. Menges & M. D. Svinicki (Eds.), *College teaching: From theory to practice* (pp. 27–37). New directions for teaching and learning, No. 45. San Francisco: Jossey-Bass.

Svinicki, M. D. (Ed.) (1999). *Teaching and learning on the edge of the millennium: Building on what we have learned*. New directions for teaching and learning, No. 80. San Francisco: Jossey-Bass.

Taba, H. (1965). Teaching of thinking. *Elementary English*, *42*, 534.

Thoms, K. J. (1998). Critical thinking requires critical questioning. *Teaching Excellence*, *10*, 7.

U.S. Congress (1994). *Goals 2000: National Goals for Education Act*. Washington, DC.

Vernon, D. T. A., & Blake, R. L. (1993). Does problem-based learning work? A meta-analysis of evaluative research. *Academic Medicine*, *68*, 550–63.

Weiss, C. A. (1992/1993). But how do we get them to think? *Teaching Excellence*, *4*, 5.

Weissinger, P. A. (2003). Critical thinking skills of first-year dental students enrolled in a hybrid curriculum with a problem-based learning component. Doctoral dissertation, Indiana University, Bloomington.

White, R. W. (1970). Foreword. In W. G. Perry, *Forms of intellectual and ethical development in the college years* (pp. v–vii). New York: Holt, Rinehart and Winston.

Wolcott, S. K. (1999). Developing and assessing critical thinking and lifelong learning skills through student self-evaluations. *Assessment Update*, *11*, 4–5, 16.

Wood, P. K. (1997). Assessment measures: Critical thinking assessment at the University of Missouri, Columbia. *Assessment Update*, *9*, 11–13.

Woods, D. R. (1994). *How to gain the most from problem-based learning*. Waterdown, Ontario: Donald R. Woods.

Woolfolk, A. (2001). *Educational psychology* (8th ed.). Boston: Allyn and Bacon.

CHAPTER 4

Exploring the Cognitive Processes of Problem-based Learning and Their Relationship to Talent Development

William Y. Wu
Victor Forrester

Problem-based Learning and Talent Development

A common feature among countries open to globalization is a movement within education reforms toward talent development. In Hong Kong, the movement is detectable by the formal defining of generic skills that are held to facilitate individual student learning (Hong Kong Curriculum Development Council, 2001). Such movements toward prioritizing the talent development of individual students mark a move away from assimilation theories of learning, where students amass and assimilate taught knowledge, toward constructivist theories of learning, where students actively construct their own knowledge.

With the change in the underpinning educational theory, there follows a change in pedagogy. One pedagogic approach that appears to facilitate the active construction of knowledge—and for this reason has aroused keen interest—is problem-based learning (PBL).

PBL: Definitions and Characteristics

PBL exists under various guises, ranging from the definitive nature of Biggs and Moore (1993), "Learning declarative and procedural knowledge in a context that has defined a need for that knowledge," to the comprehensiveness of Fogarty (1997), "PBL is a curriculum model designed around real-life problems that are ill-structured, open-ended, or ambiguous. PBL can be applied across the entire curriculum."

Whatever their definitive guises, PBL approaches are seen to display a range of common characteristics:

- All PBL approaches begin with a problem or question (Duffy & Cunningham, 1996; Grabinger, 1996).
- The process of PBL involves clarification, definition with reframing, analysis, and summary with synthesis (Tan, 2003).
- Students assume primary responsibility for analyzing the problem and making inquiry (Slavin, Madden, Dolan, & Wasik, 1994).
- The teacher's role is primarily facilitative (Stepien & Gallagher, 1993).

Enveloped by these common PBL characteristics, students find themselves in a learning context that apparently requires them to (Fogarty, 1997, 3):

- meet the problem
- define the problem
- gather the facts
- generate questions
- make hypotheses
- rephrase the problem
- generate alternative solutions
- present the solutions, preferably with justifications

Within this learning context, the prescribed role of students is to assume primary responsibility for their learning—a role that has linked PBL with self-directed learning.

PBL and Self-directed Learning

The cognitive processes of self-directed learning are delineated in a model by Eggen and Kauchak (2001): Students first assess their own knowledge base with regard to the problem presented to them. They then identify their knowledge or information gaps. Finally, plans are developed to address their knowledge or information gaps. When sufficient information is gathered, the problem is solved. Where insufficient information is available, the deficiency stimulates the development of new learning strategies. Within these twin cognitive processes, the role of the teacher is to raise facilitative questions, such as: What do you already know? What additional information do you need? Where can you find this information?

For Eggen and Kauchak (2001), one of the goals of PBL is specifically the development of self-directed learning, which enables learners to become "aware of and take control of their learning progress" (p. 229). The claim that PBL is linked specifically to self-directed learning is significant, for it elevates both concepts from being considered at the level of cognition to also being validly considered at the level of metacognition.

Theoretical support for a metacognitive view of PBL in the development of self-directed learning skills is drawn from information processing theories of transfer as well as sociocultural theories such as cognitive apprenticeship (Hmelo & Lin, 2000). Such theoretical support is appealing, for information transfer and cognitive apprenticeship imply that learning is active and progressive, that the processes involved in active learning are integrated and directly evidential of individual talent development.

This attractive logic is further extended by claims that, in PBL, students continually apply their knowledge and accordingly are gaining incremental practice of their self-directed learning strategies. Such common ground between problem solving and incremental self-directed learning suggests a naturally occurring osmosis that predicts not only talent growth but also talent growth that is transferable across novel problems (Hmelo & Lin, 2000). In other words, PBL offers a form of learning that is transferable.

PBL: A Cognitive Apprenticeship?

The view that PBL offers a form of learning that is transferable has become embedded in both the vocabulary and the methodology of PBL. The vocabulary of PBL includes the educational notion of *scaffolding*, a descriptive term describing that part of the PBL methodology that emphasizes the role of context. For example:

> An appropriate context forms a basis or scaffolding within which learners can receive the information they need to know (Coles, 1997, 316).

Context and *scaffolding* are therefore interchangeable for they serve the one common need in learners for some form of initial support. This view of context and scaffolding serving a common initial need is elaborated in the following:

> In the early stages of a course, or where the information is novel and complex and perhaps from a variety of distinct sources, the information could be suitably packaged and provided for students. Later in courses, or in the areas where students have some background experience and knowledge, they can independently identify sources of the necessary information (Coles, 1997, 318).

With the assumptions of cognitive apprenticeship and transferable learning, the active learner's needs will appear to change: what was a need becomes "background experience" and, in turn, this background experience appears to serve as a prompt or guide empowering the learner to independently access "the necessary information."

This view of an active learner serving a cognitive apprenticeship is appealing. However, it is a view that remains as yet unsupported by substantive evidence. According to Marincovich (2000), the research base is not yet firm enough for PBL advocates to state unequivocally that PBL results in improved student learning. The challenge highlighted by Marincovich is significant: although PBL may promote learning activity, there is as yet little evidence to relate that activity to specific learning outcomes. In the murky world of cognitive processes, there is always a risk of confusing correlation with causation.

Multiple Intelligences

Shining a light into the murky world of cognitive processes is our current understanding of multiple intelligences (MI). Armstrong (2000) offers a classification of MI into eight categories (p. 4):

1. *Linguistic:* sensitivity to the sounds, structure, meanings, and functions of words and language (e.g., writer)
2. *Logical–mathematical:* sensitivity to, and capacity to discern, logical or numerical patterns; ability to handle long chains of reasoning (e.g., mathematician)
3. *Spatial:* capacity to perceive the visual–spatial world accurately and to perform transformations on one's initial perceptions (e.g., artist)

4. *Bodily–kinesthetic:* ability to control one's body movements and to handle objects skillfully (e.g., athlete)
5. *Musical:* ability to produce and appreciate rhythm, pitch, and timbre; appreciation of the forms of musical expressiveness (e.g., composer)
6. *Interpersonal:* capacity to discern and respond appropriately to the moods, temperaments, motivations, and desires of other people (e.g., counselor)
7. *Intrapersonal:* access to one's own feelings and the ability to discriminate among one's emotions; knowledge of one's own strengths and weaknesses (e.g., psychotherapist)
8. *Naturalist:* expertise in distinguishing between members of a species; recognizing the existence of other neighboring species; and charting out the relations, formally or informally, between several species (e.g., biologist)

These eight categories are neither exclusive nor indivisible (Armstrong, 2000); rather they may be viewed as learning nodes through which an individual may both acquire and express learning.

MI have been described in terms which emphasize that they are naturally occurring phenomena (Armstrong, 2000, 8–9):

- Each person possesses all eight intelligences.
- Most people can develop each intelligence to an adequate level of competency.
- Intelligences usually work together in complex ways.
- There are many ways to be intelligent within each category.

From this viewpoint, if MI are indeed naturally occurring, the argument arises that effective education is that which accesses and engages all eight intelligences. It is in this way—as a measure of educational adequacy— that current interest in MI has been aroused. To measure educational adequacy, it appears logical to evaluate current educational practice not in terms of its measurable output but, more revealingly, in terms of its ability to offer an input that addresses the full range of an individual's ability to learn. When the input addresses an individual's full range of intelligences, then that individual is deemed to be learning at maximum capacity. Although as yet unsupported by evidence, this reasoning retains an a priori validity. It is in this light that we now consider the interactive view afforded by MI and the input offered by a PBL approach to education.

MI and PBL

Weber (2000) has adapted MI into a Multiple Intelligence Teaching Approach model. This model comprises five phases:

1. Questions and dialogue to solve key problems around the required subject content
2. Identification by students and teachers of specific learning objectives, stated in doable and measurable terms
3. Requirement of the class to create a rubric that shows exactly how assignments will be graded to ensure that specific objectives are attained and content understood
4. Choice by students of an assessment task that allows them to demonstrate multiple approaches to expressing deep understanding of their topic
5. Student reflection

Such categories, though helpful, might be questioned as oversimplifying the underlying complexity. The five phases are discrete and clearly targeted (e.g., solve key problems, then identify specific learning objectives); in contrast, MI have been described as usually working together in complex ways (Armstrong, 2000). Though attractive, the five-phase model is open to the challenge that it is an artifice imposed on, rather than freely drawing from, individual students' capacity to learn through a range of interacting MI.

In contrast to the five neat phases, PBL has been more objectively described as starting with an ill-structured mess (Gardner, 1983). It is from addressing this initial "mess" that students use their many intelligences—through discussion and research—to determine the real issue at hand (Fogarty, 1997). This description of the PBL process—a progression from addressing a mess to determining the real issue—captures the elements of MI as interconnected work. For example, students can use their bodily–kinesthetic intelligence through experiential, hands-on learning, their interpersonal intelligence to interview others, their intrapersonal intelligence to reflect on the problem, and their logical–mathematical intelligence to reason logically (Fogarty, 1997).

Drawing from this view of PBL, it is now possible to depict the potential relationship between MI and PBL, as shown in Figure 1. In the figure, a potential relationship is posited indicating that PBL may work in tandem with our understanding of MI. In sum, PBL offers a mess or problem, the

Multiple intelligences	Problem-based learning
An interaction between	An interaction with a "mess" requiring the use of
• linguistic • logical–mathematical • spatial • bodily–kinesthetic • musical • interpersonal • intrapersonal and • naturalist intelligences produces evidence of learning*	• linguistic • logical–mathematical • spatial • bodily–kinesthetic • musical • interpersonal • intrapersonal and • naturalist intelligences produces evidence of a solution that is taken to embody evidence of learning†

* Where all intelligences are engaged and activated, then it is assumed that what occurs is capacity learning.

† A PBL mess that engages and activates all intelligences is assumed to produce an outcome that represents the individual's capacity learning.

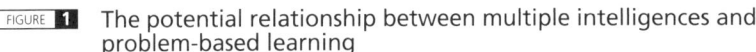 FIGURE **1**   The potential relationship between multiple intelligences and problem-based learning

solution to which fully engages MI. The close relationship between PBL and MI is explored in Table 1 with reference to one possible PBL example, which shows that resolving the PBL problem appears to fully engage MI.

The Roles of Questioning and Visualization

Where resolving a PBL problem appears to fully engage MI, we can now refine our understanding of the twin roles of questioning and visualization in cognitive processes. First, we consider the potential roles of questioning, which are set out in Table 2.

Questioning within PBL appears to take the form of six roles: to remember, understand, apply, analyze, evaluate, and create (Anderson & Krathwohl, 2001). Each appears to have a discrete role within the cognitive processes activated by PBL.

These six roles have been placed into one of two subsets. The first subset includes questions that are labeled broad or divergent; the second includes questions that are considered narrow or convergent. Broad or

TABLE **1** An example of the potential relationship between multiple intelligences and problem-based learning

	Problem-based learning		
Intelligence	Planning	Data collection	Result presentation
Linguistic	Examine the meaning of words and terminologies used in the questions given	Read relevant books	Present findings in written form and storytelling
Logical–mathematical	Break down and calculate the quantities of questions to be solved	Create codes for data collected	Present findings logically and sequentially
Spatial	Use mind map to capture brainstorming	Draw charts, graphs, diagrams, and maps	Use computer graphics to present findings
Bodily–kinesthetic	Consider body language	Evaluate body language	Employ effective body language
Musical	Locate harmony and disharmony	Establish a working rhythm	Communicate the harmony of discovery
Interpersonal	Use group brainstorming	Involve the community	Cooperate to present findings
Intrapersonal	Record own ideas through journal keeping	Make private spaces for reflecting on data	Include one-minute reflection periods
Naturalist	Be aware of environmental influences on the content matter	Draw on own experience	Connect to environmental thinking

TABLE **2** Potential roles of questioning in problem-based learning

Role of questioning	Problem-based learning		
	Planning	Data collection	Result presentation
Remember	What are the major characteristics of . . . ?	How should I store/record my data?	What key prompts serve my presentation needs?
Understand	What question(s) does the set problem pose?	What categories could it be classified into?	Who is my target audience?
Apply	Do I have relevant prior knowledge?	How is . . . related to . . . ?	What style of presentation is appropriate?
Analyze	How is the problem constructed?	What evidence can I list for . . . ?	What sequence "tells this story"?
Evaluate	What is required to address this problem?	What is the relevance of this data to my problem?	Is this where I should be in the light of what I have done so far?
Create	What additional knowledge do I require?	How can I visualize this data?	What do you suggest if you are asked to produce a new . . . ?

divergent questions encourage thinking that moves in many directions and on a broad front. In contrast, narrow or convergent questions encourage thinking to narrow down, to focus on a particular point. The significance of these question subsets is that, in general, they appear to call on different levels of thinking. Broad or divergent questions, it has been argued, are more likely to utilize higher-order thinking. In contrast, narrow or convergent questioning is more likely to activate lower-order thinking (Sweeting, 1992). It has further been argued that these orders of thinking indicate a thinking aristocracy—for example, thinking of a lower order is taken to involve only memory or observation—with the implication that higher-order questions should be more educational (Sweeting, 1992).

However, from the perspective of MI, there is no thinking aristocracy, for thinking is no longer separate and divisible; rather it is a symptom of MI in action. From this MI perspective, the apparently six discrete roles of questioning within PBL represent six roles of the same cognitive activity. The engaged student utilizes each questioning role in terms of its contribution to the problem's resolution. In short, PBL appears to generate a questioning pragmatism.

We now turn to the potential roles of visual tools in cognitive processes. It is suggested that there are three roles for visual tools in cognitive processes:

1. *Organizing information:* The human mind organizes and stores information in a series of networks (Ausubel, 1968; Hyerle, 2000). Visual tools include visual depictions resembling networks that enable students to add or modify their background knowledge by seeing the connections and contradictions between existing knowledge and new information.

2. *Understanding information and relationships:* Visual tools serve as mental tools to help students understand and retain important information and relationships (Vygotsky, 1965; Rice, 1994).

3. *Depicting knowledge and understanding:* Visual tools provide an optional way of expressing knowledge and understanding, so they are particularly beneficial for students who have difficulty with expressing relationships in written format (Hong Kong Education Department, 2001).

Given these three roles for visual tools, the question arises as to how PBL activates this visual generation, change, and communication of information.

TABLE 3 Visual tools in problem-based learning

	Problem-based learning		
Visual tool	Planning	Data collection	Result presentation
Brainstorming webs	✓	✓	✓
Graphic organizers	✓	✓	✓
Thinking process maps	✓	✓	✓

First, it is helpful to recognize that *visual tools* is an umbrella term for different mental mapping techniques (Hyerle, 1996). These visual mapping techniques have been described as including (Hyerle, 2001, 402):

- brainstorming webs (e.g., clustering, mindscaping, and mind maps)
- graphic organizers (e.g., Bloom's "one-shot thinking")
- thinking process maps (e.g., thinking patterns, conceptual development)

Such visual tools, for Hyerle, offer "open systems for thinking outside of the box" (2001, 403). The potential of such visual tools for PBL is illustrated in Table 3, which shows that visual tools may play a role not only at all levels of PBL activities but also in complementary and mutually supportive ways. For example, brainstorming webs may be utilized along with graphic organizers and/or thinking process maps to promote further planning. In this respect, PBL appears to embrace both questioning and visual tools with an open pragmatism that considers and prioritizes all forms of learning—all forms of MI—in terms of their contribution to problem resolution.

Schema for PBL

Incorporating our current understanding of the potential relationships between PBL, MI, and the tools of visualization and questioning, we can now construct a schema for PBL, as depicted in Figure 2.

The schema posits a full activation of MI in the individual's progression from perceiving a mess to being able to present a solution. Integral to this positive progression are the tools of both questioning and visualization. The "outcome" in the figure refers to both the solution and the entire process, both of which are held as evidence of learning.

An interaction with a (problem-based learning) "mess" activates the use of (multiple intelligences)
- linguistic
- logical–mathematical
- spatial
- bodily–kinesthetic
- musical
- interpersonal
- intrapersonal and
- naturalist intelligences

which accentuates the tools of questioning and visualization and produces an outcome (a solution) that is taken to embody evidence of learning

FIGURE **2**   A schema for problem-based learning

Implications for Theory Building

The impact of any schema or model on theory building is essentially to act as a stimulus. The proposed schema for PBL raises many questions. One question is if this schema is appropriate for capturing the essential complexity and interrelated nature of MI—where it serves to offer an overview rather than detailed workings, then perhaps this schema is justified. One may also ask if active use of MI depends on being presented with PBL. MI are actually in constant active use. The presentation of PBL provides a focus. Any one focus, by definition, will simultaneously prioritize certain facets of MI while diminishing other facets. In doing so, it is assumed that PBL draws on the complementary nature inherent within MI. There is also the question of whether the role of MI is negated by the accentuated roles of questioning and visualization. The accentuated roles of questioning and visualization need not negate any one of the MI. Where questioning and visualization are taken as wide-ranging cognitive and behavioral functions, it is possible to see their accentuated roles as evidence of a pragmatic interplay among all of the MI.

Implications for Research

The role of any schema or model for future research is essentially to act as a guide. The schema for PBL raises many possible areas for research. For example:

- Is there evidence that an interaction with a problem activates MI?
- Which form or model of a problem fully activates MI?
- What are the "normal" roles of questioning and visualization within MI?
- Which form or model of a problem fully activates the roles of questioning and visualization within MI?
- Is there evidence that a PBL outcome (a solution) embodies evidence of learning?
- Is the assumed linear relationship between PBL and MI valid?

Implications for Enhanced Practice

The implication of any one schema or model on enhanced PBL practice is essentially to empower creative pedagogic thinking. The schema for PBL raises many possible areas for enhanced PBL practice. For example, the PBL schema may raise pre-teaching awareness, first, by defining the difficulty level of the problem appropriate to the developmental stages of MI (reflected in student maturity) and, second, by relating students' prior and present learning experiences in terms of promoting students' actuation of all components of MI.

In teaching PBL, student activity can be considered in terms of fully engaging the interrelated activity of MI. Accordingly, the PBL class can involve both group and individual work where the individual's output need not be predetermined and in which the learning process prioritizes flexibility and responsiveness to situations on the part not only of the student but equally of the instructor. In this light, PBL recognizes learning that may take place both inside and outside the classroom and both within and without the traditional concepts of a timetable.

With regard to assessment, PBL need not be subject-specific nor examination-focused because, although its end product of knowledge acquisition can be formally examined, it equally promotes other educational products, such as interpersonal skill and questioning skill development. In the PBL lesson, presenting a solution may be less important than generating a question as evidence of utilization of MI. In this light, there may be no distinction between assessing PBL and assessing an individual's capacity to fully engage in lifelong learning.

Having considered some of the implications for theory building, research, and enhanced practice, we now consider what this schema may indicate about the nature of PBL.

The Nature of PBL: Relationship between Pedagogy and Philosophic Underpinnings

PBL—as displayed in the above discussion—is complex and comprehensive in nature. For example, the proposed schema for PBL illustrates something of its potential to empower creative pedagogic thinking. Where this creative process involves an accumulation of experiences, at a metaphysical level the philosophic root of PBL draws on pragmatism. However, where PBL has its focus on drawing out from students their own knowledge, then the PBL philosophic root draws on idealism (Gutek, 1997). Such potential for philosophic pluralism points to the chameleon nature of PBL.

An example of PBL's chameleon nature is the philosophic stance inherent in adopting an MI approach to PBL. The MI approach to PBL carries with it a basic philosophic stance of holistic pragmatism, for it is implicitly assumed that each individual both has and constantly has access to MI. From this pragmatic base flow several philosophic assumptions:

- that it rests on individuals to fully exercise their own MI
- that the individual learns both in isolation and in group interaction
- that learning is natural
- that education is a preparation for life
- that learning is by nature an experience-building activity
- that lifelong learning is natural
- that the classroom and life should not be polarized
- that individuals will learn better at their own pace
- that the PBL problem can be applicable to all levels and categories of learning
- that PBL is not restricted to pedagogy but rather embodies philosophic ideals

Although not exhaustive, this list serves to place any consideration and evaluation of PBL within a broad spectrum ranging from concerns with its pedagogic implementation to a recognition of PBL's chameleon nature.

Summation

This chapter has adopted both tentative and questioning personas with the intention of highlighting that the cognitive processes involved in PBL remain largely uncharted. This tentative exploration of the uncharted PBL cognitive processes has been guided by current perspectives of MI combined with an understanding of the twin tools of questioning and visualization. Informed by these, a schema for PBL has been derived. This schema then served to highlight potential implications in the areas of theory building, research, and enhanced practice with respect to PBL. From there, the pedagogy and resultant philosophic nature of PBL were considered and posited as illustrating that, where PBL is perceived through the holistic pragmatism of MI, it too offers an empowering holistic view of learning and talent development.

References

Anderson, L. W., & Krathwohl, D. R. (Eds.) (2001). *A taxonomy for learning, teaching and assessing: A revision of Bloom's taxonomy of educational objectives.* New York: Longman.

Armstrong, T. (2000). *Multiple intelligences in the classroom* (2nd ed.). Alexandria, VA: Association for Supervision and Curriculum Development.

Ausubel, D. P. (1968). *Educational psychology: A cognitive view.* New York: Holt, Reinhart and Winston.

Biggs, J. B., & Moore, P. J. (1993). *The process of learning.* Sydney: Prentice Hall.

Coles, C. (1997). Is problem-based learning the only way? In D. Boud & G. I. Feletti (Eds.), *The challenge of problem-based learning* (2nd ed., pp. 313–25). London: Kogan Page.

Duffy, T. M., & Cunningham, D. J. (1996). Constructivism: Implications for the design and delivery of instruction. In D. H. Jonassen (Ed.), *Handbook of research for educational communications and technology* (pp. 170–98). New York: Macmillan.

Eggen, P. D., & Kauchak, D. P. (2001). *Strategies for teachers: Teaching content and thinking skills* (4th ed.). Boston: Allyn and Bacon.

Fogarty, R. (1997). *Problem-based learning and other curriculum models for the multiple intelligences classroom.* Melbourne: Hawker Brownlow Education.

Gardner, H. (1983). *Frames of mind: The theory of multiple intelligences.* New York: Basic Books.

Grabinger, R. (1996). Rich environments for active learning. In D. H. Jonassen (Ed.), *Handbook of research for educational communications and technology* (pp. 665–92). New York: Macmillan.

Gutek, G. L. (1997). *Philosophical and ideological perspectives on education* (2nd ed.). Boston: Allyn and Bacon.

Hmelo, C. E., & Lin, X. (2000). Becoming self-directed learners: Strategy development in problem-based learning. In D. H. Evensen & C. E. Hmelo (Eds.), *Problem-based learning: A research perspective on learning interactions* (pp. 227–50). Mahwah, NJ: Erlbaum.

Hong Kong Curriculum Development Council (2001). *Learning to learn: Life-long learning and whole-person development*. Hong Kong.

Hong Kong Education Department (2001). *The use of graphic organizers to enhance thinking skills in the learning of economics*. Hong Kong.

Hyerle, D. (1996). *Visual tools for constructing knowledge*. Alexandria, VA: Association for Supervision and Curriculum Development.

Hyerle, D. (2000). *A field guide to using visual tools*. Alexandria, VA: Association for Supervision and Curriculum Development.

Hyerle, D. (2001). Visual tools for mapping minds. In A. L. Costa (Ed.), *Developing minds: A resource book for teaching thinking* (3rd ed., pp. 401–7). Alexandria, VA: Association for Supervision and Curriculum Development.

Marincovich, M. (2000). Problems and promises in problem-based learning. In O. S. Tan, P. Little, S. Y. Hee, & J. Conway (Eds.), *Problem-based learning: Educational innovation across disciplines* (pp. 3–11). Singapore: Temasek Centre for Problem-Based Learning.

Rice, G. E. (1994). Need for explanations in graphic organizer research. *Reading Psychology: An International Quarterly*, *15*, 39–67.

Slavin, R., Madden, N., Dolan, L., & Wasik, B. (1994). Roots and wings: Inspiring academic excellence. *Educational Leadership*, *52*, 10–14.

Stepien, W. J., & Gallagher, S. A. (1993). Problem-based learning: As authentic as it gets. *Educational Leadership*, *50*, 25–28.

Sweeting, T. (1992). *Questioning*. Teaching in Hong Kong, No. 11. Hong Kong: Longman.

Tan, O. S. (2003). *Problem-based learning innovation: Using problems to power learning in the 21st century*. Singapore: Thomson Learning.

Vygotsky, L. S. (1965). *Thought and language* (E. Hanfmann & G. Vakar, Eds. & Trans.). Cambridge, MA: MIT Press.

Weber, E. (2000). Five phases to PBL: MITA (Multiple Intelligence Teaching Approach) model for redesigned higher education classes. In O. S. Tan, P. Little, S. Y. Hee, & J. Conway (Eds.), *Problem-based learning: Educational innovation across disciplines* (pp. 65–76). Singapore: Temasek Centre for Problem-Based Learning.

CHAPTER 5

Reflective Practice and Problem-based Learning Course Portfolio

Mary Sue Baldwin
Valerie McCombs

Introduction

"Every artist dips his brush in his own soul, and paints his own nature into his pictures" (Beecher, 1887). Schon's description of the reflective practitioner is similar to Beecher's description of an artist. According to Schon (1983), the reflective practitioner looks beyond the classroom canvas to find meaning in the various phenomena, paints a picture of what he or she sees, and in turn reveals a portrait of the practitioner as an artist and scientist of education. Like the artist who displays works of art on a wall where they will inspire and incite the artist to ask the questions "why?", "so what?", and "now what?", educators can portray their works of teaching in a course portfolio so they too can ask themselves the same questions.

Being a reflective practitioner means not only asking questions but also using the information to refine one's artistry in a particular discipline and to gain greater effectiveness as an educator (Ferrarro, 2001; Schon, 1983). Preferably this process is done with the assistance of a mentor. A mentor can engage the practitioner in an examination of the latter's assumptions, values, and perspectives related to teaching and student learning. However, most educators practice in isolation, which creates a need for other means of communicating their reflections. Using a course portfolio to explore their experience in the classroom can enable educators to acknowledge and validate their quality of teaching, allow recognition from their peers, and contribute to the scholarship of teaching (SOT).

Scholarship of Teaching

The focus of discussions about the scholarship of teaching and learning (SOTL) has shifted from the definition and rationalization stage to an increasingly complex one: that of inquiry, sustainability, and documentation. Organizations such as the Carnegie Academy for the Scholarship of Teaching and Learning have been instrumental in supporting this effort by working with scholarly and professional societies to construct the vocabulary, criteria, products, and processes by which to conduct and communicate SOTL (Hutchings & Shulman, 2000). The Pew National Fellowship Program for Carnegie Scholars and the American Association for Higher Education's (AAHE) Teaching Academy Campus Program comprise the other organizations examining SOTL.

Since Boyer (1990) published his views on teaching in *Scholarship reconsidered: Priorities of the professoriate*, there seems to be a growing acceptance among institutions of higher learning that teaching does exist on equal scholarly footing as research because both roles require vigorous intellectual faculty work. No such acceptance, however, has occurred as to a precise definition of SOT nor with the appropriate method of implementing and communicating scholarly efforts. As to the latter, many faculty and administrators perceive "scholarly" work as being publishable only in traditional peer-reviewed journal articles, monographs, or books. And yet, for SOT to gain stature and solid acceptance among educators, a foundation of inquiry and knowledge must be built. Documents should not only reflect excellent teaching and SOT but distinguish between the two. Indeed, Hutchings and Shulman (1999) remarked that the "scholarship of teaching is not synonymous with excellent teaching" (p. 13). Kreber's (1999) Delphi study participants concurred with Hutchings and Shulman. In their view, SOT incorporates continual examination of the process and outcomes of teaching and learning as well as the contextual aspect of teaching. Faculty who exhibit SOT focus on change: they continually hone their teaching craft through a cycle of action, reflection, and revision. To accomplish this task, multiple and varied interdisciplinary inquiries are required to examine the effect teaching has on the depth and breadth of student learning. Identifying and evaluating SOT can be difficult as faculty generally teach within a vacuum, have limited established tools, and encounter negative connotations about "problems" in teaching. No less an issue is the documentation of these inquiries.

Along with the overall discussions on SOT, forums on the best method or approach to conducting and publishing SOT efforts have been held. The initial opinion expressed by Hutchings (2000) was that no one method or approach is the best for conducting SOT. Similarly, Hutchings and Shulman (1999) challenged the perceptions associated with the publishing of "scholarly" work and declared that no one venue has purported to be the best method for showcasing SOT. Accepting only traditional publications, in their view, hinders discussions on SOT. They and others explored alternative methods of documentation, and from these efforts the course portfolio was created and modified from the more expansive teaching portfolio. Based upon numerous studies on the content, process, and evaluation of teaching portfolios (Edgerton, Hutchings, & Quinlan, 1991; Seldin, 1991, 1993, 1997) and through their growing use as a formative and summative tool, the idea of using a portfolio as a form of documentation for demonstrating SOT became acceptable as well as adaptable. Via a course portfolio, faculty could theoretically demonstrate their activities of reflection and scholarship. The course portfolio, however, is not seen as a smaller version of the teaching portfolio, but as a distinct document. AAHE defines the course portfolio as a document in which faculty display their design, implementation, and assessment of a single course (Hutchings, 1998).

For teaching efforts to be considered examples of scholarship, they must be researched, analyzed, and shared so that others may comprehend and repeat the findings (Boyer, 1990; Shulman, 1998). The research should not be performed in isolation, nor should the analysis and results be kept private. Faculty, in publishing their activities and having these activities peer-reviewed and publicly displayed, can illustrate to other educators in the higher education community that scholarly work was accomplished. The course portfolio could be the most relevant method to showcase the evidence of SOT. According to Glassick, Huber, and Maeroff (1997), there are six standards by which to judge scholarly work: "clear goals, adequate preparation, appropriate methods, significant results, effective presentation, and reflective critique" (p. 35).

Writing a course portfolio takes time and energy, thus faculty will not automatically initiate one without some reassurance that their work will be recognized and rewarded as evidence of scholarly teaching and of advancement of pedagogical content relevant to SOT (Paulsen, 1999; Richlin, 1993). Although a course portfolio can be a formidable tool for reflection and personal growth, its ability to document SOT is still suspect. A reliable and valid tool to link course portfolios and SOT does not exist at this juncture in time, but there is an obvious need for such a tool with the increasing number of course portfolios being written and displayed (Samford University, 2000). Future studies are needed to determine the optimal guidelines and evaluation rubrics for affirming the course portfolio's link to SOT, as well as to promote the examination of teaching practices in a consistent and judicious manner.

Faculty Recognition and Rewards

The reflective practitioner role of a teacher has been examined primarily in relation to promotion and tenure processes. This is critically important as most faculty in institutions of higher education view academic advancement as being extremely important, and this impacts the manner in which administrators and faculty approach other issues, such as how to enhance student learning. Unfortunately, the current method for achieving tenure was established in the late 1960s and has not been significantly revised since then (Boyer, 1990).

According to Bosner (1992), the present method is inadequate for several reasons. For one, enrollments have grown at institutions so quickly that a strain has been placed upon the higher education system. Indeed, from 1960 to the end of the 1980s, enrollments in the United States alone increased from 3.5 million to over 13.5 million students (National Education Association, 1994). This has caused a concurrent increase in faculty numbers and an inverse relationship with their respective administrators. Assessing faculty performance, therefore, has evolved into an impersonal process and it is made more difficult by the fact that most administrators, although experts in their particular discipline, may not have adequate training in the principles of education, student learning, management, or leadership.

The Boyer report (1990) brought to the forefront the issue that teaching is equitable with research. Despite this declaration, prominent organizations such as the Ford Foundation continue to emphasize faculty research efforts, which still carry significant weight at institutions of higher learning. Increase in numbers and the push for research and publications have guided most institutions' missions and subsequent promotion and tenure systems. Unfortunately, this same combination is thought to have created a void in the assessment and documentation of teaching excellence (Ewell, 1993). This void is beginning to be filled by documents like portfolios.

Portfolios

According to Boyer (1990), the three traditional roles of a faculty member in higher education are researcher, educator, and scholar. He instead proposed the possible solution of viewing faculty work as a process of four overlapping functions: *discovery* (as in research), *integration* (synthesizing material such as in a textbook), *application* (consulting activities), and the scholarship of *teaching*. To display these functions, Edgerton, Hutchings, and Quinlan (1991) proposed a teaching portfolio. In their view, a teaching portfolio can "help document and display a conception of teaching that is indeed a 'pedagogy of substance'—recognized and valued as a form of scholarly work" (p. 2).

Teaching Portfolios

Trying to show the full extent of the relationship between teachers and students has been a challenge. Teaching exists more on a continuum that can occur beyond a finite period of time (Cerbin, 2001). This is especially true if one considers that teaching is broader than the two or more individuals involved. Teaching embodies the elements of vision, design, interactions, outcomes, and analysis (Shulman, 1998). Vision entails the description of one's goals and philosophy of teaching. Design and interaction elements portray the method and materials used to enhance student learning. What students actually learn is shown in the outcomes. It is the last section that brings the document full circle. Analysis, or reflection, of all the previous elements promotes the transformation and improvement of one's teaching. Recording these elements requires an extensive and dynamic document.

A teaching portfolio is "a factual description of a professor's strengths, accomplishments and includes documents and materials which collectively suggest the scope and quality of a professor's teaching performance" (Seldin, 1993, 2). It is not to be an "exhaustive compilation of all of the documents and materials that bear on teaching performance" (Seldin, 1997, 2). More than a collection of artifacts, portfolios can pose a teaching problem, make inquiries, and analyze the process. The range of information within a teaching portfolio allows a more complete view of the faculty member as a teacher. Going beyond end-of-course student evaluations and self-assessment survey tools, the teaching portfolio and its content detailing one's involvement in student activities, course and curriculum development, grant writing, publishing on teaching, and feedback from peers can facilitate a more comprehensive merit review. A summary or reflective section ties all the content together into a specific context, unique to the portfolio author's situation.

A teaching portfolio has the advantages of demonstrating the faculty member as a scholarly teacher, displaying evidence of the quality of one's teaching practice, exploring the practice of teaching, improving one's comprehension of teaching, and contributing to SOT. The potential disadvantages include the time needed to compile and organize the various material, having the material open to public scrutiny, and possibly not receiving adequate recognition. These portfolios can be cumbersome. Another possibility exists for faculty to showcase their teaching abilities. That would be to utilize a portion of a teaching portfolio, the portion that looks intensely at one aspect of a faculty's role: teaching a course.

Course Portfolios

As an entity, a course is fairly self-contained. It comprises specific goals and objectives, teaching methods, and classroom assignments designed for students to comprehend certain content and concepts. A fairly new device, the course portfolio can allow faculty to display their scholarly and pedagogical dimensions along with the opportunity to reflect upon their goals and experiences in teaching a specific course (Bass, 1998). AAHE defines course portfolios in contrast to teaching portfolios and states that "the course portfolio focuses on the unfolding of a single course, from conception to results" (Hutchings, 1998, 15). According to AAHE, a course portfolio is compiled to accomplish four goals: to facilitate the retaining of information and process within a course; to encourage scholarly inquiry; to reduce feelings of isolation; and to be rewarded for excellence in teaching.

Of these goals, Cerbin (2001), who first introduced the idea of course portfolios, stresses the second and concludes that a course is like an experiment. The goals of a course dictate its design. The design may not be fully apparent in a syllabus, but one can note the course calendar and assignments for the method in which the "experiment" is implemented. The outcomes of the experiment are shown in the values and ideas students grasp at the completion of the course (Hutchings, 1998). Performing research in this capacity can be considered a process of discovery, a scholarly endeavor according to Boyer (1990); and therefore documenting in a course portfolio this process and the teaching strategies used during the discovery should constitute a scholarly endeavor. Analysis of the entire process is essential to complete the experiment. This in-depth and systematic inquiry into one's teaching can improve not only one's teaching but students' learning as well.

Most faculty have an innate desire to foster comprehension and lifelong learning in their students. They will seek advice from their peers, query their students, and attend workshops and seminars on relevant teaching strategies. However, for the educator or a faculty peer to truly understand and support his or her teaching requires more than a snapshot of the course. Classroom observations can be of assistance, but they are neither always timely nor contiguous enough to allow the observer a true feel of the teacher's capabilities. A portfolio, on the other hand, can provide a panoramic view, from the peaks to the valleys of the course. It can be a mechanism for faculty to investigate and document their knowledge and teaching abilities that can contribute to stronger and deeper student learning. The course portfolio allows faculty to literally connect pedagogy with their students' learning by outlining the anatomy, natural history, ecology, or laboratory history of a course.

Depending on the author's discipline, the course portfolio can comprise a number of items from before, during, and after the course. Defining elements from these items are excerpts from a course inquiry and highlights of student learning. What singles out the course portfolio as a scholarly tool is the inclusion of the author's reflections (Hutchings, 1998). These reflections can add to the community of teaching practice and to SOT.

According to Barkley (2001), course portfolios can provide a template for displaying the concepts of SOT, allow for the "messy complexity" (p. 2) of teaching and learning, and convey the full implementation and transformation of a course. Furthermore, the course portfolio pushed Barkley to go beyond intuition and anecdotal information to a "culture of evidence" (p. 4). Faculty may wish to explore issues and concerns encountered in their course, critique their teaching methods, display evidence of student learning, facilitate revision of the course, share insights, or enhance the possibility of being recognized for excellence in teaching. Course portfolios can also encourage individual teachers to pose new questions, explore these questions, and then share their results with the greater teaching community. These approaches will be regulated by their respective audience. Obviously, portfolios written for oneself may vary significantly from those written for promotion and tenure, merit review, professional organizations, or even students.

Suggested content for a course portfolio varies as well. Hutchings (1998) recommended three particular sections: design, enactment, and results. Possible items to include in each section are given in Table 1. To be a reflective portfolio, however, Hutchings stressed that the author must reflect upon every item within each of these sections; and Schon (1996) strongly recommended that the author utilize a "coach" or "mentor" to guide the process.

A mentor can assist the author in ensuring the course portfolio is not a catch-all document. The key is to document the interaction between course design, implementation, and results. Although the course portfolio's content, format, and evaluation have not been firmly established, thus leaving its value to speculation, it can provide a clear, holistic view of teaching and learning.

Cognitive Approach to Problem-based Learning Course Portfolios

Armed with the tools of educational science, teachers can approach classroom problems with a variety of teaching and learning strategies. Continually pondering the effectiveness of these strategies promotes the process of transformation. The essence of transformation erupts from teachers' ability to transform their own learning. Transformational learning allows teachers to augment their knowledge base and create extensive shifts in their own comprehension and visions as teachers (Portnow et al., 1998). According to Hamilton (2002), this deep level of reflective thinking leads to significant contributions to the art and science of teaching. Teachers need to examine and delineate all the actual and potential circumstances and consequences that can impact learning in the classroom. Organizing all these aspects into a common framework and document enlightens the reflected experiences. Creating meaning out of the random chaos that can

TABLE 1 Course portfolio components

Component	Definition	Materials	Reflection
Design	Course vision or dream	Syllabus Course calendar Course description Course goals and objectives Course topics Learning outcomes Course rationale Curricular position	What is the vision for the course? What problem/issue is addressed in the course? How does this course fit in the overall curriculum? What is the history and evolution of the course? What expectations of student learning are made? What are the strengths and weaknesses of the course? What enhancers and obstacles exist for the enactment of the course? Why was this course selected for documentation in a course portfolio?
Enactment	Implementation of the course	Readings Assignments Audiovisual materials Lecture notes Evaluation tools Study questions Peer observations Web page	How does this course begin and end? What is the role of the teacher in this course? What is the role of the students in this course? Why are the assignments arranged in a particular order? What is the most important assignment in this course? What are the best and the worst assignments in this course? Which course element should be highlighted in the portfolio?
Results	Evidence of student learning	Learning outcomes Student essays Tests/quizzes Presentations Lab reports E-mail/chat rooms Surveys Evaluation rubrics Grades Self-assessments Peer evaluations	What learning outcome(s) did most of the students achieve? What learning outcome(s) did most of the students fail to achieve? What was the most surprising result of the course and why? What results were the most pleasing? What results were the most disturbing? What feature(s) of the course will be retained? What feature(s) of the course will not be retained and how will it be revised?

Adapted from Hutchings (1998).

occur with any teaching experience allows one to comprehend the past and to plan future actions, decisions, and achievements.

Using problems as the organizing focus for the instruction of the content and concepts of a course is a key component of problem-based learning (PBL). The premise inherent in PBL revolves around ill-structured, complex real-world problems and the resulting cognitive dissonance that stimulates students' collaborative learning and inquiry (Boud & Feletti, 1997). Through carefully constructed open-ended problems, students work to develop and refine critical thinking, research, and communication skills so that they can apply these same skills to contextually rich situations in the future beyond the boundaries of their present-day classroom experiences (Coles, 1997; Dunkhase & Penick, 1990).

Schmidt (1993) outlined three principles from cognitive psychology that support the use of PBL. First, PBL requires students to activate prior knowledge to address the "new" problem posed. Second, using their baseline knowledge, the students, working in teams, must discuss and formulate the association between concepts. Creating these multiple cognitive links between "old" and "new" ideas enhances the students' ability to retrieve and utilize information from memory. Finally, since PBL problems are presented as "real-world situations," students' learning occurs in a context similar to the one in which the problems will be applied. The problem and its resolution cue the learner when similar problems arise in practice. These cues are necessary to access the prior relevant knowledge embedded in one's memory.

Documenting students' and one's own experiential learning from PBL is an essential component to becoming a reflective and scholarly practitioner. Scholarly contributions to pedagogical content knowledge can arise from the practice of, reflection on, and codification of teaching (Paulsen, 2001). This can be a daunting task without a delineated process. Guidelines for writing a course portfolio can provide a stepping-off place for writing one's ideas and concerns about teaching a certain concept and content (see Appendix A for an example of guidelines). By facilitating the process of reflection, the guidelines can encourage educators to ponder and to develop a deeper understanding of their practice. These reflections can be approached in several ways: reflection-on-action, reflection-in-action, or via a conceptual framework.

Reflective Models

Reflection-on-action involves a retrospective examination of one's current abilities, knowledge, competencies, and practice (Schon, 1983). Modifications to the teaching process and enhancement of student learning can only occur with subsequent courses. Conversely, reflection-in-action is a dynamic process and promotes reflection while in the midst of teaching a class or course. Facilitating this latter process can be by having frequent discussions with one's mentor and/or by keeping a reflective diary. Regardless of either approach, encouraging educators to reflect and document their reflections at some point in their teaching is the ultimate goal.

For some educators, a model or conceptual framework may assist in the stimulation, guidance, and documentation of reflective practice. One model to consider is the Johns (1994) model of structured reflection (see Table 2), which is being used in nursing to reflect upon nurse–patient interactions. Although used in a health-care setting, this model can be applicable to reflecting upon the educator–student interaction experience. Its support of the affective domain and the view of the nurse/educator's experiences from a holistic standpoint are of particular importance. Educators are adept in delineating their intellectual motivations and

TABLE **2**   Johns' model of structured reflection

Cue topic	Cue questions
Aesthetics	What was I trying to achieve?
	Why did I respond as I did?
	What were the consequences of that for the students, myself, or others?
	How were the students or I feeling?
	How did I know this?
Personal	How did I feel in this situation?
	What internal factors were influencing me?
Ethics	How did my actions match with my beliefs?
	What factors made me act in incongruent ways?
Empirics	What knowledge did or should have informed me?
Reflexivity	How does this connect with my previous experiences?
	Could I handle this better in future situations?
	What would be the consequences of alternative action for the students, myself, or others?
	How do I feel about the experience?
	Can I support others and myself better as a consequence?
	Has this changed my ways of knowing?

Adapted from Johns (1994).

processes; recognizing and documenting their intrapersonal and inter-personal reactions to the teaching–learning experience is a much more daunting task.

Reflecting upon one's teaching from a SOT approach requires a different approach. A multidimensional model for SOT developed by Trigwell, Martin, Benjamin, and Prosser (2001) offers a framework for documenting reflections in a course portfolio. Their model was designed to be consistent with the literature on SOT, allow for the diversity in faculty's teaching, and make visible the process of student learning (Ramsden, 1992). Building upon the works of Andresen and Webb (2000), Boyer (1990), Glassick, Huber, and Maeroff (1997), Rice (1992), Schon (1995), and Shulman (1993), the model was developed around four core dimensions. The dimensions' descriptions and levels are outlined in Table 3. As one can infer from the table, those faculty who exhibit level-4 behaviors clearly are practitioners of SOT.

TABLE 3 Scholarship of teaching model dimensions: descriptions and levels

Dimension	Informed	Reflection	Communication	Conception
Description	Extent faculty are aware of their own disciplines and in general the literature on teaching and learning	Ability to reflect on one's teaching and the effect on student learning and make relevant modifications	Dissemination of practice and theories related to general and discipline-specific teaching and learning	Place on continuum from a focus purely on student learning to one mainly on teaching
Level 1	Informal teaching and learning theories used	Exhibits little to no reflective activities	None	Teaching focus from a teacher-centered perspective
Level 2	Aware of general teaching and learning literature		Disseminates ideas and teaching practices informally	
Level 3	Aware of general and discipline-specific teaching and learning literature	Actively reflects	Disseminates ideas and teaching practices at national conferences	
Level 4	Conducts and links action research and adds to pedagogical knowledge base	Actively reflects and proposes relevant research to improve teaching and learning	Disseminates ideas and teaching practices in international scholarly venues	Teaching focus from a student-centered perspective

Adapted from Trigwell, Martin, Benjamin, & Prosser (2001).

Conclusion

Teachers who desire to become reflective practitioners must constantly assess their choices and behaviors in the classroom, as well as the interrelationship between students, parents, and other teaching professionals (LEARN NC, 2001). Recognizing the positive consequences from such actions, institutions around the world are encouraging teachers to be actively involved in learning communities in which discussions and documents focus on the assessment of teaching strategies (like PBL) and student learning. Within these learning forums, teachers can interact with their peers and contribute to their own professional education. By using these teaching dialogues and course portfolios to explore their teaching, teachers can demonstrate not only their skills as reflective practitioners but also their growth as scholars in teaching.

References

Andresen, L. W., & Webb, C. A. (2000). *Discovering the scholarship of teaching.* Richmond: University of Western Sydney Hawkesbury.

Barkley, E. F. (2001). From Bach to Tupac. *AAHE Bulletin*, June. http://www.aahe.org/bulletin/bachtotupac.htm.

Bass, R. (1998). A hypertext portfolio on an experimental American literature course. In P. Hutchings (Ed.), *The course portfolio: How faculty can examine their teaching to advance practice and improve student learning* (pp. 91–96). Washington, DC: American Association for Higher Education.

Beecher, H. W. (1887). Proverbs from Plymouth pulpit. In *The Columbia book of quotations*. New York: Columbia University Press (1996).

Bosner, C. F. (1992). Total quality education? *Public Administration Review, 52,* 504 12.

Boud, D., & Feletti, G. I. (Eds.) (1997). *The challenge of problem-based learning* (2nd ed.). London: Kogan Page.

Boyer, E. L. (1990). *Scholarship reconsidered: Priorities of the professoriate.* Princeton, NJ: Carnegie Foundation for the Advancement of Teaching.

Cerbin, W. (2001). The course portfolio. *American Psychological Society News and Research.* http://www.psychologicalscience.org/newsreach/tips/0401tips.html.

Coles, C. (1997). Is problem-based learning the only way? In D. Boud & G. I. Feletti (Eds.), *The challenge of problem-based learning* (2nd ed., pp. 313–25). London: Kogan Page.

Dunkhase, J. A., & Penick, J. E. (1990). Problem solving in the real world. *Journal of College Science Teaching, 19,* 367–70.

Edgerton, R., Hutchings, P., & Quinlan, K. (1991). *The teaching portfolio: Capturing the scholarship of teaching.* Washington, DC: American Association for Higher Education.

Ewell, P. T. (1993). Total quality and academic practice: The idea we've been waiting for? *Change, 25,* 49–55.

Ferrarro, J. (2001). Reflective practice and professional development. Educational Resources Information Center Digest. http://www.ericsp.org/pages/digests/reflective_practice.html.

Glassick, C. E., Huber, M. T., & Maeroff, G. I. (1997). *Scholarship assessed: Evaluation of the professoriate.* San Francisco: Jossey-Bass.

Hamilton, S. (2002). Mirror, mirror, to the mind: What we see(k) is what we find! Writing reflectively about teaching and learning. *PBL Insight, 5,* 1–4.

Hutchings, P. (Ed.) (1998). *The course portfolio: How faculty can examine their teaching to advance practice and improve student learning.* Washington, DC: American Association for Higher Education.

Hutchings, P. (Ed.) (2000). Introduction: Approaching the scholarship of teaching and learning. In *Opening lines: Approaches to the scholarship of teaching and learning* (pp. 1–10). Menlo Park, CA: Carnegie Foundation for the Advancement of Teaching.

Hutchings, P., & Shulman, L. S. (1999). The scholarship of teaching: New elaborations, new developments. *Change, 31,* 10–15.

Hutchings, P., & Shulman, L. S. (2000). Preface. In P. Hutchings (Ed.), *Opening lines: Approaches to the scholarship of teaching and learning.* Menlo Park, CA: Carnegie Foundation for the Advancement of Teaching.

Johns, C. (1994). Guided reflection. In A. M. Palmer, S. Burns, & C. Bulman (Eds.), *Reflective practice in nursing.* Oxford: Blackwell.

Kreber, C. (1999). Defining and implementing the scholarship of teaching: The results of a Delphi study. Paper presented at the Annual Meeting of the Canadian Society for the Study of Higher Education. Universite de Sherbrooke, Sherbrooke, Quebec, June.

LEARN NC (2001). *Standard 9: Reflective practice.* Chapel Hill, NC: North Carolina Teachers' Network.

National Education Association (1994). Statement on faculty reward structures. Washington, DC.

Paulsen, M. B. (1999). How college students learn: Linking traditional educational research and contextual classroom research. *Journal of Staff, Program and Organization Development, 16,* 63–71.

Paulsen, M. B. (2001). The relation between research and the scholarship of teaching. In C. Kreber (Ed.), *Scholarship revisited: Perspectives on the scholarship of teaching* (pp. 19–30). New directions for teaching and learning, No. 86. San Francisco: Jossey-Bass.

Portnow, K., Popp, N., Broderick, M., Drago-Severson, E., & Kegan, R. (1998). NCSALL's research findings. Transformational learning in adulthood. *Focus on Basics, 2,* 22–27. http://www.gse.harvard.edu/~ncsall/fob/1998/for2id.htm.

Ramsden, P. (1992). *Learning to teach in higher education.* London: Routledge.

Rice, E. A. (1992). Toward a broader conception of scholarship: The American context. In T. G. Whiston & R. L. Geiger (Eds.), *Research and higher education in the United Kingdom and the United States.* Lancaster: Society for Research into Higher Education.

Richlin, L. (Ed.) (1993). *Preparing faculty for the new conceptions of scholarship.* New directions for teaching and learning, No. 54. San Francisco: Jossey-Bass.

Samford University (2000). PBL-PR web site. http://www.samford.edu/pbl/pblpr.html.

Schmidt, H. G. (1993). Foundations of problem-based learning: Some explanatory notes. *Medical Education, 27*, 422–32.

Schon, D. A. (1983). *The reflective practitioner.* San Francisco: Jossey-Bass.

Schon, D. A. (1995). The new scholarship requires a new epistemology. *Change, 27*, 27–34.

Schon, D. A. (1996). *Educating the reflective practitioner: Toward a new design for teaching and learning in the professions.* San Francisco: Jossey-Bass.

Seldin, P. (1991). *The teaching portfolio: A practical guide to improved performance and promotion/tenure decisions.* Bolton, MA: Anker.

Seldin, P. (1993). *Successful use of teaching portfolios.* Bolton, MA: Anker.

Seldin, P. (1997). *The teaching portfolio: A practical guide to improved performance and promotion/tenure decisions* (2nd ed.). Bolton, MA: Anker.

Shulman, L. S. (1993). Teaching as community property. *Change, 25*, 6–7.

Shulman, L. S. (1998). Course anatomy: The dissection and analysis of knowledge through teaching. In P. Hutchings (Ed.), *The course portfolio: How faculty can examine their teaching to advance practice and improve student learning* (pp. 5–12). Washington, DC: American Association for Higher Education.

Trigwell, K., Martin, E., Benjamin, J., & Prosser, M. (2001). *Scholarship of teaching: A model.* http://www.clt.uts.edu.au/Scholarship/A.Model.html.

Appendix A

Center for Problem-Based Learning
Samford University

Problem-based Learning–Peer Review (PBL-PR)
Course Portfolio Project
(Supported by Samford University and the Pew Charitable Trusts)

Course Portfolio Outline
Contents

    I. Introductory Information
    II. Course Design
        A. Rationale
        B. Reflective essay on course content
        C. Reflective essay on instructional practice
        D. PBL context and application
    III. Student Understanding
    IV. Reflective Summary of the Course

(Detailed instructions for each component of the portfolio can be found in the step-by-step guide.)

Background Information
What Is a Course Portfolio?
The course portfolio is *not* an omnibus collection of all materials related to your course, but a focused look at one aspect of the course design. In general, you should think of the portfolio as a qualitative study of the course. Be clear as to the purpose of your investigation and include any material relevant and supportive of your endeavors. A good course portfolio will adhere to the same guidelines as a good scholarly article: clarity of purpose, original ideas, appropriate use of evidence, and significant conclusions. Additional information on the components of a course portfolio may be found on the Samford PBL-PR web site at *www.samford.edu/pbl*.

Compared to a "teaching" or "professional" portfolio, a course portfolio examines a particular teaching/learning experience. Although it is assumed that most faculty employ a variety of instructional methods in a course, the review board is particularly interested in the PBL activities, whether they constitute a complete course or are learning situations not formally designated as a "course." If you have concerns or questions as to your teaching/learning experience being applicable to this project, please contact the Director, Center for Problem-Based Learning.

What Is Problem-based Learning?
Course portfolios may be written for many purposes; however, the current project is limited to courses utilizing PBL. Detailed information about PBL as a pedagogical

method is available via many sources, including the Samford PBL web site at *www.samford.edu/pbl*. To summarize some of the common characteristics, PBL involves:

- student-centered learning
- use of small student groups to discuss the problem(s) and possible avenues of resolution
- teachers acting as facilitators or guides
- problems as the organizing focus and stimulus for learning
- problems that are not subject to easy or formulaic solutions (sometimes referred to as ill-structured or complex problems)
- student gaining problem-solving skills through the learning experience and acquiring new knowledge via self-directed learning

Owing to the project design, one component of the portfolio will specifically address the manner in which PBL has been used in the course. The course portfolio should clearly explain the reasons for using PBL as a teaching method.

Why Write a Course Portfolio?
Preparing a course portfolio is an intellectually demanding and time-consuming activity. Faculty should seriously consider the commitment necessary to complete the writing of the portfolio. On the other hand, a portfolio provides an excellent means of communicating publicly the labor behind good teaching. The course portfolio also allows possible external review of the scholarship of teaching, similar to a journal article making possible the review of traditional research. Increasing numbers of faculty are using course portfolios during performance reviews for tenure, promotion, and merit-based raises. For this project, exemplary portfolios will be registered on the project web site and acknowledged as a scholarly document that withstood the scrutiny of peer review.

The PBL-PR course portfolio project is one of several national initiatives currently underway to validate the scholarship of teaching. Building upon Ernest Boyer's (1990) work, Lee Shulman and Pat Hutchings, respectively the President and Senior Scholar of the Carnegie Foundation for the Advancement of Teaching, have delineated the scholarship of teaching as being public, open to assessment, and forming a basis for others to foster lifelong learning in students and to enhance the practice of teaching (Hutchings & Shulman, 1999). An important component of a document displaying the scholarship of teaching is the reflective piece. Reflection details the author's thoughts and experiences as to what worked and what did not work in the course.

For assistance in writing one's course portfolio, you may wish to review several excellent resources, including William Cerbin's (1994) "The course portfolio as a tool for continuous improvement of teaching and learning" and others displayed on the *www.samford.edu/pbl* web site. Participants in this project will be contributing to an important conversation between faculty and administrators as to how the art and science of teaching can be studied, recognized, and valorized.

How Will the Course Portfolio be Reviewed?
Each portfolio will have a preliminary review to ensure that it meets the minimum standards of the project. If these standards are met, the portfolio will be sent out for review by a specialist in the discipline and a specialist in teaching/learning strategies. Results of the reviews, which remain confidential, will be returned to the faculty

member submitting the portfolio. The faculty member will then have the opportunity to revise and resubmit the portfolio for electronic publication on the project web site. Portfolios exemplifying the scholarship of teaching will be officially registered on the project web site.

What Are the Submission Guidelines?

The portfolio review process involves several stages. The first stage of review will be done by the PBL-PR editor and a faculty member at Samford from the same discipline or a closely related one. After the course portfolio author makes revisions based on this formative feedback, the portfolio will be submitted for formal peer review by both content and PBL instructional design experts. For this phase, four print copies must be submitted, two of which should include no reference to your identity. Depending upon the reviewers' comments, further revision may be necessary. The final portfolio will then be considered for publication in Samford's course portfolio peer registry. If accepted, the portfolio will need to be submitted electronically.

Specific criteria to fulfill in developing and submitting a course portfolio include:

1. Two print copies of the completed portfolio must be received by the Center for Problem-Based Learning, Samford University, 800 Lakeshore Drive, Birmingham, AL 35229-7020, by the date specified.
2. Portfolios should be double-spaced, except in places where usage requires or permits single spacing (e.g., footnotes).
3. Paragraphs should be indented, but no additional space (i.e., beyond the normal double-spacing) should be inserted between paragraphs.
4. Margins should be set as follows:

    a. Side margins: $1\frac{1}{2}$ inches on the left and 1 inch on the right.
    b. Right margin should be unjustified.
    c. Top and bottom margins: 1 inch.

5. Every page must be assigned a page number. The page number should be placed at the top right.
6. Times New Roman, 12 point, is the preferred typeface and size.
7. Under no circumstance should legibility be sacrificed in order to pack more text into the document.
8. Scholars may follow the accepted documentation style of their discipline (e.g., APA, MLA, and *Chicago Manual of Style*).
9. Course portfolios should be no more than twenty (20) pages, double-spaced, including all appendixes and attachments. References to course materials, student products, evaluation instruments, etc., should be made by providing a web site address where these materials may be obtained. Portfolios which exceed the page limit will be returned.
10. If accepted for publication, the final submission must include a 3.5" diskette with a Microsoft Word file (version 6.0 or higher). The electronic submission must be exactly the same file that generated the printed text.

What Are the Important Dates to Remember?

If you wish to participate in the fourth round of the project, please refer to the calendar below for important dates and relevant events.

Month/Year	Date	Activity
September 2002	30	Fourth-round portfolio applications due
January 2003	31	Fourth-round portfolios due at Center for PBL, Samford University
April 2003	30	Fourth-round authors send two copies of portfolios to Center for PBL, Samford University
May 2003	30	Fourth-round portfolios have completed Samford review. Letters of acceptance/rejection sent
June 2003	30	Fourth-round revisions due (four copies)
November 2003	1	Fourth-round exemplary portfolios to be published on the project web site

Is There a Step-by-Step Guide to Preparing the Portfolio?
Yes. Use the guidelines listed below to complete your portfolio. Be sure to include all of the information requested, and in the same order. Being knowledgeable as to the context of your course will be extremely helpful to the peer reviewers.

Part I: Introductory Information
A. **Institutional**
  1. Name of college/university: _____
  2. Total enrollment: _____
  3. Is the university public or private? _____
  4. Carnegie classification: _____
     (Refer to *http://www.carnegiefoundation.org/Classification*)
B. **Individual**
  1. Your school (Arts and Sciences, Business, etc.): _____
  2. Your department/division: _____
  3. Your faculty rank: _____
  4. Highest degree earned: _____
  5. Number of years teaching at the college level: _____
  6. Awards received for excellence in teaching: _____
C. **Course**
  1. Course name (e.g., Molecular Biology): _____
  2. Course abbreviation and number (e.g., BIOL 3399): _____
  3. Number of semester/quarter (circle one) credit hours: _____
  4. Catalog description: _____
     _____
     _____
     _____
  5. Number of students typically taught in this course: _____
  6. In what year do students typically enroll in this course: freshman, sophomore, junior, senior, or graduate? (circle one)

7. This course is best described as (select one):
   a. required general education course
   b. elective general education course
   c. required course for majors
   d. elective course for majors
   e. pre-professional course for various majors
   f. other (please specify): _____

D. **Problem-based learning**
   1. What percentage of this course uses PBL? _____
   2. How long have you been teaching the course using PBL? _____
   3. Is the course designated as PBL in any official way (e.g., school catalog)?
   _____

Part II: Course Design

A. **Rationale**
The rationale should be a brief statement of your reasons for using PBL in teaching the course the way you do. This corresponds to the "thesis" or "argument" section of a research paper. Use this as a guide in writing the portfolio and cite scholarly, professional, and content references.

B. **Reflective essay on course content**
Use this section to focus on those aspects of the course content that you chose based upon scholarly research and personal judgment. If you have taught this course repeatedly, you may choose to describe the evolution of the course as you grew in your understanding of the course and the discipline. It is not necessary to address the standard information typically included in this course (e.g., that you teach "Enlightenment" in your Western Civilization course).

C. **Reflective essay on instructional practice**
Good teaching should be guided by an understanding of student learning needs and should utilize appropriate instructional practices. Discuss the methods of instruction you use, why you chose PBL in addition to other particular method(s), and how they relate to your course goals. Similar to content issues, you may wish to discuss the evolution of your teaching methods over time.

D. **PBL context and application**
State specifically how PBL is used in your course. Consider including the nature of the problem(s) you have selected, the manner in which you facilitate the problems in class, the use of student groups for problem solving, and the outcome of the PBL activities.

Part III: Student Understanding

A. **Evidence of students achieving the learning objectives**
In this section, you need to include an example (or examples) of student products created in your course. Some examples to consider are descriptions of a student's performance or a summary of group responses to a particular PBL stimulus, etc. Along with the example(s), please provide a context for this

example. Was it exceptional work or typical of what all students produced? What directions were given to guide student performance? What interaction did students have with faculty, tutors, or other students during the process? You may wish to include a web address where further evidence may be examined, if possible.

B. **Reflection on the evidence of student learning**
How does the example(s) provided confirm (or refute) the validity of the approach being used? What standards of judgment were used to evaluate student work? How successful have students been in meeting the learning objectives? What are the limitations of this evidence? As a result of this analysis, what might be changed (or has been changed) to improve student performance? Has the student outcome information been used to modify the course design?

Part IV: Reflective Summary of the Course

The synopsis of your course portfolio should briefly review the purpose of the portfolio and the outcomes of your study. This section should be written so that it could be read independently of the overall portfolio.

References

Boyer, E. L. (1990). *Scholarship reconsidered: Priorities of the professoriate.* Princeton, NJ: Carnegie Foundation for the Advancement of Teaching.

Cerbin, W. (1994). The course portfolio as a tool for continuous improvement of teaching and learning. *Journal of Excellence in College Teaching, 5,* 95–105.

Hutchings, P., & Shulman, L. S. (1999). The scholarship of teaching: New elaborations, new developments. *Change, 31,* 10–15.

Revised 02/14/02
© Samford University

CHAPTER 6

Teachers as Coaches of Cognitive Processes in Problem-based Learning

Boon-Tiong Ho

Problem-based Learning

Problem-based learning (PBL) is both a curriculum development tool and an instructional strategy (Savery & Duffy, 1998). PBL simultaneously develops problem-solving strategies, knowledge bases in multiple disciplines, and various skills by placing the learner in the active role of problem solver confronted with an ill-structured problem that mirrors real-world situations. In a PBL unit, the ill-structured problem is presented first and thereafter serves as the organizing center and context for learning. The problem is considered ill-structured in nature because of the following characteristics:

- The problem contains a "messy" situation (as in real life, where there are usually many problems embedded in each situation).
- Its nature changes with the addition of new information.
- It is not solved easily or formulaically.
- Neither is it resolved by a "right" answer.

"The starting point for learning is always the problem" (Boud, 1985, 14). A problem is considered a stimulus for which a learner does not have a ready response; it is also one that students are apt to face as future professionals (Bridges, 1992). Therefore, in PBL classrooms, learners assume the role of problem solvers, while teachers assume the role of coaches. In the teaching and learning process, information is shared but knowledge is personally constructed by the learners. Thinking is fully articulated and held to strict benchmarks. Appropriate and authentic assessment accompanies the entire learning process in the PBL approach.

Teachers as Coaches of Cognitive Processes

As an instructional strategy, PBL offers ample opportunities for learners to be engaged in various cognitive processes, such as defining a problem, gathering information, analyzing data, building and testing hypotheses, generating solutions, and evaluating their outcomes. This is largely due to the manner in which the ill-structured problem is crafted. Such ill-structured problems demand that learners activate both creative and critical thinking skills when solving them. Hence, the learners suspend the guessing game of "What's the right answer that the teacher wants?"; instead, they become more motivated and more engaged in learning since they now know and feel that they are empowered to impact on the outcome of their own investigation. Their learning experiences become meaningful, especially when they are involved in solving problems that they regard as significant. The relevance of the context for the learners offers an obvious answer to their usual questions of "Why do we need to learn this information?" and "What does schoolwork have to do with anything in the real world?"

In this sense, PBL is vastly different in its pedagogical approach to that of the traditional chalk-and-talk style of didactic teaching. At the same time, one would expect differences to also exist in other dimensions of teaching and learning, such as the roles of teachers and learners, learning outcomes, and assessment. For example, the usual paper-and-pencil mode of assessment is not appropriate in the PBL approach as PBL tends to assess learning in ways that demonstrate understanding and not mere acquisition of knowledge. In the PBL approach, since learners' prior knowledge is activated and opportunities are provided for them to elaborate and apply knowledge in contexts similar to the learning contexts, the learning outcomes often exceed expectations. Learners not only retain what they learn but they can appropriately use the knowledge they have learned:

> The advantage of such an approach is that students become much more aware of how the knowledge they are acquiring can be put to use. Adopting a problem solving mentality, even when it is marginally appropriate, reinforces the notion that the knowledge is useful for achieving particular goals. Students are not being asked to store information away; they see how it works in certain situations which increase the accessibility (Prawat, 1989, 18).

Last but not least, the role of teachers adopting the PBL approach also changes. Instead of being the "sage on the stage," they now become the "guide by the side." They function more as mentors taking on the coaching role. Coaching is a process of goal setting, modeling, guiding, facilitating, monitoring, and providing feedback to learners in order to support their active and self-directed thinking and learning. This change of role may not be obvious to teachers. Even if it is apparent, we must not assume that teachers can take on the coaching role easily. Coaching is an intense and complex process, and teachers do require training and experience, coupled with reflections, to excel in it. The role of teachers in enhancing motivation and fostering cognitive engagement as part of the coaching process includes these functions (Blumenfeld et al., 1998, 116):

- Create opportunities for learning by providing access to information.
- Support learning by scaffolding instruction and modeling and guiding students to make tasks more manageable.
- Encourage students to use learning and metacognitive processes.
- Assess progress, diagnose problems, provide feedback, and evaluate results.
- Create an environment conducive to constructive inquiry.
- Manage the classroom to ensure that work is accomplished in an orderly and efficient fashion.

Over the last two decades, many studies have been conducted to determine how teachers can best fulfill these varied roles (Brophy, 1989; Bryant & Timmins, 2000; Gallagher, Stepien, Sher, & Workman, 1995; Ho, 1999; Ho & Toh, 2001; Rosenshine & Stevens, 1986; Tan, 2000). Although research and theory have provided answers to many important questions related to the use of PBL in classroom teaching, teachers must understand the key features of the approach and be trained and equipped in order to successfully implement it. PBL is "likely to pose difficulties for teachers too. They may need help with content, with new instructional forms, and with implementation and management of projects" (Blumenfeld et al., 1998, 131). However, the critical role teachers play as coaches of cognitive processes in the successful implementation of a PBL unit cannot be overlooked:

> Project-based learning requires considerable knowledge, effort, persistence, and
> self-regulation on the part of students; they need to devise plans, gather information,
> evaluate both findings and their approach, and generate and revise artifacts. Such
> requirements are not easily met. Teachers will play a critical role in helping students
> in the process, and shaping opportunities for learning, guiding students' thinking,
> and helping them construct new understandings (p. 131).

McConnell (2000), who is professor of sport and head of the School of Sport at UNITEC Institute of Technology, Auckland, New Zealand, and author of the best-selling book *Inside the All Blacks*, commented on coaches and coaching: "Coaches are leaders" (p. 11), "Coaching does not always go smoothly" (p. 13), and "To be a successful coach, you must be a successful teacher" (p. 139). Though his comments were made with reference to sports, I believe they are equally applicable to and descriptive of the coaching process in education: Teachers are indeed leaders (see elaboration by Ho, 2001, and Ho & Toh, 2002), and they do need to modify their lesson plans to suit particular teaching contexts. There will be interruptions and surprises in class that teachers have to learn to manage or solve. In fact, I would say that "to be a successful teacher, you must be a successful coach."

The coaching role of teachers in conducting a PBL unit has been likened to that of a sports coach. As coaches, teachers assume a supporting sideline role. They must know when to offer help as it is needed and to provide guidance in building and testing strategies. The learners are the key players in the game. Teachers as coaches merely support the players. The key considerations are knowing and deciding when to let the players play and when and how to intervene. In PBL, teachers coach a variety of tasks, ranging from communication (how learners receive, share, and make sense of what they read, write, speak, and hear) to information gathering (from the library, the Internet, and experimentation) and autonomous learning habits (self-initiative and self-direction). All coaching and learning in PBL are done in the context of the problematic situation and of the disciplines in which the problem applies.

Costa and Garmston (1994) introduced another metaphor for coaching. They envisioned it as a conveyance, something like a stagecoach. From their notion,

> to coach means to convey a valued colleague from where he or she is to where he
> or she wants to be. Skillful cognitive coaches apply specific strategies to enhance
> another person's perceptions, decisions, and intellectual functions. Changing these

inner thought processes is prerequisite to improving overt behaviors that, in turn, enhance student learning (p. 2).

Two aspects of this definition support the salient features of the PBL approach. Firstly, the mention of the valued colleague places the learner in center stage of the PBL approach instead of focusing on a set of propositional statements as knowledge in a discipline to be imposed upon the learner. In its truest sense, the PBL approach is learner-centric and constructivist in nature. In fact, the first step in designing any PBL unit is to know the students. Only their interests and needs will drive their learning through PBL.

Secondly, the emphasis on changing inner thought processes as a prerequisite to improving overt behaviors is testimony to what most teachers, and learners alike, experience when they first encounter PBL. In the early stages, teachers tend to be uncomfortable with coaching PBL, feeling "a lack of control" over the direction and development of the lesson. Often learners also find that they "do not learn much." However, once they are able to make the mindset shift to concentrate on the learner and the PBL process, then they begin to recognize the associated benefits. Indeed, the roles of coaching and coaches are so essential that "few educational innovations achieve their full impact without a coaching component" (Costa & Garmston, 1994, 7).

The Three Levels of Coaching

It has been observed in teacher development workshops that, while coaching has to be the most pervasive activity in PBL, it is also the least familiar and least automatic to teachers. Many teachers simply do not have enough evaluated experience in coaching PBL. Kitchener (1983) described three levels of coaching: cognition, metacognition, and epistemic cognition.

In coaching cognition, we are not concerned with teaching any particular type of thinking. Instead, the emphasis and practice are on fostering "thoughtfulness" (Newmann, 1990) through the use of interpretation, analysis, application, and manipulation of information in order to address a "messy" problem, a mental challenge of sort that cannot be addressed through routine application of previously learned information. Here, cognition involves the application of higher-order thinking. Beyer (1997) suggested that, to provide compelling opportunities for higher-order thinking in the classroom, teachers need to do the following:

- Frame learning with thoughtful questions.
- Provoke puzzlement or dissonance.
- Engage students in knowledge-producing activities.
- Structure learning around knowledge-producing strategies.

Asking thoughtful questions is part of coaching cognition. "A thoughtful question is clearly not a question that can be answered simply by recall or with a single word or phrase" (Beyer, 1997, 32). It is also one to which there is no preferred or "right" answer. What it does is to stimulate thinking beyond the mere recall of facts. "Answering a thoughtful question necessitates finding and reorganizing information and data as well as evaluating the data and the questions derived from or based on them" (p. 32). Specifically, Wiggins (1987) listed several criteria that characterize a thoughtful question (p. 12):

- It deals with the most controversial and important topics or issues of a discipline or subject.
- It has no obvious, single, prescribed correct answer.
- It requires analysis, evaluation, and/or synthesis, as well as other types of complex thinking.
- It allows personalized responses because there is no one correct way to go about developing an adequate response.
- It requires the production or construction of new knowledge— knowledge presumably unknown to the students prior to receiving the question.
- It advances students toward a deeper understanding of the subject on which they focus.

The following are examples of questions useful for coaching cognition:

Challenging questions
- Are you sure? Have you considered . . . ?
- Do you have enough facts to suggest . . . ? How reliable is . . . ? How valid is . . . ? How reasonable is . . . ?
- Does anyone believe/know this to be true? If what Daniel and Mary say is true, do you still believe . . . ?

Probing questions
- Tell me more. Can you say more about that?
- What about . . . ? Who else? What if . . . ?

- How so? Why?
- What do you mean? What does this mean for the problem?

Cognitive questions
- What is your hypothesis, hunch, your best guess about this?
- What is going on here? What seems important?
- Where does this fit in? What does this information tell you?

Metacognition, as described by Costa (2001, 82), is a mental processing that

> involves knowing what we know and what we don't know. It is our ability to devise a plan for producing whatever information is needed, to be conscious of our own steps and strategies during the act of problem solving, and to reflect on and evaluate the productiveness of our thinking. . . . Probably the major components of metacognition are developing a plan of action, keeping that plan in mind over a period of time, and then evaluating the plan upon its completion. Mapping out a strategy before embarking on a course of action helps us consciously track the steps in the sequence of planned behaviors for the duration of the activity.

Therefore, coaching at the level of metacognition involves monitoring the progress of the cognitive processes that learners are engaged in. Teachers might consider using the following questions to help them coach PBL at the level of metacognition:

Challenging questions
- Are you sure? Have you considered . . . (process or strategy)?
- How reliable is . . . (process or strategy)? How valid is . . . (process or strategy)?
- Do you really know or . . . ?

Monitoring questions
- How are things progressing? What still needs to be done? What else still needs attention?
- What, if anything, in your goals and strategies needs to change? What has been helpful to you so far? Have you reached your goal?
- What conclusions have you drawn? What solutions are emerging? Where do you see inconsistencies, gaps, ambiguities, or failures?

Metacognitive questions
- Where can we start? How do we proceed? What is your strategy?
- Why is this (process or strategy) important?

- How could we go about this? Who will do this?
- How can we learn more about this?

At the next level, coaching for epistemic cognition, we are more concerned about the recognition and application of the limits of knowledge, the certainty of knowing, and the criteria of knowing. The following are examples of questions to coach learners at this level:

Probing questions
- What makes you say that?
- If . . . , then . . . ?
- Can you say more about that?

Epistemic cognitive questions
- How do you know?
- What can we know? To what degree of certainty?
- Why do we need to know more? What is at stake here?

All of these questions serve as exemplary verbal cues for teachers to engage learners at these different levels of coaching. It has been widely acknowledged that the single most important teaching act is asking questions. Asking good, thoughtful questions is never as easy and straightforward as the questioning techniques themselves. Questioning techniques such as wait-time I and wait-time II, using nonverbal cues (eye contact, proximity, gestures), and intonation, which fall in the domain of skills, can be enhanced through practicing. Asking thoughtful questions, however, is a different matter. While it is possible and encouraged for teachers to prepare their questions before asking them, subsequent follow-through questions will depend on learners' responses to the first question asked. Often teachers would have to phrase their follow-through questions on the spot, and this requires skill and evaluated experience. An easy-to-remember guiding principle is this:

- *Pause:* listen attentively and emphatically to the learner.
- *Paraphrase:* summarize, rephrase, translate, or give an example.
- *Probe:* seek clarification whenever necessary.

Try using all these three levels of cognitive questioning, but they must be appropriate to the specific coaching events. Begin by questioning less and listening more to establish learners' ownership and empowerment of the entire PBL process.

Principles of Effective Coaching

Like the law of gravity acting on an object, a principle holds true under all situations regardless of the context. Therefore, principles are powerful laws or truths governing the behaviors and/or outcomes of the objects or events within which they operate. Similarly, in coaching PBL, there are certain principles that teachers should be cognizant of. These principles of effective coaching include both general and specific ones.

Specific coaching principles for a PBL unit include the following:

- Plan a PBL unit that will engage students, meet curriculum requirements, and develop students' problem-solving skills.
- Prepare students for their role as active problem solvers and self-directed learners.
- Interest learners in the ill-structured problem.
- Coach building of hypothesis, reasoning, and construction of meaning.
- Coach problem definition.
- Coach information gathering and sharing.
- Encourage generation of solutions.
- Coach "fit" of solutions to the problem.
- Develop and implement authentic assessment of student learning.
- Debrief the process.

More general coaching principles include these:

- Avoid "yes" or "no" questions and questions that require one-word answers.
- Avoid excessive restating.
- Resist the temptation to correct immediately or to interrupt.
- Diagnose learners' needs and engagement through careful observation.
- Encourage participation of all students.
- Encourage justification of ideas.
- Extend learners' thinking using thoughtful questions.
- Embed appropriate instruction and mentoring in the PBL unit.
- Facilitate goal setting and strategy building, while encouraging openness, patience, enthusiasm, initiative-taking, in confronting ill-structured, ambiguous, and incomplete problems.
- Maintain appropriate levels of challenge throughout the PBL unit.

- Monitor reasoning, communication, and interpersonal relationships, and provide appropriate and reasonably immediate feedback.
- In teaching collaboration, ask who does what, when, and why, and consider the implications of doing this the same way or differently from day to day.

While both lists may seem overwhelmingly long, it is through constant practice with feedback and reflection that these principles become embedded in us. The key to becoming an effective teacher-coach lies in our willingness and ability to reflect and learn from our experiences. Not everyone learns from experience; there are people who do not learn, so that even when they go through similar experiences a second or third time they behave very much in the same way as before. We often assume that we learn from our experience and that experience is the best teacher. This is an inaccurate conception. The truth is that only *evaluated* experience is the best teacher. Merely going through an experience does not guarantee that we learn from it, although an experience might be the starting point of our learning. "Our day-to-day experiences as we confront challenges, incidents, and problems in our lives are rich sources of learning … if accompanied by reflection on action" (Butler, 2001, 1). Hence, teachers need to engage in reflective practice in order to become effective in coaching cognitive processes.

In coaching overt behaviors, teachers should be mindful that these behaviors are "the products and artifacts of inner thought processes and intellectual functions. To change the overt behaviors of instruction requires the alteration and rearrangement of the inner and invisible cognitive behaviors of instruction" (Costa & Garmston, 1994, 16). Teacher-coaches will have to adopt the role of mediators. As mediators, trust-building becomes an essential component of the coaching process. Therefore, besides the principles of effective coaching, teachers will also have to match learners' nonverbal cues in attempting to build rapport and trust in the longer term. Nonverbal cues to be matched include posture, gesture, inflection, pitch, volume, rate of speech, language choice, and even breathing.

Teachers' Experiences as Coaches

A group of 15 secondary school teachers participated over a four-month period (April to July 1999) in a project involving the use of PBL in classroom teaching. These teachers formed three heterogeneous groups from three different schools with teaching experiences ranging from 3 to 20 years and in various disciplines, such as English language, Chinese language, science (physics and chemistry), mathematics, and history. Together they formed a rich and diverse working group for developing an interdisciplinary problem for a PBL unit. The project was undertaken as part of a larger framework of the Teachers' Network known as the Learning Circle. The Learning Circle, a primary activity of the Teachers' Network, involves "teachers who want to better understand educational issues and concerns of common interest, or teachers who are keen to further develop an idea or teaching strategy" (Ministry of Education, 1998, 2).

The feedback from the participants was very positive. Generally, the teachers felt that their involvement in this project had been an enriching learning experience. In fact, one teacher noted that students' learning transcended the learning of content knowledge and skills; it was learning to learn that had impacted the students:

> In terms of, maybe, not just content, it will be more of the nontangible [*sic*] things. Questioning, be able to question concepts, establish ideas, developing interest for science, and to play a more active role in learning. Not just sitting back and receiving. So these are the values which I think are useful (interview transcript 8, July 22, 1999).

These benefits came about because teachers had changed their role and adopted a more facilitative teaching style. However, commenting on the need for a more facilitative style, a beginning teacher with only one year of teaching experience described her own fear of this changed role:

> The teacher also needs a change. I won't be able to cope with it if you suddenly dump me in this kind of situation. I don't know what is within my control and what is not within my control. I really don't know (interview transcript 2, July 7, 1999).

Similar findings from other studies (Doyle, 1977; Rich, 1993) reveal that this change does not happen easily. In fact, teachers feel threatened when using new models of pedagogy because of a feeling of incompetence and being out of control. As a result, they would often revert to more familiar strategies, such as the didactic style of the traditional teacher talk, that they are already comfortable with. "When faced with insecurity in the complex environment of the classroom, teachers tend to revert to methods they know to be effective in rendering the situation manageable" (Baumfield & Oberski, 1998, 48).

On a separate occasion, because of the discomfort with this changed role and the accompanying lack of confidence in coaching, the same teacher actually expressed doubt that the PBL approach could enable students to achieve their desired learning outcomes:

> So actually I'm … quite happy with what I'm seeing at the moment. So hopefully, on Thursday, when I give them the test, everything is OK. To me, a lot depends on the test results. At the end of the day when I mark the scripts, then we will see how [things go] (interview transcript 9, July 26, 1999).

Apart from the concern over students' performance in tests, this teacher was quite satisfied with the PBL experience. Ironically, this concern is exactly the central thrust of the PBL approach: that students be developed from being passive recipients of knowledge through to being active inquirers to becoming productive problem solvers (see Figure 1). This is the challenge in our education system in the knowledge-based economy. In this new era, along with rapid technological advances, changes are swift and inevitable. Indeed, the attitude of "why fix things when they ain't broken" can no longer be a justification for contending with the status quo. Teachers and students alike must be prepared for changes and indeed must change. In the next section, a framework is proposed with an example in physical science to look into how teachers can make this paradigm shift in mindset.

What's Next after Coaching? A Framework to Develop Learners as Active Inquirers

Conventionally, when a teacher sets a task requiring students to, say, calculate the specific heat capacity of a given solid, the learning objective is to be able to define what specific heat capacity of a solid is. The mindset of the teacher is to focus on the product, on academic rationalism, on getting the one correct answer (see Table 1).

When teachers begin to redesign the learning task and ask students "How do you find the specific heat capacity of a solid?", the learning objective now becomes "to discover different methods" of determining the specific heat capacity of that solid. We begin to focus our minds on possibilities instead of being confined to the one correct answer. Next, instead of insisting that students learn about the specific heat capacity of a given solid, if teachers were to ask "What might you want to know about this solid?", we change the learning objective again. We begin to encourage students to make observations, ask questions, form hypotheses, and test

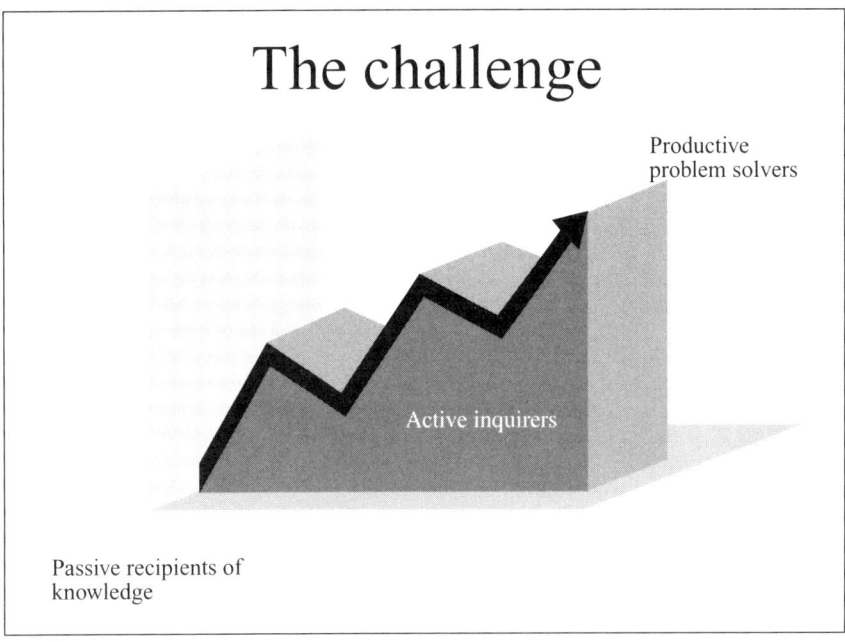

The challenge

Productive
problem solvers

Active inquirers

Passive recipients of
knowledge

FIGURE 1   The challenge in education

them. In essence, we deepen their inquiry skills. The focus is then on the process.

Finally, as in most research work, there will be no given object, no prescribed method, and students have to learn to pose their own problems. In order to solve them, they will have to learn to become productive problem solvers. At this stage, the focus is on people as individual learners. When we reach this stage, we would have arrived at the pinnacle of learning through the PBL approach.

TABLE 1   Shift in question design, objective, and mindset

Question	Objective	Mindset
Find the specific heat capacity of a solid: Amount of heat, $Q = mc\theta$	To define specific heat capacity of solid	Product
How do you find the specific heat capacity of a solid?	To discover different methods	Possibilities
What might you want to know about this solid?	To deepen inquiry skills	Process
No given object. No given method. Find your own problem.	To develop problem solvers	People

References

Baumfield, V., & Oberski, I. (1998). What do teachers think about thinking skills? *Quality Assurance in Education*, *6*, 44–51.

Beyer, B. K. (1997). *Improving student thinking: A comprehensive approach*. Boston: Allyn and Bacon.

Blumenfeld, P. C., Soloway, E., Marx, R. W., Krajcik, J. S., Guzdial, M., & Palincsar, A. (1998). Motivating project-based learning: Sustaining the doing, supporting the learning. In R. Fogarty (Ed.), *Problem-based learning: A collection of articles* (pp. 103–39). Arlington Heights, IL: SkyLight.

Boud, D. (Ed.) (1985). Problem based learning in perspective. In *Problem based learning in education for the professions* (pp. 13–18). Sydney: Higher Education Research and Development Society of Australasia.

Bridges, E. M. (1992). *Problem based learning for administrators*. Eugene, OR: ERIC Clearinghouse on Educational Management.

Brophy, J. (1989). Advances in research on teaching. In *Teaching for understanding*, Vol. 1. Greenwich, CT: JAI Press.

Bryant, S. L., & Timmins, A. A. (2000). Using portfolio assessment as an innovation to assess problem-based learning in Hong Kong schools. In O. S. Tan, P. Little, S. Y. Hee, & J. Conway (Eds.), *Problem-based learning: Educational innovation across disciplines* (pp. 155–68). Singapore: Temasek Centre for Problem-Based Learning.

Butler, J. (2001). Reflection: Images of the self in action. Paper presented at the Ninth International Conference on Thinking. Auckland, New Zealand, January.

Costa, A. L. (Ed.) (2001). Habits of mind. In *Developing minds: A resource book for teaching thinking* (3rd ed., pp. 80–86). Alexandria, VA: Association for Supervision and Curriculum Development.

Costa, A. L., & Garmston, R. J. (1994). *Cognitive coaching: A foundation for renaissance schools*. Norwood, MA: Christopher-Gordon.

Doyle, T. (1977). Learning the classroom environment. *Journal of Teacher Education*, *28*, 51–55.

Gallagher, S. A., Stepien, W. J., Sher, B. T., & Workman, D. (1995). Implementing problem-based learning in science classroom. *School Science and Mathematics*, *95*, 136–46.

Ho, B. T. (1999). Using problem-based learning (PBL) as a curriculum development tool. In *Proceedings of the Joint Malaysia–Singapore Educational Research Association Conference*. Malacca, Malaysia.

Ho, B. T. (2001). Reflective teachers as leaders: A model for quality teaching. Paper presented at the Teachers' Network Conference 2001 on Teacher Leadership. Singapore, May 30–June 1.

Ho, B. T., & Toh, K. A. (2001). Secondary school teachers' reflections on the use of problem-based learning in classroom teaching. In J. Tan, S. Gopinathan, & W. K. Ho (Eds.), *Challenges facing the Singapore educational system today* (pp. 71–82). Singapore: Prentice Hall.

Ho, B. T., & Toh, K. A. (2002). The role of teachers in the 21st century classrooms: From consumerism to trend-setting. Paper presented at the Teachers' Network Conference 2002 on the Classroom of the 21st Century—A Paradigm Shift. Singapore, May 29–30.

Kitchener, K. S. (1983). Cognition, meta-cognition and epistemic cognition: A three-level model of cognitive processing. *Human Development*, *26*, 222–32.

McConnell, R. (2000). *The successful coach*. Auckland: HarperCollins.

Ministry of Education, Singapore (1998). Leading the way: The teacher as a catalyst of change. Speech by Teo Chee Hean, Minister for Education and Second Minister for Defence at the Teachers' Network official launch on April 30. http://www1.moe.edu.sg/Speeches/300498.html.

Newmann, F. M. (1990). Higher order thinking in teaching social studies. *Journal of Curriculum Studies*, *22*, 41–56.

Prawat, R. (1989). Promoting access to knowledge, strategies, and dispositions in students: A research synthesis. *Review of Educational Research*, *59*, 1–41.

Rich, E. (1993). Stability and change in teacher expertise. *Teaching and Teacher Education*, *9*, 137–46.

Rosenshine, B., & Stevens, R. (1986). Teaching functions. In M. C. Wittrock (Ed.), *Handbook of research on teaching* (3rd ed., pp. 376–91). New York: Macmillan.

Savery, J. R., & Duffy, T. M. (1998). Problem based learning: An instructional model and its constructivist framework. In R. Fogarty (Ed.), *Problem-based learning: A collection of articles* (pp. 73–92). Arlington Heights, IL: SkyLight.

Tan, O. S. (2000). Thinking skills, creativity and problem-based learning. In O. S. Tan, P. Little, S. Y. Hee, & J. Conway (Eds.), *Problem-based learning: Educational innovation across disciplines* (pp. 47–55). Singapore: Temasek Centre for Problem-Based Learning.

Wiggins, G. (1987). Creating a thought-provoking curriculum. *American Educator*, *11*, 10–17.

CHAPTER 7

Problem-based Learning in Medical Education: Curriculum Reform and Alignment of Expected Outcomes

Matthew C. E. Gwee

The Central Mission of Medical Education

> The central mission of medical education is to improve the quality of health care delivered by doctors and we must never fail to remember the central role played by patients as the ultimate recipients of our skills—what doctors do, and how and when they do it, depends on the quality of medical education. We need to get it right (Bligh & Parsell, 2000).

Whether patients will live or die, and the quality of life they will have upon recovery from an illness or disease, is critically dependent upon what doctors do and how and when they do it. Moreover, the degree of faith, trust, and respect that patients have for their doctors depends much upon what doctors do and how they do it in initiating and maintaining the doctor–patient relationship. In a similar context, what medical teachers teach and how and when they teach it impact strongly on the quality of the education that they provide to students and, consequently, on the quality of medical graduates when they take on their professional roles in practice. Thus, in preparing the medical students of today to become the competent and caring doctors of tomorrow, medical teachers need to get it right.

The Traditional Medical Curriculum: Entrenchment, Entrapment, and Soul Searching

> Medical education, with its intensive pattern of basic science lectures followed by an equally exhausting clinical programme, was rapidly becoming an ineffective and inhumane way to prepare students, given the explosion in medical education and the rapidly changing demands of future practice (Boud & Feletti, 1997).

Undergraduate medical education has been deeply entrenched and entrapped in tradition over many decades. Major critics of traditional medical education have often come from within the medical profession. This has prompted medical educators to engage in periodic soul searching for over a century in their attempts to design an effective and relevant curriculum for preparing medical students for their future practice. More importantly, the criticisms also have often provided the impetus for curriculum reforms in medical education (General Medical Council, U.K., 1993).

Identifying Major Shortcomings: Pedagogical Sins of Commission and Omission

Three pedagogical limitations (the unholy trinity) have been identified as the major shortcomings in traditional undergraduate medical education:

1. Highly lecture-based instruction
2. Highly discipline-specific curricula
3. Highly teacher-centered education

A criticism of the highly lecture-based instruction is that "the scarcely tolerable burden of information that is imposed taxes the memory but not the intellect. The emphasis is on the passive acquisition of knowledge, much of it to become outdated or forgotten, rather than on its discovery through curiosity and experiment" (General Medical Council, 1993). In such an educational environment, students become passive recipients of abundant and often inert content knowledge that causes information overload. Student learning and thinking, therefore, are often not curiosity-driven nor grounded in understanding (deep learning). Instead, students resort to rote learning (memorize, recall, regurgitate) as a survival skill to pass examinations that test mainly recall of facts. Knowledge acquisition is therefore the main outcome of this mode of instruction. As Meyers and Jones (1993) have commented, "a steady diet of lecturing leads to intellectual anaemia."

Miller (1961) has clearly pointed out that "each department is responsible for some part of the education of a medical student, but no department should forget that it is no more than a part of the whole school which is responsible for the education of a whole student and the fulfillment of the overall objectives." Unfortunately, the highly discipline-specific traditional medical curriculum created the great preclinical–clinical divide leading to the departmentalization of the medical disciplines, which vie for time and dominance without due regard for the goals of the overall curriculum. Abrahamson (1978) characterized this situation as "curriculosclerosis," one of nine diseases of the medical curriculum, which tends to stifle and inhibit curriculum development and function with a design that reflects "more a power-struggle than an educational venture."

Students on such a curriculum undertake compartmentalized learning that borders on the education of "mini-specialists" in multiple disciplines! Consequently, medical students often lack the ability to integrate and apply knowledge from different disciplines, especially in the transfer of basic science knowledge to the disease process and to patient care. The serious consequences of pedagogically separating knowledge and understanding from action and practice in medical education have been clearly pointed out by Margetson (1999). The need to ensure greater unity (integration) in diversity of the undergraduate medical curriculum is now well recognized as a priority in curriculum reforms implemented in medical schools worldwide.

In the traditional teacher-centered education, the dominance of the teacher as the know-all and the sage in center stage creates in students a high dependency state, relying on their teachers to decide for them what, when, and how to learn, including a strong predisposition toward an addiction to lectures. Medical students, therefore, often lack the skills, the confidence, and the motivation to undertake self-directed learning, for which they need to take greater initiative for their own learning and to develop skills for appraising the accuracy of information obtained from various sources. Boud (2001) has cautioned that we teachers can potentially "deskill" students by unrealistically mediating all that they need to know.

The Need for Medical Education Reform

> ... we can at best strive to educate doctors capable of adaptation to change, with minds that can encompass new ideas and developments and with attitudes to learning that inspire the continuation of the educational process throughout professional life (General Medical Council, 1993).

Global events emerging in this digital age of information explosion, along with the rapid advances made in science, technology, and the information and communication field, have had a major impact on the setting of priorities and strategies at all levels of education. More importantly, education today must enable students to meet the growing challenges and the increasingly more complex demands of the work environment and of daily living in this new millennium. Similarly, major reform of the undergraduate medical curriculum is necessary to cope with changes in the medical field, such as the changing patterns of diseases (including the emergence of more chronic ailments of old age) and of health-care delivery; exponential growth in medical knowledge and rapid advances in medical technology; higher expectations of more educated patients, who are better informed about health matters; and greater emphasis on preventive and community health care. Thus, student learning in the knowledge, skills, and attitudinal domains in medical education need to be redefined to closely reflect the changing needs and demands required of good medical practice in the years ahead (Dent, 2001).

It is imperative for educators to reappraise the undergraduate medical curriculum to align the education of students with the desired outcomes in the context of the medical and health-care needs in this new millennium. An educational strategy known as the SPICES model (Harden, Snowden, & Dunn, 1984) offers a useful approach to planning and designing an undergraduate medical curriculum that can overcome many of the major shortcomings identified in traditional medical education. Several of the major educational elements of the SPICES model—which is a student-centered, problem-based, integrated, community-based, elective, systematic approach—are incorporated in the problem-based learning (PBL) strategy. Moreover, incorporating the PBL strategy in medical education will more effectively address the concerns expressed by the General Medical Council (1993) that "the doctors of tomorrow will be applying knowledge and deploying skills which are at present unforeseen," a philosophy that must guide educators in designing the undergraduate medical curriculum of today.

Problem-based Learning: An Innovative Pathway to Learning in Medical Education

Problem-based learning (PBL) is grounded in the belief that learning is most effective when students are actively involved and learn in the context in which the knowledge is to be used (Boud & Feletti, 1997).

The contextual theory has often been claimed to be the main pedagogical underpinning of PBL. The basic premise is that when material is learned in the context in which it is to be applied, learning—and therefore the ability to use that information—is enhanced. More recently, Albanese (2000) has criticized this theory as one of the least compelling theories in support of PBL, since almost the entire clinical education is in the relevant context of patient care. Albanese proposed four other theories as the major pedagogical underpinnings of PBL:

- The *information processing theory*, which relates to prior knowledge activation, encoding specificity (i.e., learning in context), and knowledge elaboration (i.e., creating opportunities for active discussion).
- The *cooperative learning theory*, which relates to mutual cooperation and support in group learning with the aim of achieving common goals.
- The *self-determination theory*, which relates to conditions that are more likely to promote intrinsic (autonomous) motivation, as in a PBL environment (in contrast to the extrinsic or controlled motivation that is likely to occur in a traditional curriculum).
- The *control theory*, which relates to influencing behavior through satisfying an individual's basic needs for survival, belonging and love, power, freedom, and fun. From a pedagogical viewpoint, the PBL small-group learning design seems to correlate well with this theory.

The Role of PBL in Medical Education

PBL is a learning system design that incorporates several complementary pedagogical elements in a strategic alliance that is employed in medical education to enhance and optimize student learning, not only in the acquisition of knowledge but also in the development and acquisition of more enduring and transferable process and professional skills required for medical practice. In its operational context, PBL can be defined as the learning that results from the process of working toward the understanding or resolution of a problem (Spaulding, 1969; Barrows & Tamblyn, 1980; Barrows, 1996).

Essentially, then, PBL represents a major shift in educational paradigm to problem-based, process-oriented, discipline-integrated, and student-centered learning in collaborative small groups. It creates excellent opportunities for students to engage in regular practice in the problem-solving process so essential to medical practice. PBL in medical education also focuses on learning, not only about a patient's disease but also about the patient's "dis-ease" (discomfort) and about the impact and implications of the disease on the patient's family, the community, and the population. PBL, therefore, offers a more holistic approach to medical education that incorporates learning about the population, the behavior, and the life sciences in relation to diseases.

Expected Educational Outcomes of PBL in Medical Education

KNOWLEDGE ACQUISITION

An important intended outcome of PBL in medical education is to enhance the problem-solving skills of students in preparation for their future role as doctors; and this, according to Norman (1997), will require students to acquire an optimum knowledge base. An immediate aim of PBL, therefore, must be to ensure that learning results in enhanced knowledge acquisition. Earlier studies reported that, when compared to students from conventional medical curricula, PBL students did not perform much better, or even slightly worse in some cases (Albanese & Mitchell, 1993; Berkson, 1993; Vernon & Blake, 1993; Norman & Schmidt, 2000). However, a more recent study provided more convincing evidence that medical students from PBL curricula performed better than students from traditional curricula in the United States Medical Licensing Examination (USMLE) (Blake, Hosokawa, & Riley, 2000).

BEYOND KNOWLEDGE ACQUISITION: ENHANCING PROCESS, PROFESSIONAL, AND LIFE SKILLS

Apart from knowledge transfer, medical students should also be inculcated with attitudes of mind and of behavior that befit a doctor, together with qualities appropriate to their future responsibilities to patients, colleagues, and the community in general (General Medical Council, 1993). Learning in small social groups (or learning communities) is the main instructional design used in the delivery of PBL curricula. Such a structure creates opportunities for students to practice and develop transferable skills useful to their future practice and professional development. Central to the goals of PBL in medical education is the nurturing and enhancement of the *problem-solving skills* of students with the expectation of the transfer of these skills to the clinical management of patients in their future practice. The PBL strategy creates excellent opportunities for students to regularly practice and learn the problem-solving process early in the course.

PBL also fosters the development of *self-directed learning skills*, which will lay the foundation for, and is fundamental to, nurturing the habit of lifelong continuing self-education so essential to ensuring continued professional competence in medical practice. Medical students consistently report that they enjoy their learning experience in a PBL environment, and Albanese (2000) suggested that such an environment is more likely to motivate students to undertake lifelong learning. The need to inculcate in students the habit of lifelong engagement in learning is clearly stated in the recommendations of the General Medical Council (1993).

Medical students need to develop *critical thinking skills*, which are vital for the clinical decision-making process. PBL is expected to help students learn how to analyze, evaluate, integrate, and apply information through their active involvement in learning together in small groups. The PBL tutorial, therefore, creates an "all teach, all learn" educational setting for students to engage in peer teaching and learning through constructive dialogue (brainstorming, argumentation, exchanging viewpoints, seeking clarification and justification), which, according to Abercrombie (1960), promotes clinical judgment. "Discussion in a group does for thinking what testing on real objects does for seeing. . . . Instead of seeing our own mistakes by contrast with the statements of an unquestioned authority as in the traditional pupil–teacher relationship, we see a variety of interpretations of the same stimulus pattern, and the usefulness of each must be tested in its own right" (Abercrombie, 1960). Moreover, Brookfield (1987) pointed out that, when like-minded students learn together through mutual exploration and critical discussion, the process provides "a powerful psychological ballast to critical thinking efforts."

PBL also fosters the development of *reflective learning* through feedback sessions, and this helps develop self-awareness and hence encourages self-initiated remedial action (i.e., metacognition). Consequently, students can develop personal insights of their strengths and limitations relating to a given area of learning, an attribute that characterizes critical thinkers (Halpern, 1996; Maudsley & Strivens, 2000).

The PBL small-group learning also provides students with opportunities to develop their *communication skills*. Doctors have to be able and willing to communicate effectively, an attribute that the General Medical Council (1993) recommends must be developed throughout the undergraduate course and beyond. There is now an even greater need for doctors to communicate effectively with and display a more caring attitude toward patients. Today's patients are more educated and better informed about health matters, as such information is now readily available at the click of a button, and they also have greater expectations about what doctors can and should do for them. Skills in effective communication are critical to initiating and maintaining an optimum doctor–patient relationship, and the General Medical Council (1993) observed that a high proportion of complaints and misunderstandings result from the lack of communication skills among doctors. This lack of communication, resulting in misunderstanding, could lead to unnecessary litigation (*Medical Alumni Newsletter*, 2001).

Interpersonal and teamwork skills are also essential for doctors working in a health-care team. Small-group learning in PBL promotes the development of such skills, as it is underpinned by cooperative learning principles characterized by "joint goals, mutual rewards, shared resources, and complementary roles among the members of a group" (Albanese, 2000). Qin, Johnson, and Johnson (1995) concluded from a meta-analysis that higher-quality problem solving is achieved through cooperation than through competition (effect size = 0.55): "The average person (at the 50th percentile) in the cooperation condition solved problems better than 72.5% of the participants in the competitive condition."

A consistent finding in the medical literature is that students and teachers express more joy in learning together through the PBL process, when compared to those learning through more conventional curricula, and that PBL provides a more collegial environment for learning (Albanese, 2000). In his commentary on PBL in medical education, Federman (1999) made the point that "the benefits of contact between student and student, and between student and tutor, need no statistical confirmation." The PBL strategy, therefore, creates a conducive learning environment that builds partnerships and bonding in learning between students and their tutors and among students. Students learn through social interaction in an educational setting, and they also learn to comply with the "code of practice" for working in groups. In the process, they develop mutual trust and respect as well as provide support to one another. Consequently, students can be expected to develop useful interpersonal skills required of health-care practitioners working as a team. According to a Canadian study, PBL graduates from McMaster Medical School showed a greater desire for affiliation in their choice of medical careers and specialties, thus providing evidence that PBL does have a strong impact on the learning environment (Woodward, Ferrier, Cohen, & Goldsmith, 1990).

Return on Investment in PBL in Medical Education

The strategic alliance of complementary pedagogical elements employed in the PBL approach offers great expectations. The PBL way to medical education is expected to lead to more effective acquisition and transfer of knowledge, skills, and attitudes that will equip students with desirable abilities and attributes required of a competent and caring doctor throughout his or her professional life. However, there appears to be a serious mismatch between the high expectations of the outcomes and the results of outcome measures of PBL in medical education.

Two meta-evaluations (Albanese & Mitchell, 1993; Vernon & Blake, 1993) and a study (Berkson, 1993) showed that only small, short-term gains in medical knowledge and clinical skills were achieved through PBL. Colliver (2000) interpreted the findings as clear evidence that PBL does not improve knowledge base and clinical performance to the extent that is to be expected considering the commitment of resources. The main thrust of Colliver's arguments is that the theoretical basis (of the contextual learning theory) underpinning PBL is weak and that the effect sizes produced by studies of PBL approaches in medical education were less than 0.8 and thus did not live up to expectations (of 0.8 to 1.0).

Citing the review of Nendaz and Tekian (1999) for support, Rothman (2000) pointed out that assessment in PBL is still unsatisfactory, without any specific model to follow, and lacking in psychometric scrutiny. He also raised doubts about the value of implementing PBL in the clinic, since there would be difficulties encountered as a consequence primarily of differences in the culture and environment of the preclinical and the clinical contexts, as described by Gresham and Philip (1996). Rothman concluded that it may be time to acknowledge that there are serious limitations of the PBL approach.

The arguments so far seem to suggest that the PBL approach in medical education has little pedagogical advantage to offer in terms of educational outcomes, especially in view of the demands made on the resources of an institution in the implementation of PBL. Thus, the return on investment in PBL would seem rather uncertain in medical education, raising some genuine concerns among educators that need to be addressed urgently.

Insights and Perspectives on the Educational Outcomes of PBL in Medical Education

Several counter-arguments have been advanced that criticized Colliver's (2000) interpretation and conclusion that there is no convincing evidence for the educational benefits of PBL in medical education. Agreeing with Colliver that the contextual theory is weak, Albanese (2000) proposed four other theories (information processing theory, cooperative learning theory, self-determination theory, and control theory—which were described earlier in this chapter) that he considered could provide stronger theoretical underpinnings for PBL and better explain and predict the effectiveness of the various elements of PBL. He also offered some plausible explanations for the apparent mismatch between the expected educational outcomes of PBL and the results of outcome measures.

Albanese (2000) considered it unrealistic to expect knowledge gain by medical students on a PBL curriculum to reach statistical significance with a large effect size of 0.8 or greater as perceived by Colliver since, firstly, "many very commonly used and accepted medical procedures and therapies are based upon studies that had effect sizes even below 0.5." Moreover, medical students generally are already very high achievers and, consequently, top medical students who receive high grades in examinations cannot be expected to go much higher whatever innovative curriculum they may be subjected to. The operation of such "ceiling effects" will therefore make it difficult to show significant gains in knowledge in such comparative studies.

Albanese also drew attention to "system issues" related to the prior learning experience of students when in school, as this would have a considerable influence on the outcome measures of such comparative studies. He pointed out that, throughout their schooling, medical students have been nurtured and selected by a traditional educational approach in which they have excelled and, therefore, expecting them "to suddenly excel in a different type of milieu seems to be overly optimistic." Albanese also commented that the selection process of medical students itself guarantees that they will survive well in a traditional curriculum, and to expect such students to perform better in PBL would seem like "transporting a T. rex from the Jurassic period to modern times and expecting it to thrive in a petting zoo"!

Additionally, Albanese pointed out that it would be difficult to interpret with any accuracy the results of the outcome measures used in evaluating the effectiveness of PBL in medical education, since the assessment strategies used to measure performance generally have been designed for the conventional curriculum. Consequently, performance in PBL would mean that it has not only to outperform the former curriculum in meeting the old goals but to meet the goals of the new curriculum too. Such confounding and conflicting aims and procedures cannot therefore generate the effect sizes expected. Moreover, as discussed above, the effect sizes are also likely to be attenuated by system issues.

Similar arguments were put forth by Norman and Schmidt (2000), who observed that "educational trials are ill-founded and ill-advised" since it is not possible to ensure blinding, either among students or among teachers, in such interventions. Thus, success or failure cannot be attributed solely to a given intervention. The authors also highlighted the futility of seeking cause and effect relationships in respect of the PBL curriculum, as PBL represents not just a single curricular intervention but an alliance of several curriculum components (e.g., group size and dynamics, quality of problem case, tutor characteristics, overall curriculum goals). Thus, in estimating the effectiveness of PBL, it is important to take into account the possibility of complex interactions among the various components.

Toward a New Generation of PBL Strategies in Medical Education

PBL has been one of the most successful innovations in medical education and has established credibility. It is time to step back to reflect on "accepted practice" and to develop the next generation of PBL (Kaufman, 2000).

While recognizing some of the shortcomings of its expected educational deliverables, the PBL strategy's inherent pedagogical strength still makes a strong case for reflection, retention, and its renewal in medical education. Albanese (2000) drew attention to the fact that there is compelling evidence that PBL is doing something useful, in view of the fact that it has spread so widely within and beyond medicine. Kaufman (2000) also provided strong support to several of the arguments advanced by Albanese. The most consistent benefit, and the ultimate outcome, of PBL relates to the creation of a conducive learning environment enjoyed by both students and teachers (Norman & Schmidt, 2000; Albanese, 2000). "PBL does provide a more challenging, motivating and enjoyable approach to medical education. That may be a sufficient raison d'être, providing that the cost of implementation is not too great" (Norman & Schmidt, 2000).

A more recent study comparing graduates from the traditional and from the PBL curricula clearly showed gains in scores for the PBL group, based on their performance in the USMLE (Blake et al., 2000). It is noteworthy that the design strategy of this examination has changed: questions now increasingly test knowledge application in the clinical context. Thus, this study clearly demonstrates the need to ensure that the design of the quality control system for appraising the effectiveness of any innovative curriculum change employs performance measures that are appropriate for and relevant and sensitive to (and not distort) the intended outcomes to be measured (Albanese, 2000).

Kaufman (2000) has therefore proposed that we critically reflect on the pedagogical issues in PBL that impact strongly on the achievement of the intended outcomes of PBL in medical education, especially in regard to enhancing the psychometric scrutiny of assessment in PBL through more relevant and more insightful research, as well as "bridging the gap between the PBL approach used in the pre-clinical and clinical settings with actual patient problems seen by learners" with the specific aim of developing the next generation of PBL strategies.

Conclusion

> Even if knowledge acquisition and clinical skills are not improved by PBL, the enhanced work environment for students and faculty that has been consistently found with PBL is a worthwhile goal (Albanese, 2000).

PBL has certainly endured the test of time since its inception more than three decades ago. It continues to flourish and to spread widely beyond the discipline of medicine and in many continents, including Asia, which is now experiencing a rapid rise in the acceptance of PBL, especially in medical schools. More recently, the return on educational investment in PBL has been questioned, giving rise to serious concerns among educators about the value and benefits of PBL in medical education. At the same time, there are strong arguments that support the continued use of PBL in medical education. There is good reason to be optimistic: as noted by Albanese (2000), "change may be in the offing," in his reference to the compelling evidence of PBL students scoring better in the USMLE. The need for more relevant and insightful research in PBL that will further enhance its status as a value-added, quality-enhancing, and more holistic pedagogical strategy in medical education is also well recognized.

It is indeed likely that the best is yet to come from PBL in medical education, as "it will probably take a change in the entire educational process leading up to medical school before PBL (or any similar innovation) will be likely to reach its true potential" (Albanese, 2000). The serious concerns notwithstanding, PBL can certainly claim to provide an innovative pathway to learning in medical education with clear accruing benefits in the humanistic aspects of medicine: "But isn't that, enriched by science, what medicine is?" as Federman (1999) so aptly observed.

References

Abercrombie, M. L. J. (1960). *The anatomy of judgement.* Harmondsworth: Penguin.

Abrahamson, S. (1978). Diseases of the curriculum. *Journal of Medical Education, 53*, 951–57.

Albanese, M. A. (2000). Problem-based learning: Why curricula are likely to show little effect on knowledge and clinical skills. *Medical Education, 34*, 729–38.

Albanese, M. A., & Mitchell, S. (1993). Problem-based learning: A review of literature on its outcomes and implementation issues. *Academic Medicine, 68*, 52–81.

Barrows, H. S. (1996). Problem-based learning in medicine and beyond: A brief overview. In L. Wilkerson & W. H. Gijselaers (Eds.), *Bringing problem-based learning to higher education: Theory and practice* (pp. 3–12). New directions for teaching and learning, No. 68. San Francisco: Jossey-Bass.

Barrows, H. S., & Tamblyn, R. N. (1980). *Problem-based learning: An approach to medical education.* New York: Springer.

Berkson, L. (1993). Problem-based learning: Have the expectations been met? *Academic Medicine, 68* (Suppl.), 79–88.

Blake, R. L., Hosokawa, M. C., & Riley, S. L. (2000). Student performances on Step 1 and Step 2 of the United States Medical Licensing Examination following implementation of a problem-based learning curriculum. *Academic Medicine, 75*, 66–70.

Bligh, J., & Parsell, G. (2000). Taking stock . . . *Medical Education, 34*, 416–17.

Boud, D. (2001). Introduction: Making the move to peer learning. In D. Boud, R. Cohen, & J. Sampson (Eds.), *Peer learning in higher education.* London: Kogan Page.

Boud, D., & Feletti, G. I. (Eds.) (1997). *The challenge of problem-based learning* (2nd ed.). London: Kogan Page.

Brookfield, S. D. (1987). *Developing critical thinkers: Challenging adults to explore alternative ways of thinking and acting.* San Francisco: Jossey-Bass.

Colliver, J. A. (2000). Effectiveness of problem-based learning curricula: Research and theory. *Academic Medicine, 75,* 259–66.

Dent, J. A. (2001). Teaching and learning medicine. In J. A. Dent & R. M. Harden (Eds.), *A practical guide for medical teachers.* Edinburgh: Churchill Livingstone.

Federman, D. D. (1999). Little-heralded advantages of problem-based learning. *Academic Medicine, 74,* 93–94.

General Medical Council, U.K. (1993). *Tomorrow's doctors: Recommendations on undergraduate medical education.* London.

Gresham, C. L., & Philip, J. R. (1996). Problem-based learning in clinical medicine. *Teaching and Learning in Medicine, 8,* 111–15.

Halpern, D. F. (1996). *Thought and knowledge: An introduction to critical thinking* (3rd ed.). Mahwah, NJ: Erlbaum.

Harden, R. M., Snowden, S., & Dunn, W. R. (1984). Some educational strategies in curriculum development: The SPICES model. *Medical Education, 18,* 284–97.

Kaufman, D. M. (2000). Problem-based learning—Time to step back? *Medical Education, 34,* 510–11.

Margetson, D. B. (1999). The relation between understanding and practice in problem-based learning. *Medical Education, 33,* 359–64.

Maudsley, G., & Strivens, J. (2000). "Science," "critical thinking" and "competence" for tomorrow's doctors: A review of terms and concepts. *Medical Education, 34,* 53–60.

Medical Alumni Newsletter, Singapore (2001). Communication, May, 1–2.

Meyers, C., & Jones, T. B. (1993). *Promoting active learning strategies for the college classroom.* San Francisco: Jossey-Bass.

Miller, G. E. (Ed.) (1961). The objectives of medical education. In *Teaching and learning in medical school.* Cambridge, MA: Harvard University Press.

Nendaz, M. R., & Tekian, A. (1999). Assessment in problem-based learning medical schools: A literature review. *Teaching and Learning in Medicine, 11,* 232–43.

Norman, G. R. (1997). Assessment in problem-based learning. In D. Boud & G. I. Feletti (Eds.), *The challenge of problem-based learning.* London: Kogan Page.

Norman, G. R., & Schmidt, H. G. (2000). Effectiveness of problem-based learning curricula: Theory, practice and paper darts. *Medical Education, 34,* 721–28.

Qin, Z., Johnson, D. W., & Johnson, R. T. (1995). Cooperative versus competitive efforts and problem solving. *Review of Educational Research, 65,* 129–43.

Rothman, A. I. (2000). Problem-based learning—Time to move forward? *Medical Education, 34,* 509–10.

Spaulding, W. B. (1969). The undergraduate medical curriculum (1969 model): McMaster University. *Canadian Medical Association Journal, 100,* 659–64.

Vernon, D. T. A., & Blake, R. L. (1993). Does problem-based learning work? A meta-analysis of evaluative research. *Academic Medicine, 68,* 550–63.

Woodward, C. A., Ferrier, B. M., Cohen, M., & Goldsmith, C. (1990). A comparison of the practice patterns of general practitioners and family physicians graduating from McMaster and other Ontario medical schools. *Teaching and Learning Medicine*, *2*, 79–88.

CHAPTER 8

Collaboration, Dialogue, and Critical Openness through Problem-based Learning Processes

Moira G. C. Lee
Oon-Seng Tan

Introduction

The 21st century is often described as the knowledge-based era. Knowledge is proliferating at an increasing pace. We will not be able to effectively harness the power in all that knowledge if we do not know how to integrate learning from different disciplines and sources through collaborative inquiry and synthesis. Problem-based learning (PBL) is an attempt to achieve that goal: it entails learning to deal with situations where we are uncertain about data, information, as well as the solutions, and mastering the art of harnessing intelligence through self-directed as well as collaborative learning (Tan, 2003).

In PBL classes, learning is done in small groups. Small-group learning provides opportunities for students to actively engage in interactive inquiry and group learning, with the aim to:

- gain a deeper understanding of the knowledge (content and process) being acquired
- learn problem-solving processes

- learn to benefit from team perspectives
- develop interpersonal and communication skills
- learn to be effective team contributors

This chapter focuses on the key psychological aspects of collaboration, dialogue, and critical openness in PBL processes.

Collaborative Learning

Collaborative learning is often used as an umbrella term for a variety of educational approaches involving joint intellectual effort by participants, or participants and facilitators together (Bosworth & Hamilton, 1994; Bruffee, 1984, 1987, 1993; Gamson, 1994; Goodsell et al., 1992; MacGregor, 1990; Matthews, 1996; Whipple, 1987; Wiener, 1986). There is wide variability in collaborative learning activities, but in PBL participants' active exploration of new knowledge, peer learning, and collective inquiry and deliberations are directed toward the resolution of the given problem. In PBL, simulated or real-world problem scenarios are often selected and designed to motivate the formation of a learning community through partnership, working in small groups and networking with people. Questions, problems, or the challenge of discovering something "new" drives the collaborative learning activity.

There are four essential elements in the collaborative learning approach. First, collaborative learning promotes an active engagement with the dialogue process. It is based on the idea that learning is a naturally social act in which the participants talk among themselves. It is through talk that learning occurs. The rapid interchanges ignite a myriad of activities: exploration, clarification, shared interpretation, revelation of differences of opinions, illustration and anecdote telling, explanation through gesture, and expression of doubt.

Second, collaborative learning is based on the social constructionist theory of knowledge creation. Knowledge is regarded as intrinsically the common property of a group, and participants and facilitators are involved in a common enterprise, a mutual search for understanding. Since everyone is grappling with the material simultaneously, collaborative learning has the potential to unleash a unique intellectual and social synergy.

Third, there is a distinct shift in the locus of authority from the traditional teacher to the dynamic learning community, and the traditional classroom social structure is replaced with negotiated relationships between participants as well as between the community of participants and the facilitators. The end result of stimulating interdependence is that the learning community becomes more autonomous, articulate, and socially and intellectually mature.

Fourth, collaborative learning fosters a learning culture where there is an atmosphere of critical openness. There is a ready forum for interchange of ideas and of varying perspectives. The paradox of collaborative learning is that, through the process of interacting with others, individuals rediscover themselves and their perspective expands. If collaboration is to provide a way for participants to negotiate multiple positions, it must involve two recursive moves: a dialectical encounter with an "other" (person or idea) and a reflexive engagement with self.

Stimulating Thinking through Dialogue

Students learn in the PBL process that teamwork and collaboration are important for developing cognitive processes pertaining to scanning the environment, understanding the problem, gathering essential data and analyzing them, and elaborating on solutions. Dialogue is essential to ensure that we are not locked into our own limited or prejudiced perspectives. It is important for developing critical thinking and reflection.

In problem-based approaches, we "make our thinking and mind visible through dialogue" (Tan, 2003, 151). Dialogue is *dia-logos* in Greek, *logos* referring to the making of meaning. PBL involves creating meaningful learning through inquiry and through various channels of dialogue. Through collegial critique, self-evaluation, and reflection, we sharpen our mental tools in problem solving.

In contrast to didactic instruction, in collaborative learning everyone contributes in order to *create* something together. Through mutual exploration, meaning-making, and feedback, there might arise the "germination of an idea that neither party had at the beginning of the exchange" (Furedy & Furedy, 1985, 64). There emerges "shared creation— a situation where two or more individuals with complementary skills interact and create a shared meaning that none had previously possessed or could have come to on their own" (Schrage, 1990, 40).

Differences of opinions are part and parcel of dialogue, reaffirming that consensus should be seen in terms of differences and not just of agreements, as the result of conflicts and not as a monolith. The creative sparks that might be ignited through dialogue move the collaborative learning community to "a different place and level." Growth, movement, and vitality mark the synergistic energy of these communities. A life of its own emerges, and new depths of insight and learning are generated. According to Bohm (1996) and Isaacs (1994), dialogue is given space to emerge within a "life of its own," while Freire's (1993) concept of dialogue is about confronting oppressive structures that inhibit the empowerment of participants. Dialogical education is an integral component in collaborative learning. Wallis and Allman (1996) emphasized that students engaged in dialogical education are not only developing critical understanding but also experiencing and learning a way of communicating that seems extremely appropriate for all types of democratic participation: "Because dialogue is the seal of the transformed epistemological and ontological relations, it develops both critical thought and trusting, harmonious relations between those who engage in it. In an educational context, this means authentically transformed student–teacher relations" (p. 177).

Collaborative learning and dialogue in PBL require an enlightened understanding and effective mediation and facilitation (Tan, 2003). Poor dialogue can happen when PBL groups lack the foundation knowledge and skills, prerequisite experiences, and maturity. The result of poor collaborative learning could be a "pooling of ignorance."

The concept of "generative listening" plays an integral role in the dynamics inherent within collaborative learning communities. Listening attentively and taking in the other's meaning is part of learning. On the other hand, there is a risk of being influenced by what is heard. In this sense, listening gives dialogue its relational and transformative power. Through mutual reflection, dialogue begins to clarify the places where assumptions are tangled or seem to contradict. The act of attentive listening elicits people's true voices and inner wisdom. Pockets of silence might make it easier for the learning community to become "observers of one's own thinking" (Senge, 1993). There might then arise an increased understanding of the participatory nature of thought.

It might be useful to make a subtle distinction between the terms *dialogue* and *discussion*. *Discussion* shares its root meaning with *percussion* and *concussion*, both involving breaking things up. Specifically, the term *discussion* stems from the Latin *discutere*, which means "to smash to pieces." In dialogue, there is the free and creative exploration of complex issues, a deep listening to one another, and suspension of one's own views. By contrast, in discussion, different views are presented and defended and the best view is sought to support decisions that must be made. Dialogue and discussion are potentially complementary, but it seems necessary to distinguish between the two and to move consciously between them. In our opinion, the term *dialogue* is more consonant with the discursive relational dynamics of collaborative learning; there is a constant movement toward shared minds rather than a single overpowering position.

In the field of organizational theory, Bill Isaacs, Director of the Massachusetts Institute of Technology's Dialogue Project, has conducted pioneering research in dialogue process, emphasizing that dialogue differs markedly from the casual discourse of daily life, persuasive discussion, negotiation, or formal debate. Dialogue is most useful for learning about complexity where no one has "the right answer." Rather than trying to understand an issue by breaking it into parts, the practice of dialogue draws attention to the whole. As each person offers a unique contribution to the dialogue, the intent is not to persuade but to explore from another perspective (Bohm, 1996; Isaacs, 1994; Senge et al., 1994).

As conceived by Bohm (1996), dialogue is a multifaceted process that explores the manner in which thought is generated and sustained on a collective level. Such an inquiry calls into question deeply ingrained assumptions about culture, meaning, and identity. Bohm suggested that four elements permeate the dialogue process. First, there is suspension of assumptions. To suspend one's assumptions means to hold them, as if they were hanging in front of you, constantly accessible to questioning and observation. This does not mean throwing out assumptions, suppressing them, or avoiding their expression. Rather, it means being aware of them and holding them up for examination. This cannot be done if one is defending one's opinions. Nor can it be done if one is unaware of one's own assumptions, or unaware that one's views are based on assumptions rather than incontrovertible facts.

In Bohm's second element, the spirit of inquiry involves an open space in which to ask questions about where a particular assertion, belief, or idea comes from. In dialogue, a person who is making broad generalizations can be subject to inquiry. How did he get there? Can he provide others with the data that supports his conclusions? There is greater possibility for deeper understanding arising from the inquiry.

Third, generative listening involves letting go of "building my case" when someone is speaking from a different point of view. It involves listening for understanding rather than preparing to convince the other person that he or she is wrong.

Fourth, holding tension of opposites is an essential element of dialogue. Maintaining a space for polarity and opposites is an acknowledgment of the wide variation in views usually present in a diverse group. There is a container built that respects differences and enjoys and cultivates the energies among diverse elements.

Cultivating Critical Openness

Participants in PBL groups bring their own diverse experiences and learning, which in turn stimulate their own thinking and self-assessment. Entering into critical appraisal with others of one's findings and presentation helps develop the spirit of critical openness and critical reflective thinking.

In a learning community, critical thinking is not relegated to just the cognitive dimension; it has relational and emotional dimensions. The quality of relationships affects the extent to which participants engage in critical openness. "Emotions are central to the critical thinking process. As we try to think critically and help others to do so, we cannot help but become aware of the importance of emotions to this activity. Asking critical questions about our previously accepted values, ideas, and behaviors is anxiety-producing" (Brookfield, 1987, 7).

The process of critical thinking entails an iteration between collaboration (shared world) and reflection (private world) for the purpose of assessing new ideas and perspectives through experience and relationships (Brookfield, 1987; Dewey, 1933; Freire, 1993; Garrison, 1992). In the process of critical thinking, there is "a listening to others in mutuality and self-criticism" (Thiselton, 1995). Dewey (1933) viewed thinking as both an internal and an external process and posited that critical reflective thinking is relating abstract ideas to external things.

In the context of adult education, Brookfield (1987) suggested a five-phase model of critical thinking. The phases consist of a triggering event; appraisal of the situation; exploration to explain anomalies; development of alternative perspectives; and integration of diverse perspectives into the fabric of life. In the integration phase, individuals appraise their perspectives through dialogue with others. Thus, it is in the shared world that meaning is achieved. While constructing meaning is a personal responsibility, the process of critical thinking also includes the application of meaning structures to the specifics of the context. The further grasp of concepts is enhanced through collaborative action, which necessitates sharing control of the process.

Mezirow (1991) has written extensively on reflective learning, a term that he uses synonymously with critical thinking. According to him, meaning is always an interpretation from a contextually defined perspective. Meaning is about one's experience, which guides further action and the revision of meaning schemes. Focusing on communicative learning, Mezirow (1978) posited that through discourse there is the potential for assessing evidence and arguments to consensually arrive at a provisional judgment about the justifiability of the idea. It is through the process of critical discourse that contested meanings are confirmed or negated.

In reflecting on the phrase *critical openness*, Watson (1987) raised three concerns: the problem of critical openness being used to mean the opposite of a committed approach; the unfortunate negative and "destructive overtones" that are sometimes associated with "critical"; and the varying capacity of people to think critically. She suggested an alternative in the phrase *critical affirmation*. For her, critical affirmation is a warmer phrase than critical openness. Its primary meaning is to make firm, strengthen, support, and confirm. It has a positive ring and synergizes with conviction, commitment, and certainty. According to Watson, critical affirmation encompasses five dimensions: the desire to find insights; the expectation that probably insights are to be found; the determination to try to uncover them; the rigorous use of critical faculties in so doing; and the desire to make other people's insights one's own.

In our opinion, Watson's concept of critical affirmation does not get at the "appreciation of differences" nor at "suspension of judgments" that are enmeshed within the concept of critical openness. Additionally, Watson's fifth proposition about making other people's insights one's own implies a unity that is elusive. It is possible to learn from other people's insights, but they will always be "other" to one's own insights. Contrary to Watson's view, Thiessen (1993) recommended that the phrase *normal critical openness* be used. He suggested that adding the word *normal* guards against the negative adversarial connotation some read into the word *critical*. For Thiessen, normal critical openness entails having a disposition to form and revise one's own views in the light of evidence and arguments. This is not incompatible with having strong convictions, so long as there remains "the permanent possibility of reopening even settled issues" (Hare, 1979, 30).

The Value of Questions

Learning involves dealing with uncertainty and ambiguity. It is about inquiry and deliberation, becoming critically minded and intellectually curious. Usher, Bryant, and Johnston (1997) observed that "difficulty, uncertainty and error are not necessarily flawed states to be overcome but ongoing conditions of the educational process itself. . . . they are educationally beneficent correctives to arrogance and complacency" (p. 25).

In PBL, facilitators often intentionally engage in challenging participants with questions and more questions. Facilitators do not present themselves as "experts" having answers to every issue. The message to participants is often that they have to go away and do more work on it and that we are leaving you with more questions to ponder over as a result of the interaction.

PBL facilitators are often confronted with participants' discontent with "an amalgamation of what others think" and inchoate conclusions. It is often argued that facilitators deliberately leave issues open-ended because they believe that the nature of the reality we are dealing with is open-ended and the nature of collaborative learning is open-ended too. To be left with questions is to leave further learning open.

In realizing that others also wrestle with questions, a corresponding openness in voicing one's own questions might arise. There is a growing awareness that questions are a vital part of learning and growing. In PBL, participants realize that others have the same doubts, questions, and difficulties that they have. They learn that it is all right not to have all the answers, and for them to ask questions and to have doubts. In a collaborative learning community, participants work through questions together and they will come to realize that it is all right to live with unanswered questions.

The importance of questions has been raised. MacMurray (1957) remarked: "The rationality of our conclusions does not depend alone upon the correctness of our thinking. It depends more upon the propriety of the questions with which we concern ourselves. The primary and critical task is the discovery of the problem. If we ask the wrong questions, the logical correctness of our answer is of little consequence" (p. 21). Questions always bring out the undetermined possibilities of something: "To understand the questionableness of something is already to be questioning" (Gadamer, 1996, 375).

The value of raising provocative questions is a pivotal feature in the philosophy underpinning radical adult education. While most educational philosophies, such as that of humanistic adult education, attempt to mobilize education to reform society, the radical approach proposes profound changes at the root of the system. Thomas (1982) explained that "radicalism is the expressed intention to attack the foundations of a system, complemented by a visible, manifold effort to do so, whether or not that effort is successful" (p. 13). The radical approach questions the assumptions on which organizations, institutions, and society rest. Radicals claim that wrong questions are asked mainly because they are not sufficiently basic.

Conclusion

In PBL, learning is transformed into an active process where participants are mutually engaged in dialogue, often fueled by questions and a meaningful sharing of roles and responsibilities. Learners are exposed to the richness of critical openness, which makes them more discerning and wise. It is important for PBL practitioners to reflect on the notions of collaboration, dialogue, and critical openness. Collaboration as a competence includes inter- and intrapersonal skills and effective communication and social skills. The ability to work in teams and to collaborate effectively is critical for all professionals today. Globalization calls for effective communication across cultures as well as working with others for mutual benefit and the achievement of goals. Moreover, with increasing complexity and specialization of tasks, we need to share resources and optimize on the different strengths of people in a group. Dialogue and openness are important to making thinking visible to people we work with.

References

Bohm, D. (Ed.) (1996). *On dialogue* (L. Nichol, Ed.). London: Routledge.

Bosworth, K., & Hamilton, S. J. (Eds.) (1994). *Collaborative learning: Underlying processes and effective techniques*. New directions for teaching and learning, No. 59. San Francisco: Jossey-Bass.

Brookfield, S. D. (1987). *Developing critical thinkers: Challenging adults to explore alternative ways of thinking and acting*. San Francisco: Jossey-Bass.

Bruffee, K. A. (1984). Collaborative learning and the conversation of mankind. *College English*, *46*, 635–52.

Bruffee, K. A. (1987). The art of collaborative learning. *Change*, *19*, 42–47.

Bruffee, K. A. (1993). *Collaborative learning*. Baltimore, MD: Johns Hopkins University Press.

Dewey, J. (1933). *How we think*. Boston: D. C. Heath.

Freire, P. (1993). *Pedagogy of the oppressed*. New York: Herder and Herder.

Furedy, C., & Furedy, J. (1985). Critical thinking: Toward research and dialogue. In J. G. Donald & A. M. Sullivan (Eds.), *Using research to improve teaching* (pp. 51–70). New directions for teaching and learning, No. 23. San Francisco: Jossey-Bass.

Gadamer, H.-G. (1996). *Truth and method* (2nd rev. ed., J. Weinsheimer & D. G. Marshall, Trans. & Rev.). London: Sheed and Ward.

Gamson, Z. F. (1994). Collaborative learning comes of age. *Change, 26*, 44–49.

Garrison, D. R. (1992). Critical thinking and self-directed learning in adult education: An analysis of responsibility and control issues. *Adult Education Quarterly, 42*, 136–48.

Goodsell, A., Maher, M., Tinto, V., Smith, B. L., & MacGregor, J. (1992). *Collaborative learning: A sourcebook for higher education*. Pennsylvania: Pennsylvania State University, National Center on Postsecondary Teaching, Learning and Assessment.

Hare, W. (1979). *Open-mindedness and education*. Montreal: McGill–Queen's University Press.

Isaacs, W. (1994). Dialogue. In P. M. Senge, A. Kleiner, C. Roberts, R. B. Ross, & B. J. Smith (Eds.), *The fifth discipline fieldbook* (pp. 357–64). London: Nicholas Brealey.

MacGregor, J. (1990). Collaborative learning: Shared inquiry as a process of reform. In M. D. Svinicki (Ed.), *The challenging face of college teaching* (pp. 19–30). New directions for teaching and learning, No. 42. San Francisco: Jossey-Bass.

MacMurray, J. (1957). *The self as agent*. Atlantic Highlands, NJ: Humanities Press (1991).

Matthews, R. S. (1996). Collaborative learning: Creating knowledge with students. In R. Menges, M. Weimer, & Associates (Eds.), *Teaching on solid ground* (pp. 101–24). San Francisco: Jossey-Bass.

Mezirow, J. (1978). Perspective transformation. *Adult Education, 28*, 100–10.

Mezirow, J. (1991). *Transformative dimensions of adult learning*. San Francisco: Jossey-Bass.

Schrage, M. (1990). *Shared minds: The new technologies of collaboration*. New York: Random House.

Senge, P. M. (1993). *The fifth discipline: The art and practice of the learning organization*. London: Doubleday Dell.

Senge, P. M., Kleiner, A., Roberts, C., Ross, R. B., & Smith, B. J. (Eds.) (1994). *The fifth discipline fieldbook*. London: Nicholas Brealey.

Tan, O. S. (2003). *Problem-based learning innovation: Using problems to power learning in the 21st century*. Singapore: Thomson Learning.

Thiessen, E. J. (1993). *Teaching for commitment: Liberal education, indoctrination and Christian nurture*. Leominster, Herefordshire: Gracewing.

Thiselton, A. (1995). *Interpreting God and the postmodern self*. Edinburgh: T & T Clark.

Thomas, J. E. (1982). *Radical adult education: Theory and practice*. Nottingham: Department of Adult Education, University of Nottingham.

Usher, R., Bryant, I., & Johnston, R. (1997). *Adult education and the postmodern challenge: Learning beyond the limits*. London: Routledge.

Wallis, J., & Allman, P. (1996). Adult education, the critical citizen and social change. In J. Wallis (Ed.), *Liberal adult education: The end of an era?* (pp. 163–79). Nottingham: Continuing Education Press, University of Nottingham.

Watson, B. (1987). *Education and belief*. Oxford: Basil Blackwell.

Whipple, W. R. (1987). Collaborative learning: Recognizing it when we see it. *American Association of Higher Education Bulletin, 40*, 3–7.

Wiener, H. S. (1986). Collaborative learning in the classroom: A guide to evaluation. *College English, 48*, 52–61.

CHAPTER 9

Facilitating Collaborative Inquiry: A Case Illustration

Ruth O. Beltran
Shane John Merritt

Introduction

Collaborative inquiry was defined by Bray, Lee, Smith, and Yorks (2000, 6) as "a process consisting of repeated episodes of reflection and action through which a group of peers strives to answer a question of importance to them." According to them, this kind of inquiry was based on the model of cooperative inquiry developed by John Heron and elaborated by Peter Reason. They pointed out that there are three parts to their definition of collaborative inquiry. These are cycles of reflection and action, peers as co-inquirers, and the inquiry question. Collaborative inquiry involves a four-phase process. These phases are not necessarily discrete, fixed, and autonomous structures. The process is fluid and is offered as a guide and not a dogma for conducting collaborative inquiry. The process begins with the first phase, forming a collaborative inquiry group, followed by creating the conditions for group learning. The third phase, which is central to the process, is acting on the inquiry question. The final phase is making meaning by constructing knowledge. The same authors suggested that collaborative inquiry is a strategy that has potentials for adult education and as a form of research.

Much as we facilitate and encourage our students to reflect on their experiences to enhance learning, as educators we also seek to learn about and enhance our teaching by reflecting on our teaching experiences. This chapter is a case study of the process of reflection of our teaching within the framework of collaborative inquiry and in the context of facilitating students' exploration of Indigenous mental health issues. The question that drove us through this five-year collaborative process was how learning about Indigenous health issues could be facilitated so that students would be equipped to deal with Indigenous clients in their practice.

We will discuss how we introduced and explored these issues within a two-year professional preparation course for occupational therapists. Firstly, we will give an overview of the Master of Occupational Therapy (MOT) course. Secondly, we will discuss the principles and processes we used in facilitating students' understanding of Indigenous health issues. Thirdly, we will discuss the feedback provided by the students about this learning experience and our reflections on this feedback; and finally, we will discuss the developments that were initiated as an outcome of this feedback. These discussions will be framed in the context of collaborative inquiry as developed by Bray, Lee, Smith, and Yorks (2000).

The Curriculum: Capability Professional Education

In 1998, the School of Occupation and Leisure Sciences, Faculty of Health Sciences, University of Sydney, introduced for the first time an MOT degree. This is a two-year professional master's preparation program in occupational therapy for graduates from a variety of undergraduate programs. In the last five years, students who enrolled in the course had come from a variety of first-degree backgrounds, including nursing, medicine, economics, nutrition, psychology, sociology, anthropology, sports science, leisure and health, and other related disciplines. These students bring with them a wealth of specialized knowledge and skills learned from their undergraduate education, which they can access in the process of learning and subsequently contribute to the profession.

The curriculum's conceptual framework is based on capability professional education (Stephenson & Weil, 1992). It incorporates elements of various approaches to learning, including adult learning (Boud & Feletti,

1991), reflective learning (Boud, Keogh, & Walker, 1985; Schon, 1987), and self-directed learning (Knowles, 1975). In accordance with a capability professional education framework, students assess their own entry level against a list of expected outcomes they must achieve at the end of the course. At the beginning of the first semester, students in the first year of the course undertake six weeks of fieldwork with occupational therapists in order to identify for themselves the capabilities of occupational therapists. Based on their self-assessment of their entry level, students determine their learning program in consultation with an academic adviser. This self-assessment is an ongoing process throughout the course. All students enroll in the six core subjects and some elective units and are required to complete integrated assessments related to the core subjects. The type of independent learning that each student requires to support their progress through the six subjects will differ depending on the nature of their first degree and experience. This component of their learning is negotiated with the relevant teaching staff. For example, a student who did not do human biological sciences in their undergraduate course may opt to do an independent study or an elective unit on the anatomy of the hand in order to successfully deal with the dysfunction that a particular case scenario presents on rehabilitation of hand trauma.

Six capabilities of an occupational therapist were identified as important for students to develop (School of Occupational Therapy, 1997). It is expected that the students will be able to:

- assess a client's ability to perform daily activities (problem identification)
- assess daily activities appropriate to the client's roles (taking into account biocognitive and psychosocial factors as well as client contexts and the impact these have on the roles)
- implement occupational therapy intervention, including adapting daily activities to achieve the client's goals (taking into consideration the occupational therapy process from setting goals to implementing selected interventions)
- evaluate and research their practice critically and reflectively (including the evaluation of intervention effectiveness as well as of research and programs)
- use a range of strategies to maximize their ability to manage and work competently within a variety of work contexts (including health-care systems, teamwork, ethics, professional behaviors, management theory and skills, and the university's generic attributes)

- critically articulate the theoretical and practice rationales that underpin the occupational therapy process as outlined in the first four capabilities above (using documentation, verbal presentation, and written presentation for the audience of other health professionals, clients, and students)

These capabilities form the basis for the core subjects in the course. The core subjects are problem identification, activity analysis and adaptation, occupational therapy intervention, evaluation and research, professional management, and professional presentation. Each of these subjects integrates information from four streams: occupational therapy theory; contextual (contexts of the occupational therapist and the clients, including fieldwork); biocognitive (including biological sciences and psychology); and psychosocial–cultural (including behavioral and social sciences). Figure 1 illustrates the organization of the subjects and the streams.

The subjects are taught using problem-based case scenarios and issues-based content. These scenarios are structured around the domains of occupational therapy, namely daily activities appropriate to client roles. In order to ensure that a broad range of client concerns and issues is addressed in the course, the following variables are considered when developing the range of scenarios and issues for the two years of the course in both campus-based and fieldwork settings: age, roles, type of disability, populations and community-based groups, culture, socioeconomic status, gender, occupational therapy worksites, environments, and type of intervention (e.g., individual, group, community, or population based).

Problem-based Case Scenario: Indigenous Mental Health

Considering the above variables, one of the case scenarios introduced in the first-year curriculum is on Indigenous mental health. The current undergraduate and graduate curricula in occupational therapy in the University of Sydney are limited in exposing students to Indigenous health issues. Occupational therapists are constantly challenged with these issues in a variety of practice contexts. One of the strategies identified in the *New South Wales Aboriginal mental health policy* as essential in determining, administering, and providing health services in relation to all mental health issues affecting Aboriginal people is that "education is an integral aspect of the workplace for both aboriginal and non-aboriginal people" (NSW Department of Health, 1997, 22). The inclusion of a problem-based case

Stream	OT theory	Biocognitive	Psychosocial–cultural	Contextual
		• Biomedical sciences • Psychology	• Psychology • Social sciences	Client: • Roles • Family • Work • etc.
Core subject				
Problem identification	*	*	*	
Activity analysis and adaptation	*	*	*	
Occupational therapy intervention	*	*	* #	
Evaluation and research			#	#
Professional management				
Professional presentation				

OT = occupational therapy. The intersections of boxed areas represent the crossovers between subjects and streams. For example, some problem-based learning case scenarios may focus more on the combination of subjects and streams such as the ones with *, while other scenarios may focus more on other combinations such as those with #, and so forth.

FIGURE 1 Organization of subjects and streams in the master's program in occupational therapy

Source: School of Occupational Therapy (1997).

scenario on Indigenous mental health in the MOT curriculum is in response to this strategic direction. The process of case scenario development, implementation, and evaluation will now be described using the collaborative inquiry framework.

The Collaborative Inquiry Process

Phase I: Forming a Collaborative Inquiry Group

CONSULTING WITH AN INDIGENOUS PERSON

In the process of developing the case scenario and the learning experiences that students need to encounter in order to gain an understanding of Indigenous mental health issues, the case coordinator (R. Beltran) consulted with an Indigenous person who is also a health professional with expertise on Indigenous mental health (S. Merritt). The case coordinator, who is of a migrant background and has practiced as an occupational therapist in mental health and has taught undergraduates and graduates in this area of practice, recognized that one needs more than knowledge and experience to have a real understanding and appreciation of mental health issues within the Australian Aboriginal community. It was therefore important to consult with an Indigenous person who has insider knowledge of the issues. This started the collaboration between the two authors, which was to become a cyclical series of experiencing, reflecting on these experiences, and acting together (Heron, 1996).

INQUIRY QUESTION

In our planning and subsequent reflective processes, the question we constantly asked ourselves was: How can learning about Indigenous health issues be facilitated so that students would be equipped to deal with Indigenous clients in their practice? The inquiry question should fulfill two basic principles: one, that the inquirers can explore the question through their experiences; two, that inquiry members are equal peers in terms of their ability to address the question (Bray et al., 2000).

Phase II: Creating the Conditions for Group Learning

Critical in this phase is agreeing on the structure for collaboration (Bray et al., 2000). For us, it was important that our roles as case coordinator and resource person, respectively, were clear to each other and that both were committed to pursuing answers to the inquiry question as peer learners ourselves. In addition to these roles, we were aware of the fact that we were facilitators of our students' learning.

SETTING THE SCENE: DEVELOPMENT OF A PROBLEM-BASED CASE SCENARIO

Our aim here was to develop a scenario that is representational and true, a composite case that does not present a stereotype picture of the issues nor breach confidentiality. We decided that, for confidentiality reason, it was safer to use a published case than to write a new one. We searched the literature and decided to use the case history published in the *New South Wales Aboriginal mental health policy* document (Swan, 1997) as the basis for the case scenario. We reviewed published cases to ensure that specific problems and issues embedded in the case scenario represent the current Indigenous condition. The case history provides the framework by which the history and context of Indigenous health, specifically mental health and well-being, can be outlined for the MOT students. The aim is for students to develop an understanding of Indigenous issues in a broader sense and to be aware of cultural and individual differences of clients in order to be a more effective health professional.

INDIGENOUS PERSON AS A RESOURCE

It is important to enlist an Indigenous person as a resource to guide some of the learning experiences of the students. This person's insider view provides credibility, authenticity, and better understanding of the issues. Additionally, our faculty has a School of Indigenous Health Studies, which has expertise in and a strong commitment to Indigenous health.

At this point, we reviewed the chosen case history and brainstormed on possible issues that might be raised by students as well as how they might be addressed by the Indigenous resource person. For example, we identified that Aboriginal history, mental health problems, and grief and loss might be raised.

We also attempted to preempt possible barriers to learning, such as students' stereotypes of what it might mean to be Aboriginal, what an Aboriginal is, what grants or subsidies that "blacks" get off the government, and so on. We then determined which of these issues could be directly addressed by the Indigenous resource person.

Phase III: Acting on the Inquiry Question

INITIAL EXPLORATION OF ISSUES

On the initial presentation of the case scenario, students are asked a few focus questions (see later). The use of these focus questions is consistent with the principles of problem-based course construction (Bouhuijs & Gijselaers, 1993). Scenario Part A is given to students in the first session of this curriculum:

Scenario—Part A

You are an occupational therapist in a large psychiatric hospital in the Central Sydney Area Health Service. You are a member of the In-patient Rehabilitation Service. One of the referrals you received during the week was June, a 43-year-old female of Aboriginal descent, who was admitted to hospital eight days ago. You decided to read June's chart, and the following is the information that you learned about her.

June lives in a housing commission unit, which she was able to obtain a few weeks after she was released by the Corrective Services. She was referred from the Aboriginal Medical Service. She apparently had been feeling anxious and depressed for the last six months since her children, Mira, 8, and Richard, 11, were placed under the care of the Community Services. She became worse three months prior to admission with loss of appetite and weight. She had been treated with medications without response. Two days prior to admission, her behavior changed; she became labile, excitable, and restless. She was also noted to be thought disordered with loosening of association and pressure of speech. She was constantly verbalizing about her dreams of her children being taken by four large animals and that she last saw them riding on the back of these strange-looking animals at a vacant land near La Perouse.

June has no past psychiatric admission. For her family and developmental history, see attached.

On admission, June was unable to give a detailed history. However, her sensorium was clear and was oriented. She denied auditory hallucinations; however, there was evidence of loosening of association and pressure of speech. She also spoke briefly of feeling in the past few days that something special was about to happen to her and her children. She would frequently associate these special events with circumstances around her, for example, believing that when the phone rang it would be someone with special news just for her. She also appeared to be elated and was restless and energetic.

June was admitted with a provisional diagnosis of bipolar disorder (manic phase) and was commenced on medications. Her mood quickly stabilized, and it became apparent that she was extremely insightful and was quick to grasp ideas and open about her personal concerns. Her serum lithium level was 0.6 mmol/L.

Over time, as her mood stabilized, it became apparent that she continued to have an underlying depression. She often found it difficult to speak of painful things and her smile, although frequent, was not congruent with the content of her thoughts.

Focus Questions

- What issues and key concepts do you need to know to deal with this situation?
- Given your background and experiences and previous cases that you have studied, what are the things that you already know?
- What resources will you need to find out the things that you don't know?
- Since June is referred to you in the Rehabilitation Service, how would you go about assessing June's needs and concerns?

With this case scenario, we aimed to tap students' current knowledge and experience. Based on students' responses to the focus questions, it appeared that they were able to identify questions and specific issues related to the therapy management of the case. They also identified that they needed a broader understanding of the sociocultural, political, economic, and historical factors that have a significant impact on Indigenous health. This response has been more or less consistent in the last five years that we have been teaching this curriculum.

BREAKING DOWN STEREOTYPES

Introducing the notion of stereotype is necessary to help students gain a broader understanding of factors influencing Indigenous mental health. It is important to facilitate a forum that has a respectful and nonjudgmental atmosphere and is accepting of every member's beliefs and opinions. It is crucial to acknowledge that everyone has certain stereotypes that impact on one's perceptions of people. By presenting this issue in a nonthreatening way and putting it in the agenda, students become prepared to look at their stereotypes of Indigenous people without fear of being judged. One exercise that facilitates this process is the question posed by the facilitator: What do you think of when you think about Aboriginal health? The stereotypes about black skin versus white skin are also presented supplemented with an understanding of the psychosocial, cultural, and economic consequences of white policy on the Aboriginal community and its impact on the health of the community. However, breaking down stereotypes may not always work, as our experience in one of the years suggests. This is discussed later in the chapter.

IMPARTING KNOWLEDGE OF HISTORY

It is important for facilitators to encourage students to read and update their knowledge of Aboriginal history in Australia and to challenge some of the stereotypical views that may have filtered through in the Anglo-Saxon view of history as presented in some sectors of society. The Indigenous resource person also presents an insider's view of history, which broadens and challenges students' knowledge and views. This was ascertained from the first round of evaluation of the curriculum.

RESOURCE SESSIONS ON ABORIGINAL MENTAL HEALTH ISSUES

The curriculum content covering Aboriginal mental health issues was developed based upon students' identification of what they considered to be relevant issues. Occupational therapy academics, clinicians, and researchers with expertise on such issues are invited to speak on topics such as community approaches with Indigenous people, occupational therapy and Indigenous mental health in the context of a psychiatric hospital, parenting and vocational issues, culture and mental health, and mental illness.

STUDENTS' DETERMINATION OF LEARNING NEEDS

Within the capability professional education framework, students take an active role in determining their own learning needs. For example, they are given the option of identifying whether they need extra sessions with the Indigenous and other resource persons. They also are asked to identify which topics they want to pursue. These additional sessions (if asked for) are then negotiated between the resource persons and the students.

FEEDBACK FROM STUDENTS

As part of standard practice in the provision of higher education, student feedback is sought in relation to teaching and learning. In the MOT course, students are asked for their written feedback after each case scenario. A feedback sheet was developed for this purpose by the MOT team. Students are asked to reflect on the case that they have just finished and to write their responses on the form. Feedback is not compulsory for students. Appendix A is the standard feedback form used for all case scenarios in the MOT course.

Feedback is collated and reflected upon, as a matter of course, by the curriculum team. This feedback helps us in future curriculum development.

Selected excerpts from feedback forms are included here to give a sense of students' views and perceptions and to illustrate how useful these comments can be in relation to curriculum development.

- QUESTION: **Describe an aspect of the case which has been most useful in terms of your learning.**

In general, students found almost all the learning experiences related to the case useful. In particular, the feedback reflected change that had happened to the students because of this case study. They commented on change in attitude and a broadening of their views. The case is an "eye-opener" for them.

> "It is a joy to be exposed to so much new learning about aboriginal issues in mental health, parenting, community occupational therapy. Thank you. It has been an experience to 'open my mind'!"

> "Learning about Aboriginal mental health is an issue that I didn't realize was as significant as I do now."

> "Having my myth of mental health, and what OTs do in mental health, dispelled."

> "Made me aware I do have stereotypes but now I am reshaping these."

> " . . . which opened my mind about aboriginal people and their culture."

> "This was a most interesting case. I enjoyed it so much and it was such an eye opener. Having Shane Merritt was probably the most useful aspect. I'm 27 and I've only just learned about these issues. That is a national disgrace. Every Australian should be taught about the Aboriginal perspective when at school."

> "The case as a whole made me question my stereotype (which has been formed from a very selected knowledge) and the cultural awareness related to Aboriginal people (and other groups of people)."

Among students' comments on the lectures and lecturers, most notable were those on the challenge brought by an insider's as well as experts' perspectives.

> "Every lecture was fantastic, thought provoking and very interesting."

"Having Shane lecture us was fantastic because of his own personal background and experience, as well as his knowledge basis."

"Particularly liked the four hours spent with Shane; liked the way he challenged our views—really gave me something to think about."

"Session with Shane Merritt (1st session) about indigenous people . . ."

"Especially good were lectures by Shane, plus the panel of three on parenting and the . . . hour on OT in mental health . . ."

"[the lecturer from OT] on community rehabilitation. This provided me with a real sense of excitement as to what OTs can provide people who are not so fortunate."

"Also session by [name omitted] on community-based rehab in India was an eye opener about how OTs can really help indigenous people."

Students commented on the case coordinator's input and role, as well as the way the focus questions were framed, which directed them on the relevant issues to pay attention to and challenged them to identify what other learning they needed to pursue.

"Focus questions, which directed Part B of the case scenario."

"The focus questions given to us gave us opportunities to explore the issues and what we already know of Part B."

"Consulting with Ruth about our concerns about what we would learn and having these worries addressed. . . . Ruth really heard what we were concerned about and acted on this even if we were too hasty!!"

"Great in that Ruth sat in on each of the sessions, this is very encouraging as often the coordinators don't attend lectures."

Students commented strongly on the teaching/learning process used in class. These comments centered around the benefit of making the content relevant, the manner in which students were urged to exercise self-determination in their own learning, and the encouragement that they be active learners.

"Being introduced to Aboriginal health in a very practical, realistic manner."

"Consulting with Ruth about our concerns about what we would learn and having these worries addressed. Good lesson in being up front about issues in an assertive manner. Consequently I got heaps out of nearly all the lectures . . . I felt the lecturers really involved us in the learning."

- QUESTION: **What would you add or change in this case?**

Students suggested, among other issues, introducing the case study in the undergraduate program; expanding the discussion on therapy intervention; extending the session on parenting; covering experiential components; and including speakers from other indigenous groups. One of the issues identified by students in relation to the case "Stolen Generation" was parenting—the repercussions of poor parenting and how to facilitate development of parenting skills in people who have not experienced love and care from their own parents.

"I would add this whole case study to the undergraduate program."

"ADD it to the undergraduate course!!"

"How to actually attempt to implement some of the intervention."

" . . . roles of community health in Aboriginal communities in more depth."

" . . . maybe just a little bit more on intervention."

"More about appropriate intervention for aboriginal people. Maybe OT more specifically involved with Aboriginals."

"More time for the session on parenting."

"Have a longer session with [names omitted] on parenting."

"Another hour to parenting issue session."

"Have more practical component in Aboriginal issues? For example, talking to mothers who lost their children."

"Maybe add a speaker outside of aboriginals, i.e. Torres Strait Islanders, etc., for their view."

- QUESTION: **Indicate (on the scale) how confident you would feel dealing with a similar case in practice? What leads you to mark your level of confidence where you have on the scale?**

Students assessed their confidence level from the midpoint of the scale up toward the "very confident" level. Among their answers for their level of confidence were increased awareness; better understanding of issues, approaches, and resources; realization of the importance of the case study; and agreement of the case study with occupational therapy philosophy.

"More awareness of the culture and people and awareness of my attitudes etc."

"More aware of aboriginal people but still very unsure of appropriate intervention to help a client such as June."

"Have a much better understanding of problems involved with Aboriginal Mental Health and approaches to take plus resources available to help—people plus community places such as . . ."

"I feel confident that I would be more open and understanding of the possible issues of an aboriginal client. However, I being white, will still not ever be able to fully help an indigenous person, because I am not aboriginal."

"The readings as well as Shane's lectures brought out the issues in Aboriginal Mental Health. I feel confident in discussing them to a certain extent."

"This information has just provided me with a base understanding about Aboriginal issues so that I am in a better position to provide appropriate OT services."

"Feel I have a much better understanding as to why this case has been included and its importance. Excellent case!!"

"What we have been taught fits in beautifully with OT philosophy re providing intervention for the individual."

- QUESTION: **What advice would you give future students about this case?**

Students' recommendations ranged from reading and listening to keeping an open mind.

"Read lots."

"Read more about Aboriginal history and health issues."

"Read the poems and stories from the stolen generation."

"Listen and hear."

"Attend every lecture."

"Have 2 sessions with Shane (like we did) because they both were so valuable to my understanding."

"Watch the recommended videos. They help quite a bit."

"Use this case as an introduction for being aware of indigenous issues. So that we can change the general attitude of the health profession in treating indigenous people."

"Soak this case up. It is fascinating. It should be a part of every high school student's education not just MOT . . ."

"To use this case as an opportunity to learn about the people (not only aboriginal people in this country) and their beliefs and attitudes about the issue."

"Important to keep a real open mind and challenge the views that you have about Aborigines and their state of mental health."

"Keep an open mind."

"Enjoy it and keep an open mind."

"And to be open to all the lecturers' views regardless of the present view of others (i.e. students)."

It can be noted above that some students suggested that perhaps there should be more input on specific occupational therapy intervention built into the case. However, one particular feedback highlights the importance and the priority of understanding the history and the broader contexts of Aboriginal mental health issues first *before* specific therapy interventions:

"Don't be concerned about not learning so much the intervention. Very important to obtain the background/history such as the Stolen Generation."

Perhaps an understanding of the issues, on the part of health-care professionals, may be sufficient in itself to make changes or interventions possible. Changes or interventions may not necessarily come from health-care professionals but can arise from people's self-determination.

Phase IV: Making Meaning by Constructing Knowledge

This phase centers around capturing our experiences as facilitators, understanding and interpreting our experiences, and sharing them with colleagues and students. It is also during this phase that we seek validation of our experiences and celebrate meaningful collaboration (Bray et al., 2000).

INTERPRETING OUR EXPERIENCES

Our decisions and actions taken in the teaching of this case scenario relied heavily on our evaluation of the feedback that we gathered every year for the last five years. Table 1 tabulates the total enrollment in the MOT course and the number of feedback responses received. Table 2 presents a comparison of the general trend in the evaluation from 1998 to 2002.

TABLE 1 Total number of enrolled students and student feedback received by year

	1998	1999	2000	2001	2002
Number of students	11	14	19	17	17
Number of responses	8	12	14	15	10

TABLE 2	Comparison of student feedback, 1998–2002
1998	• Overall, feedback was extremely positive. • Students felt very confident about dealing with similar cases in the future because they felt they now understood the issues. • Many comments were along the lines of the content being "such an eye-opener." • No negative comments.
1999	• Overall, feedback was negative. • Students felt that Shane had a "hidden agenda." • Students felt that the content was not sufficiently related to the assessment task. • Many comments seemed to illustrate disinterest in the issues discussed.
2000	• Feedback was again positive. • Students felt that more time dealing with Indigenous mental health would be beneficial. • Many comments on how important it was to gain information on cultural issues. • No negative comments.
2001	• Mostly positive feedback. • Students felt that the information presented was useful and relevant. • Many comments were along the lines of the content being "enlightening." • One negative comment: "too many poems & quotes."
2002	• Overall, positive feedback. • Students felt that the content highlighted Indigenous inequalities with regard to health. • Some students commented on the "lecturer's passion" for the topic and that all lecturers should be like that. • Most students listed the inclusion of Aboriginal issues as the most useful in terms of their learning with the case scenarios.

Overall, the evaluation throughout the five years suggests a positive experience for the students, except for 1999. A total reversal seemed to have occurred that year in comparison with the other years. The general feeling that year seemed to have changed from "Why weren't we told [about Indigenous history]?" in other years to "I don't want a history lesson." This issue was shared with peers at a curriculum conference (see next section). Throughout the past five years, the curriculum basically stayed the same with very minor revisions.

COMMUNICATING OUR EXPERIENCES IN THE PUBLIC ARENA

At various stages throughout the process of this curriculum development, part of the cycle of action and reflection is communicating our work to peers in the faculty (Research Forum, School of Indigenous Health Studies, October 1999) and in the wider university (Faculty of Medicine Curriculum Conference, University of Sydney, December 1999), as well as at state and international conferences (New South Wales Aboriginal Mental Health Conference, Sydney, September 1999; the 26th Biennial Congress of the

World Federation of Mental Health, Vancouver, July 2001). We also provided subsequent cohorts of students with relevant information about feedback from past students about the case scenario. At the Faculty of Medicine Curriculum Conference, we discussed with curriculum experts in the audience, in a workshop setting, about the negative feedback in 1999. We were encouraged to leave the curriculum as it was and to see how evaluation in subsequent years would fare.

CELEBRATING MEANINGFUL COLLABORATION:
OUTCOME AND DEVELOPMENTS

As an outcome of our experiences in facilitating this case and based on the feedback of students, we maintain an ongoing commitment to address the issues of Indigenous mental health in the occupational therapy curriculum. The Indigenous case scenario is one of the core learning units for MOT students. Indigenous mental health is now included in the undergraduate occupational therapy course, although in a different format to that of the MOT course. Students are encouraged to undertake fieldwork placement with Indigenous health workers and with Indigenous communities.

Implications and Recommendations

Figure 2 illustrates and summarizes the process adapted for the collaborative inquiry used to reflect and act on the development, implementation, and evaluation of the Indigenous mental health curriculum within the MOT program.

Collaborative inquiry is an action-based inquiry method that has wide-ranging implications as a strategy for adult learning and as a research method (Bray et al., 2000). As a strategy for adult learning, we have illustrated in this chapter its use to enhance our learning within the context of our various roles as curriculum planners, case coordinator, resource persons, and facilitators. Collaborative inquiry can be used as a framework for reflecting and acting on the planning, implementation, and evaluation of a curriculum. As is the case with this method of inquiry, the process of reflection and action is driven by an inquiry question. As stated earlier, our inquiry question was how we could facilitate learning about Indigenous health issues so that students would be equipped to deal with Indigenous clients in their practice. From our experience, this process certainly was not linear. At various phases, we kept going back to where we started: the inquiry question. Consistent with the findings of Gamble, Chan, and Davey (2001), we have found that

I. Forming a Collaborative Inquiry Group

- Consulting with an Indigenous person
- Inquiry question
- Action and reflection

II. Creating the Conditions for Group Learning

- Setting the scene: development of a case scenario
- Indigenous person as a resource
- Action and reflection

III. Acting on the Inquiry Question

- Initial exploration of issues
- Breaking down stereotypes
- Imparting knowledge of history
- Resource sessions on Aboriginal mental health issues
- Students' determination of learning needs
- Feedback from students
- Action and reflection

IV. Making Meaning by Constructing Knowledge

- Interpreting our experiences (including reflections on evaluation data)
- Communicating our experiences in the public arena
- Celebrating meaningful collaboration: outcome and developments
- Action and reflection

Forming (or Re-forming)

- The curriculum is reformulated if necessary, in line with the process and in response to student feedback.
- What other answers do we have regarding our inquiry question? Go back to the inquiry question.

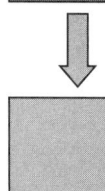

FIGURE **2** Collaborative inquiry as a tool for reflection, action, and making meaning

Adapted from Figure 1.1: A four-phase framework of the collaborative inquiry process. In J. N. Bray, J. Lee, L. L. Smith, & L. Yorks (2000). *Collaborative inquiry in practice: Action, reflection, and making meaning*, p. 14. Thousand Oaks, CA: Sage.

critical to the use of collaborative inquiry as a tool for reflection is the condition of trust between collaborators and between peers who may be part of the public arena. For us, the MOT team has certainly played an excellent sounding board for our reflections, decisions, and actions.

As a research method, we have used collaborative inquiry as a framework for this case study in which we attempted to narrate our experiences of a five-year collaborative process. A critical aspect of collaborative inquiry as a research process is the production of meaning and knowledge for the public arena (Bray et al., 2000). We have been conscious of this from the very start as evidenced by the presentations we have made at various levels with the hope of generating critical debate, new insights, and enhanced understanding.

An important recommendation and an action worth pursuing that arose from this case study is to use collaborative inquiry as a learning strategy for students, which can run parallel with its use as a learning strategy for teachers (as illustrated in this chapter) within the same curriculum context.

Collaborative inquiry as a strategy for adult learning and as a form of research has facilitated our understanding of our experiences and enabled us to make informed decisions about our teaching. So far the outcome has veered toward the positive side, which strengthens our commitment in facilitating students' understanding of Indigenous mental health issues in the context of society, culture, personality, economics, politics, and history.

Acknowledgments

We would like to thank our respective schools for their support of the MOT curriculum, the MOT team for their collegiality, and all the MOT students— past, current, and future—whose enthusiasm for learning makes our experiences and insights possible.

References

Boud, D., & Feletti, G. (Eds.) (1991). *The challenge of problem-based learning*. London: Kogan Page.

Boud, D., Keogh, R., & Walker, D. (Eds.) (1985). *Reflection: Turning learning into experience*. London: Kogan Page.

Bouhuijs, P. A. J., & Gijselaers, W. H. (1993). Course construction in problem-based learning. In P. A. J. Bouhuijs, H. G. Schmidt, & H. J. M. van Berkel (Eds.), *Problem-based learning as an educational strategy* (Chap. 5). Maastricht: Network Publications.

Bray, J. N., Lee, J., Smith, L. L., & Yorks, L. (2000). *Collaborative inquiry in practice: Action, reflection, and making meaning.* Thousand Oaks, CA: Sage.

Gamble, J., Chan, P., & Davey, H. (2001). Reflection as a tool for developing professional practice knowledge expertise. In J. Higgs & A. Titchen (Eds.), *Practice knowledge and expertise in the health professions* (Chap. 15). Boston: Butterworth-Heinemann.

Heron, J. (1996). *Co-operative inquiry: Research into the human condition.* London: Sage.

Knowles, M. (1975). *Self-directed learning: A guide for learners and teachers.* New York: Association Press.

NSW Department of Health, Centre for Mental Health (1997). *New South Wales Aboriginal mental health policy.* Sydney.

Schon, D. A. (1987). *Educating the reflective practitioner.* San Francisco: Jossey-Bass.

School of Occupational Therapy, Faculty of Health Sciences, University of Sydney (1997). Course proposal for the Master of Occupational Therapy, Draft 7. Sydney.

Stephenson, J., & Weil, S. (1992). *Quality in learning: A capability approach in higher education.* London: Kogan Page.

Swan, P. (1997). 2000 years of unfinished business. In NSW Department of Health, *New South Wales Aboriginal mental health policy.* Sydney.

Appendix A

School of Occupation & Leisure Sciences
Master of Occupational Therapy

Student Feedback Sheet

We are seeking your feedback about the learning experiences which have been part of the MOT. Your ideas will help us to strengthen future cases in which you and other students participate.

Thank you for your time and for your comments.

Case number/title: _____

Please reflect on the case which you have just finished as part of your MOT studies and answer the following questions.

1. Describe an aspect of the case which has been MOST useful in terms of your learning.

2. Describe an aspect of the case which has been LEAST useful in terms of your learning.

3. What would you ADD or CHANGE in this case, within the 1½-week time frame?
   (a) I would add . . .

   (b) I would change . . .

4. Indicate (on the scale) how confident you would feel dealing with a similar case in practice?

   _____
   Not very confident   Very confident

   What leads you to mark your level of confidence where you have on the above scale?

5. What advice would you give future students about this case?

School of Occupation & Leisure Sciences
Master of Occupational Therapy

Student Feedback Sheet—Procedures

Following each case, the case coordinator is responsible for arranging for students to provide feedback about the case.

Provide copies of the attached blank form to be distributed *by another member of staff* not involved with the case as soon as possible after the case has finished.

Allow about 15 minutes for students to complete and return the form.

Students are not obliged to provide feedback; however, indicate that we are grateful to those who do.

Return the feedback forms to the case coordinator, who will then summarize key issues raised and make recommendations for future modifications to the case.

It is highly desirable that the summary and recommendations be documented by the case coordinator as a record for the future development of the case.

CHAPTER 10

Toward a Model for Web-enhanced Problem-based Learning

Barbara Grabowski
Younghoon Kim
Tiffany Koszalka

Introduction

In this chapter, we merge the conceptual frameworks from two major projects funded by the National Aeronautics Space Administration (NASA)—Web-enhanced Learning Environment Strategies and Kids as Airborne Mission Scientists—to create a model for web-enhanced problem-based learning (Grabowski, Koszalka, & McCarthy, 2000). This model is supported by and built upon research in two areas: (1) problem-based learning (PBL) and the associated cognitive processes involved during learning, and (2) web-enhancement of classroom instruction. The intent of the model is to suggest a means for teachers, and to encourage them, to consider the richness of the Web in supporting PBL in their classrooms. Given that teachers, science teachers most notably, are resources-poor (O'Sullivan, Weiss, & Askew, 1998) and the Internet is resource-rich, this merger offers a very practical opportunity to capitalize on learning processes that research has shown to be effective for improving problem-solving ability, teamwork, communication skills, and interpersonal skills (Tan, 2002).

Web-enhanced Problem-based Learning Model

The model shown in Figure 1 conceptualizes web-enhanced problem-based learning (W-PBL) within the current learning-centered paradigm (see, e.g., Reigeluth, 1999). The model is read from the inside out, with each ring identifying the factors and their attributes involved in a PBL event. Each area between the spokes represents a phase of the learning event that shows the interrelationship of the factors. The central feature of this model is the "learner as problem solver" (Tan, 2002). From this notion, every other part

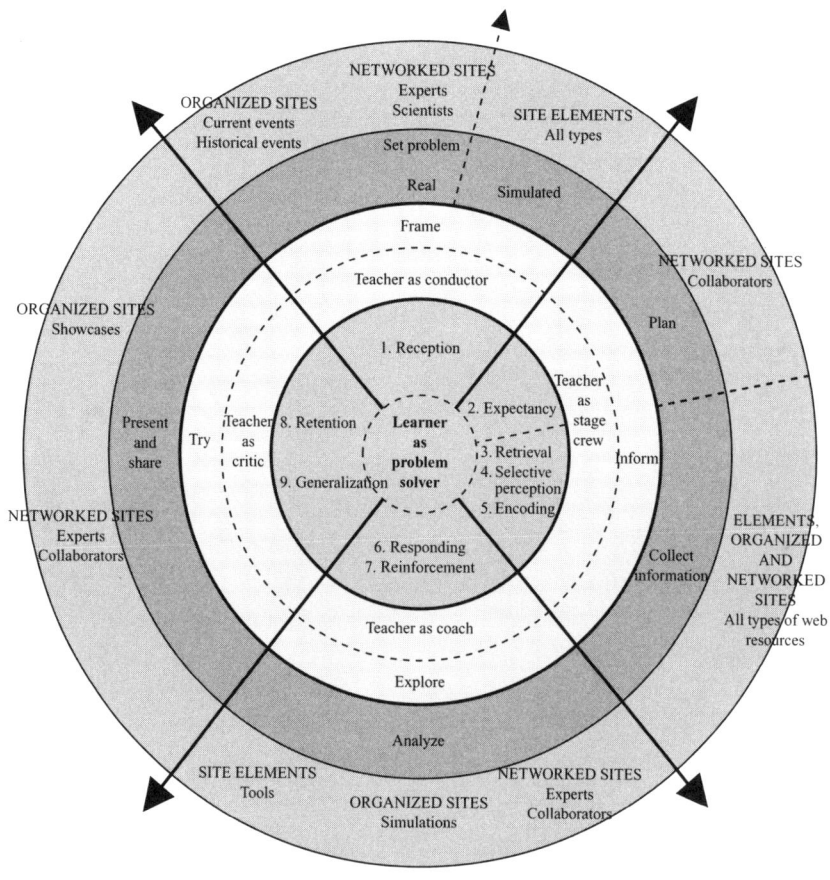

Ring 1: Learner as problem solver
Ring 2: Learner's cognitive functioning
Ring 3: Teacher's roles
Ring 4: Web-enhanced learning environment strategies
Ring 5: Problem-based learning process
Ring 6: Web resources

FIGURE **1**   A model for web-enhanced problem-based learning

emerges. The nine cognitive processes surrounding the learner are those stimulated in any independent or formal learning event (Gagne, 1985). The next ring brings the learning event into a formal classroom setting by defining four changing roles of the teacher engaged in a standard four-phased lesson. These lesson phases, as noted in the companion ring by the dotted circle (ring 4), are named by the web-enhanced learning environment strategies: frame, inform, explore, and try (Grabowski et al., 2000). Ring 5 overlays the teaching methodology—that of PBL—onto the framework. Finally, the types of web resources recommended for each phase flow from the last ring.

The teacher and learner move in tandem through the PBL stages. The responsibility of the learner remains as problem solver throughout, but the amount of control varies depending on the phase. A major assumption captured in the third ring is that the teacher serves in four different roles, determined by the phases of the learning event. In some cases, it is important for the teacher to take a leadership role, and at other times a less visible role. Using an arts metaphor, the teacher begins the learning event like a conductor. In this role, the teacher frames the lesson and selects the problem to be presented to the learners. The learners and the teacher work in tandem to develop an understanding of the problem. The teacher then moves into the role of stage crew, setting up a rich environment. The learners are able to assume a central role in deciding what they know and what they don't know and then planning how they will go about gathering the information in the next PBL phase of collecting information. When the learners begin the analysis phase, the teacher becomes a coach, guiding them through the experiments and analyzing their results. Finally, during the present-and-share-information phase, the teacher is a critic, providing important feedback to the learners.

A second important assumption of W-PBL is that the teacher in some situations, the learner in others, and both together in still other situations engage dynamically in selecting and using information from the Web to enrich the learning event and experience. Depending on the goal of the phase, they can choose from the varied sources on the Web. These sources are categorized into information and human resources, from a three-category taxonomy: site elements, organized sites, and networked resources. Site elements are resources that represent the raw materials from the Web. They include numbers, narratives, lists of references, still images, animations, video clips, sounds, and tools. Organized sites are resources that are generally developed with a specific purpose in mind, such as to entertain, present current or historical events, provide background information, instruct, or encourage hands-on activities. These resources include information, databanks, interactive events, current events, historical events, showcases, simulations, and tutorials. Networked resources are those that connect people electronically to enable shared interactions with experts, leaders, scientists, role models, and collaborators via e-mail, listservs, newsgroups, chat rooms, audioconferencing, and videoconferencing (Grabowski et al., 2000).

PBL and Cognitive Processing

The PBL model we selected has been well documented in the literature and is supported theoretically and empirically by other chapters in this book. The model in this chapter applies this foundational understanding and builds a rationale from this base.

PBL is a teaching methodology for posing realistic and interesting problem situations to learners. The methodology challenges learners to direct their own learning and resolve self-identified problems. Knowledge construction results from learners experiencing cognitive dissonance because of exposure to the problem scenario (Tan, 2002). By engaging in a variety of activities to understand and explore the identified problems, the learners attempt to reduce this dissonance and thus develop a deeper understanding of the knowledge domain.

PBL includes five key characteristics (Barrows, 1986, 1992; Hmelo & Evensen, 2000; Savery & Duffy, 1995; Schwartz, Brophy, Lin, & Bransford, 1999):

1. Real-world problems are used to set the learning context and act as a motivational driver for learners. These problems are used to help focus learners and stimulate them to get involved in the learning activity. The problems can be taken from actual or simulated scenarios.

2. Students set their own learning goals by questioning what they know and do not know about the problem scenario and then plan how to gather and learn the information relevant to solving the problem.

3. Multiple resources are provided for students to explore. These may include media, print, electronic, or human resources. With access to rich and varied resources, students can develop a deep understanding of the content related to the problem.

4. Students actively engage in problem solving through experimentation, data collection, reflection, collaboration, and communication
   with teachers, peers, and others who are key to investigating the
   problem. By being engaged in this way, students share their different
   perspectives and exhibit skills in reflective thinking, collaboration,
   and communication, which are essential for effective problem
   solving.

5. The teacher's role is that of a facilitator, to support the learning
   process and problem-solving activities rather than to directly teach
   what learners should know and how they should solve problems.
   However, we believe that, like a facilitator, the teacher's actions and
   visibility change based on the learning phase and the needs of the
   students, from conducting, creating a rich learning environment,
   coaching, to critiquing.

Much PBL research and evaluation has been conducted in diverse content
domains, such as medicine, business education, social studies, and science.
Most of the research, however, has focused on medical education, college
or graduate school, and professional education settings. Some studies in
medicine compared the effectiveness of a PBL program with conventional
instruction. According to Hmelo and Evensen (2000), medical students who
engaged in PBL were able to solve problems and transfer their learning
better than students who studied under a conventional program. Albanese
and Mitchell (1993) conducted a meta-analysis of the PBL literature from
1972 to 1992 and found that PBL helped medical students construct basic
clinical and science knowledge and enhanced their reasoning skills when
compared with a traditional instructional approach.

The research conducted in higher education and adult learning contexts
prompted the development of PBL programs for middle and high schools.
The Jasper Woodbury problem-solving series developed by the Cognition
and Technology Group at Vanderbilt (1990, 1991, 1992) has been
successfully implemented in middle school science and mathematics
teaching. The Jasper series was based on anchored instruction with a PBL
perspective and video-based programs. It was found to enhance students'
construction of knowledge, transfer of problem-solving skills, and
motivation. The use of an authentic problem in the Jasper series was
especially powerful in promoting students' interest in and positive attitude
toward mathematics and science learning.

Achilles and Hoover (1996) investigated middle and high school teachers' feedback from their PBL experience. In this study, teachers reported that PBL made learning more exciting and was a useful model for promoting students' communication and social skills, which were necessary for working with peers in a learning group. Faulkner (1999) reported that middle school science students who learned under a PBL model performed better in solving a near transfer problem than those who learned using worked examples. In addition, West (1992), studying the use of PBL in secondary school science classrooms, concluded that PBL could be an effective instructional strategy for stimulating students' interest in science, enhancing knowledge construction and problem-solving skills, and integrating science with other knowledge domains.

A five-phase PBL framework (Barrows, 1986, 1992; West 1992) drawn from these characteristics and research parallels the cognitive development processes (Gagne, 1985; Tan, Parsons, Hinson, & Sardo-Brown, 2003) that correspond to each learning event of the learning process (Gagne, 1985). These phases are set problem, plan, collect information, analyze, and present and share.

During phase 1, learners are presented with a problem scenario. The purpose of the scenario is to gain the learners' attention, thus activating sensory reception, the first stage in cognitive development. Without gaining and maintaining attention, there can be no learning (Keller, 1983). During phase 2, learners articulate what they know and do not know about the problem and create a plan for how to proceed. These tasks prompt learners to develop learning objectives that aid in solving the problem, thus activating expectancy control in cognitive processing. During phase 3, learners collect the information and study potential solutions to the problem as specified in the plan. Further, during phases 2 and 3, prior knowledge is retrieved that contributes to initial understanding of what is already known. Through activating selective perceptions, learners review multiple resources in an attempt to sort out the information and learn more about the problem as well as potential ways to solve it. Finally, as key information that is deemed relevant is found, learners encode it, that is, they organize the information in a way that is meaningful to them and that allows easy retrieval.

During phase 4, learners analyze the collected information, evaluate its usefulness to solving the problem, and draw conclusions. These tasks require learners to act upon the information they have learned, and the process activates the responding and reinforcing cycle of cognitive processing. Given the results of their experimentation, original ideas are reinforced or revised and new information is assimilated or tuned (Rummelhart & Norman, 1978). Finally, during phase 5, students are tasked with presenting their solutions and sharing their ideas with others, who may provide additional insights from different perspectives. These tasks activate retrieval of new knowledge in the context of the problem solution, retention of new knowledge, and, potentially, generalization of the new knowledge based on insights gathered from the different perspectives offered by the audience.

In summary, this five-phase PBL framework parallels the cognitive processing stages of reception, expectancy, retrieval, selective perception, encoding, responding, reinforcement, retention, and generalization during learning. The PBL process takes learners through the five learning stages, each of which activates cognitive processing and therefore prompts learning. Thus, well-designed and well-executed PBL environments encourage learners to develop a deep understanding of a knowledge domain while they practice and develop problem-solving skills (Duffy & Cunningham, 1996; Hmelo & Evensen, 2000).

Web-enhanced Learning Environment Strategies (WELES) and PBL

Today, Internet technology enables the integration of web resources into classrooms to enhance the interactive and social nature of instruction. In recent years, researchers have investigated Internet, intranet, and extranet interactive learning strategies (Geyer, 1997), interactive collaboration with scientists (Federman & Edwards, 1997), electronic discussion groups (Karayan & Crowe, 1997; Papert, 1997), multiuser object-oriented virtual spaces for sharing ideas and developing solutions to problems (Conlon, 1997), electronic learning communities (Lieberman, 1996), and general use of Internet resources in the classroom (Koszalka, 1999). This field of research is rich. Findings suggested that these interactive and technology-enhanced learning strategies engaged learners more fully in instruction and facilitated their ability to comprehend and to construct personal knowledge. Evidence also showed that the use of Internet technologies in the classroom promoted openness, sharing, and involvement in students' own learning; raised academic achievement; helped the development of social skills; aided in the mainstreaming of handicapped students; reduced ethnic tensions; increased self-esteem; and predicted students' interest in science careers (Kagan & Widaman, 1987; Koszalka, 1999; Sharan & Kussell, 1984; Slavin,

1983). These studies have demonstrated that the possibilities for web use in the classroom extend far beyond the individualized drill-and-practice and entertainment scenarios of the past.

Just because web resources can be used, or have many possibilities for use in schools, it does not mean that they will be. Recent statistics showed that, although upwards of 98 percent of schools in the United States were reported to be wired for some type of Internet access and over 70 percent of classrooms had Internet connections, only 21 percent of educators acknowledged using the Internet to a small extent and 31 percent to a moderate or large extent with their students (National Center for Educational Statistics, 2000a, b). One reason might be that more technology funds in schools are being spent on equipment rather than on supporting educators' professional development and efforts to create learning environments that integrate such resources into teaching and learning (Department of Education, 2000; Ronnkvist, Dexter, & Anderson, 2000). Supporting educators' professional development in technology integration may provide a key to increasing the incorporation of technology resources into teaching practices and learning environments. Implementing interventions that are flexible and are able to help a variety of educators adopt these new technologies in their own classrooms is crucial.

The WELES reflection tool, shown in Figure 2, provides educators with a road map through the myriad of resources available on the Web, as well as a framework for reflecting on how these different types of resources may be used with six methods of teaching using four key lesson strategies. The resulting four central WELES follow a typical lesson sequence: framing a lesson; informing learners; providing for content exploration by learners; and allowing learners to try out newly acquired skills, knowledge, and inclinations. This reflection tool, along with an accompanying lesson planner, is provided to educators as an overview of the conceptual interrelationship between teaching methodology and web resource categories. Educators can often see from this overview a broader conception of how the Web can be integrated into their classroom teaching. For example, a sixth-grade earth science teacher who prefers a presentation teaching method to frame lessons and motivate students may choose to present a series of web-based pictures and video clips of erupting volcanoes to his or her students to begin a lesson on volcanology. A high school physics teacher who prefers hands-on active learning may find a velocity and motion simulation for his or her students to use during the exploration of motion principles.

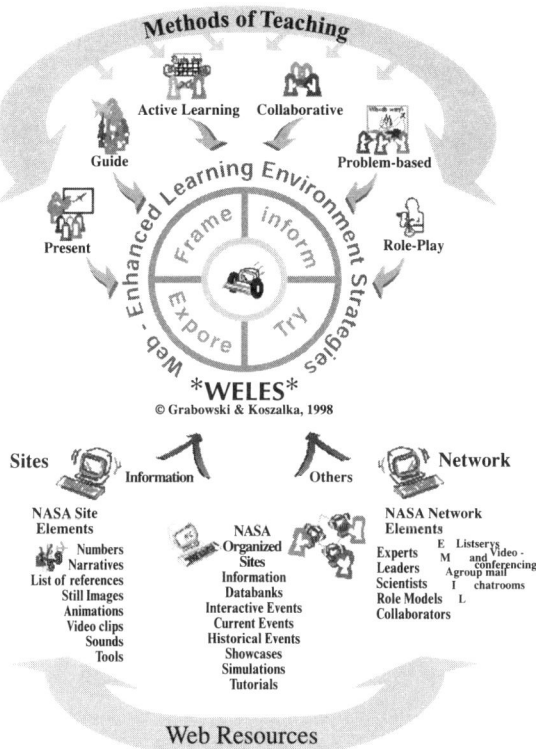

FIGURE 2 Web-enhanced learning environment strategies (WELES) reflection tool

Source: B. Grabowski, T. Koszalka, & M. McCarthy. *Web-enhanced learning environment strategies: Handbook and reflection tool* (11th ed.). © 2000 by Penn State University, Instructional Systems Program. Reproduced with permission from the authors.

The WELES tools were run through a validation process with several experts in instructional design and educational technology, modified, and then used with over 359 teachers in 23 states of the United States and in Thailand. Findings suggested that the final version of the WELES reflection tool and lesson planner was representative of the most common pedagogic approaches and technology integration strategies, helped educators think about using web resources to enhance their teaching, increased the use of Internet resources among educators who were trained in using the WELES tools, and led to greater use of different types of Internet resources in multiple subject areas using multiple methods of teaching. Thus, WELES helped educators operationalize the use of web-based resources within their

TABLE **1**   Types of web resources matched to problem-based learning (PBL) phases

	Type of web resources		
	Information resources		Human resources
PBL phase	Site elements	Organized sites	Networked resources
Set the problem Real-world		Current events Historical events	Experts Scientists
Simulated	All types		
Plan			Collaborators
Collect information	All types	All types	All types
Analyze data	Tools	Simulations	Experts Collaborators
Present and share solutions		Showcases	Experts Collaborators

technology-enhanced classrooms, based on their teaching preferences, resource and curriculum needs, and existing technology configurations (Grabowski & Koszalka, 2000).

The W-PBL model extends the merger of teaching method and resources to identify the type of web resources that would most likely enhance the various phases of the PBL experience, as summarized in Table 1. When *setting the problem*, there can be two types of problems: real-world and simulated (Tan, 2002). The resources for a real-world problem are most likely to come from organized sites containing current or historical events. These sites contain contexts that are entirely real. In these cases, learners solve the problems in a similar manner as experts would in the real situations. For a simulated problem, teachers have at their fingertips all types of site elements. They can gain immediate and easy access to authentic numbers, video and sound clips, animations, narratives, images, and tools to make the problem feel real.

In the *planning* phase, learners collaborate among themselves to assess what they themselves already know. In this case, there is no need for web resources. However, to complete the phase, the teacher, as coach, helps them refine their ideas to determine their plan of action. At this point, collaborators or experts accessible through networked web resources would serve a useful function. Once their plan of action is created, there is no limit to the possibilities of resource acquisition through the Web. Learners should be encouraged to seek out site elements, organized sites, and networked resources to *collect relevant information* and data.

In the *data analysis* phase, learners can seek out web tools (site elements), simulations from organized sites, and experts and other collaborators in order to interpret all of the information they have gathered. Finally, the Web offers one of the richest opportunities to *present and share solutions* beyond the classroom—through showcases designed specifically for this purpose. Feedback can be sought from experts and other collaborators through networked resources.

W-PBL Exemplified in KaAMS (Kids as Airborne Mission Scientists)

KaAMS, a NASA-funded development and research project, was designed using a W-PBL approach. From research on PBL, we selected four phases for the learning event as shown in Figure 3 and created web-enhanced lesson plans to guide teachers' use of this process. Using KaAMS lesson plans, teachers present a real problem and coach students through the mission as scientists as they participate in "bursts" of interactive activities culminating in the analysis of data from real NASA airborne missions.

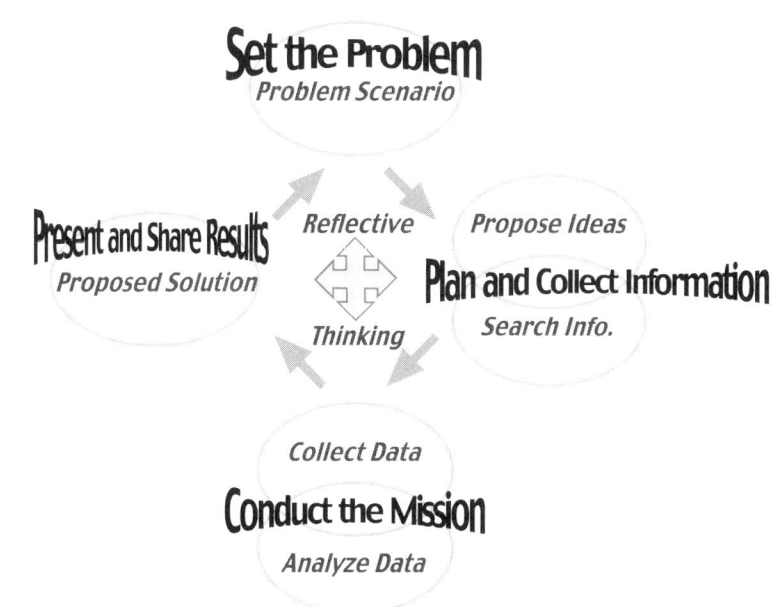

FIGURE **3** Kids as Airborne Mission Scientists (KaAMS) web-enhanced problem-based learning process

This project was realized by connecting and organizing a variety of existing web-based learning resources for teachers to use with their middle school students. With the KaAMS PBL model as a guide, four modules addressing two different environmental missions—active lava flows and the health of coral reefs in Hawaii—were developed. These missions were selected because NASA data already existed for studying the problems. In addition, the topics matched well with middle school curricula, national standards, and middle school student interests.

KaAMS Phase 1: Present Problem Scenario

In phase 1, students are presented with the problem scenario. Learning is framed by the context of one of the authentic, real-world problems noted above to gain students' attention and to motivate them to get involved immediately (Cognition and Technology Group at Vanderbilt, 1990, 1991, 1992; Duffy & Cunningham, 1996). This is the *frame* phase. In the first mission, concerning active lava flows in Hawaii, students are put in the role of airborne remote sensing scientists charged with identifying where the active lava flows are located on the Kilauea volcano. The KaAMS development team created this simulated mission from several web site elements related to volcanoes, active lava flows, and information about the Pacific Disaster Management Agency. The teacher selects this mission and begins the learning event by showing students a web-based letter requesting assistance from the Pacific Disaster Management Agency (see Figure 4). The problem scenario prompts students to explore the overall problem by having them develop an understanding of key concepts such as aeronautics, remote sensing, and airborne remote sensing. It also provides students with a sense of being airborne mission scientists who use aeronautics principles and remote sensing data to study an environmental problem of the earth. At this point, students obtain clarification about the problem from their teacher.

KaAMS Phase 2: Propose Ideas and Search for Information

During learning phase 2, students propose ideas and search for information. This is the *inform* phase, or the planning and gathering information phase of PBL. The PBL literature posits that students should create their own learning goals and be provided with access to multiple learning resources (Duffy & Cunningham, 1996; Savery & Duffy, 1995). Therefore, students are encouraged to explore rich and varied existing NASA web resources to

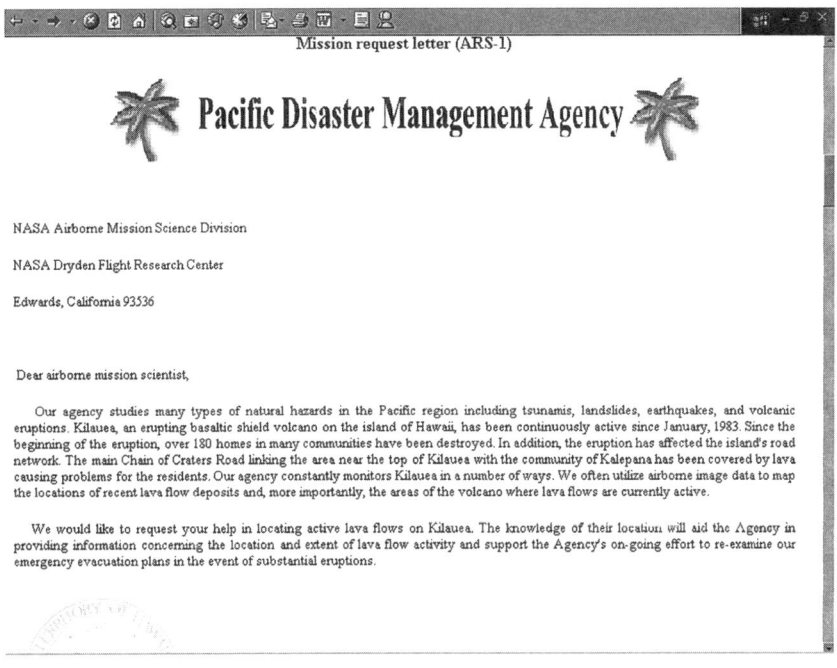

Mission request letter (ARS-1)

Pacific Disaster Management Agency

NASA Airborne Mission Science Division

NASA Dryden Flight Research Center

Edwards, California 93536

Dear airborne mission scientist,

Our agency studies many types of natural hazards in the Pacific region including tsunamis, landslides, earthquakes, and volcanic eruptions. Kilauea, an erupting basaltic shield volcano on the island of Hawaii, has been continuously active since January, 1983. Since the beginning of the eruption, over 180 homes in many communities have been destroyed. In addition, the eruption has affected the island's road network. The main Chain of Craters Road linking the area near the top of Kilauea with the community of Kalepana has been covered by lava causing problems for the residents. Our agency constantly monitors Kilauea in a number of ways. We often utilize airborne image data to map the locations of recent lava flow deposits and, more importantly, the areas of the volcano where lava flows are currently active.

We would like to request your help in locating active lava flows on Kilauea. The knowledge of their location will aid the Agency in providing information concerning the location and extent of lava flow activity and support the Agency's on-going effort to re-examine our emergency evacuation plans in the event of substantial eruptions.

FIGURE **4**   An example of the problem scenario

find the basic science necessary to solve the problem. They are asked to create a plan of study that will help them clarify issues surrounding the problem and plan for conducting a NASA mission to gather data to help them solve the problem. To support these learning activities, all types of web resources, such as information, still images, video clips, and databanks of NASA aircraft, remote sensing, and volcanoes are provided to students. A lesson plan within this phase also presents web resources related to a variety of learning activities for students to develop an understanding about who airborne mission scientists are, how they explore the world, and how these scientists work together (see Figure 5).

KaAMS Phase 3: Collect and Analyze Data

Another key characteristic of PBL is that students actively explore, experiment, analyze, and interpret information (Barrows, 1986, 1992). The third and fourth PBL phases are combined in KaAMS into one *explore* phase: conducting the mission. After searching for information and

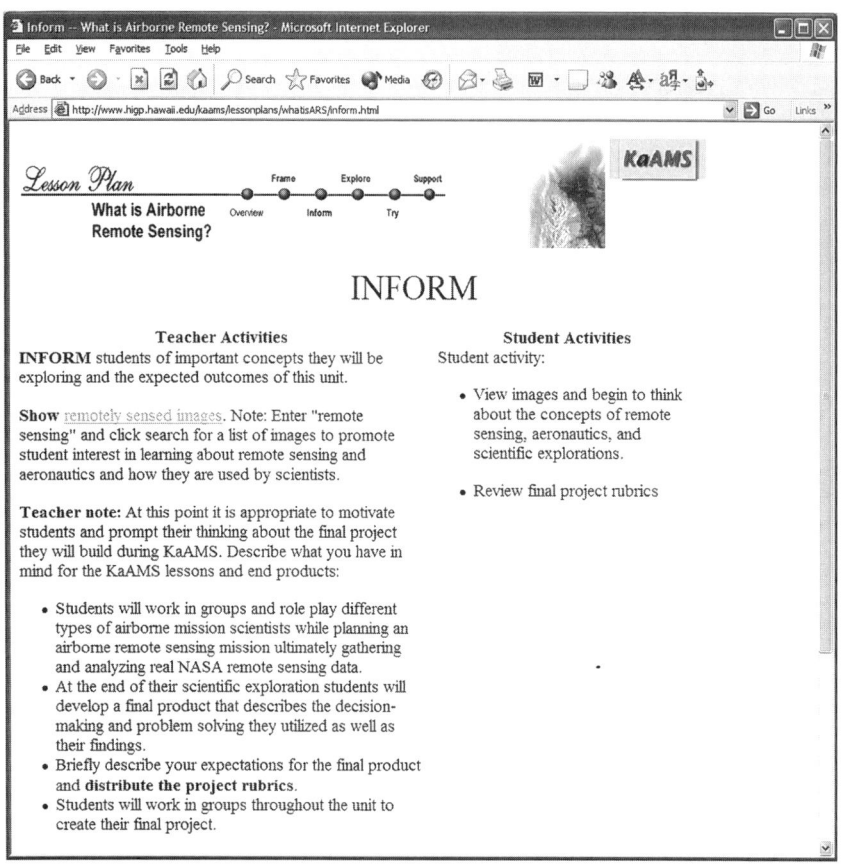

Lesson Plan
What is Airborne Remote Sensing?
Frame   Explore   Support
Overview   Inform   Try

KaAMS

INFORM

Teacher Activities

INFORM students of important concepts they will be exploring and the expected outcomes of this unit.

Show remotely sensed images. Note: Enter "remote sensing" and click search for a list of images to promote student interest in learning about remote sensing and aeronautics and how they are used by scientists.

Teacher note: At this point it is appropriate to motivate students and prompt their thinking about the final project they will build during KaAMS. Describe what you have in mind for the KaAMS lessons and end products:

• Students will work in groups and role play different types of airborne mission scientists while planning an airborne remote sensing mission ultimately gathering and analyzing real NASA remote sensing data.
• At the end of their scientific exploration students will develop a final product that describes the decision-making and problem solving they utilized as well as their findings.
• Briefly describe your expectations for the final product and **distribute the project rubrics**.
• Students will work in groups throughout the unit to create their final project.

Student Activities

Student activity:

• View images and begin to think about the concepts of remote sensing, aeronautics, and scientific explorations.

• Review final project rubrics

FIGURE **5**   An example of the *propose ideas* learning phase

developing an understanding of the problem, students are given an opportunity to select which NASA aircraft they will use to run their mission to collect actual data (see Figure 6). They are prompted to think about how data can be collected using airborne remote sensing aircraft. To support students' learning in this phase, web resources related to NASA aircraft and several simulations or hands-on activities, such as flying a kite, developing film, and analyzing data images, are provided to students.

After collecting the data, students can participate in numerous activities to learn how to analyze and interpret both visible and infrared remote sensing images. To support these learning activities, visually rich NASA web-based remote sensing images and web-based guidelines developed by NASA

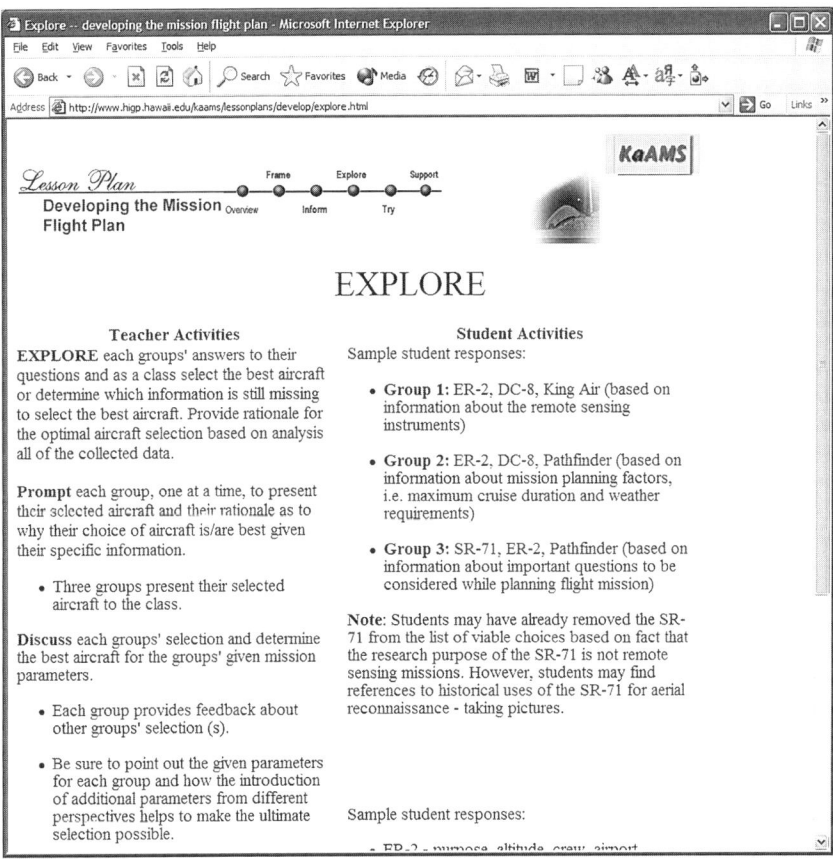

FIGURE **6**   An example of the *collect data* learning phase

scientists are provided. Students then analyze and interpret two actual NASA images of the Kilauea volcano to locate the active lava flows.

KaAMS Phase 4: Propose Solutions

In the last phase, students try out their knowledge by proposing solutions in a public forum (Go Public) (Schwartz et al., 1999). This is the *try* phase. After analyzing and interpreting the data, students write the results of their investigation for the KaAMS mission to locate active lava flows on Kilauea (see Figure 7). Each student group presents the best solution and shares it with the other students and teachers. After all the solutions are presented,

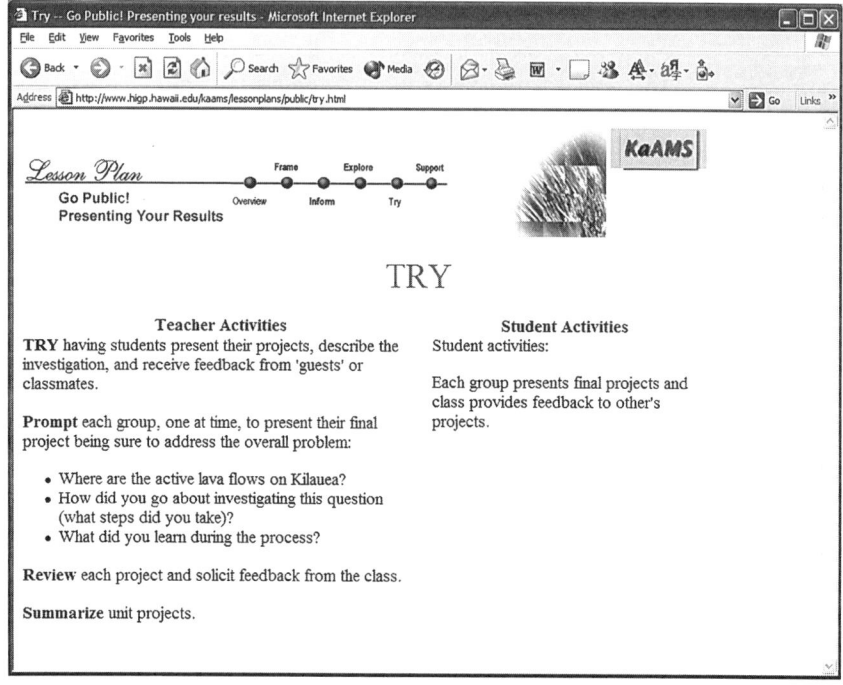

FIGURE **7**   An example of the *propose solutions* learning phase

students have an opportunity to revise their solutions based on feedback from their peers, teachers, and experts before making their final statement. With this final statement, they complete their investigation and mission.

Plans for the KaAMS site include developing a showcase interface for students to post and display their solutions and a NASA network interface that facilitates communication between students and NASA scientists.

Conclusion

A model for W-PBL merges the role of learner as problem solver and four roles of the teacher in the five phases of a PBL process. The interrelationships between the learners, their cognitive processes, teachers, learning events, and the PBL phases determine which types of information or human web resources are the most likely sources for lesson enhancement. The W-PBL model is supported by and built upon research in PBL, cognitive learning processes, and web-enhancement of classroom instruction. The model suggests a means for teachers, and encourages them, to consider the richness of the Web in supporting PBL in their classrooms.

Acknowledgments

These projects were made possible through funding from the NASA Dryden Flight Research Center and the NASA Leading Educators to Applications, Research, and NASA-related Educational Resources in Science (LEARNERS), a Cooperative Agreement Notice from the NASA Education Division and Learning Technologies Project, project number NCC5-432: Learning Using ERAST Aircraft for Understanding Remote Sensing, Atmospheric Sampling and Aircraft Technologies (LUAU II). In addition, we acknowledge a multitude of individuals who have contributed to this project, especially Dr. Marianne McCarthy, Education Officer from the NASA Dryden Flight Research Center, and Dr. Luke Flynn of the University of Hawaii, Department of Geophysics.

References

Achilles, C. M., & Hoover, S. P. (1996). *Problem-based learning (PBL) as a school-improvement vehicle* (ERIC Document Reproduction Service No. ED 401 631).

Albanese, M. A., & Mitchell, S. (1993). Problem-based learning: A review of literature on its outcomes and implementation issues. *Academic Medicine, 68*, 52–81.

Barrows, H. S. (1986). A taxonomy of problem based learning methods. *Medical Education, 20*, 481–86.

Barrows, H. S. (1992). *The tutorial process*. Springfield, IL: Southern Illinois University School of Medicine.

Cognition and Technology Group at Vanderbilt (1990). Anchored instruction and its relationship to situated cognition. *Educational Researcher, 19*, 2–10.

Cognition and Technology Group at Vanderbilt (1991). Technology and the design of generative learning environment. *Educational Technology, 31*, 34–40.

Cognition and Technology Group at Vanderbilt (1992). The Jasper series as an example of anchored instruction: Theory, program description, and assessment data. *Educational Psychologist, 27*, 291–315.

Conlon, M. (1997). MOOville: The writing project's own "private Idaho." *T.H.E. Journal, 24*, 66–68.

Department of Education (2000). Technology for Education Act of 1994, Part A—Technology for education of all students, Sec. 3111: Findings. http://www.ed.gov/legislation/ESEA/sec3111.html.

Duffy, T. M., & Cunningham, D. J. (1996). Constructivism: Implications for the design and delivery of instruction. In D. H. Jonassen (Ed.), *Handbook of research for educational communications and technology* (pp. 170–98). New York: Macmillan.

Faulkner, D. R. (1999). A comparison of worked-examples and problem-based learning on the achievement and retention of middle school student teams. Doctoral dissertation, University of South Alabama.

Federman, A., & Edwards, S. (1997). Interactive, collaborative science via the Net: Live from the Hubble space telescope. *T.H.E. Journal* (Suppl.), 20–22.

Gagne, R. M. (1985). *The conditions of learning and theory of instruction* (4th ed.). New York: Holt, Rinehart and Winston.

Geyer, R. W. (1997). Approaching ground zero with today's technology tools. *T.H.E. Journal, 25*, 56–59.

Grabowski, B., & Koszalka, T. (2000). *Learning technologies project short and long term impact study and final report: Web-enhanced learning environment strategies*. Dryden, CA: NASA Dryden Flight Research Center.

Grabowski, B., Koszalka, T., & McCarthy, M. (2000). *Web-enhanced learning environment strategies: Handbook and reflection tool* (11th ed.). University Park, PA: Penn State University, Instructional Systems Program.

Hmelo, C. E., & Evensen, D. H. (2000). Problem-based learning: Gaining insights on learning interactions through multiple methods of inquiry. In D. H. Evensen & C. E. Hmelo (Eds.), *Problem-based learning: A research perspective on learning interactions*. Mahwah, NJ: Erlbaum.

Kagan, S., & Widaman, K. (1987). Cooperativeness and achievement: Interaction of student cooperativeness with cooperative versus competitive classroom organization. *Journal of School Psychology, 25*, 355–65.

Karayan, S., & Crowe, J. (1997). Student perceptions of electronic discussion groups. *T.H.E. Journal, 24*, 69–71.

Keller, J. (1983). Motivational design of instruction. In C. Reigeluth (Ed.), *Instructional design theories and models: An overview of their current status*. Hillsdale, NJ: Erlbaum.

Koszalka, T. (1999). The relationship between the types of resources used in science classrooms and middle school students' interest in science careers: An exploratory analysis. Doctoral dissertation, Pennsylvania State University.

Lieberman, A. (1996). Creating intentional learning communities. *Educational Leadership, 54*, 51–55.

National Center for Educational Statistics (2000a). Internet access in U.S. public schools and classrooms, 1994–2000. http://nces.ed.gov/pubs2001/InternetAccess/figs.asp.

National Center for Educational Statistics (2000b). Teachers' tools for the 21st century. http://nces.ed.gov/pubs2000/2000102A.pdf.

O'Sullivan, C. Y., Weiss, A. R., & Askew, J. M. (1998). *Students learning science: A report on policies and practices in U.S. schools*. Statistical analysis report, NCES 98493. Washington, DC: National Center for Educational Statistics.

Papert, S. (1997). Educational computing: How are we doing? *T.H.E. Journal, 24*, 78–80.

Reigeluth, C. M. (1999). *Instructional design theories and models: A new paradigm of instructional theory*, Vol. 2. Mahwah, NJ: Erlbaum.

Ronnkvist, A., Dexter, S., & Anderson, R. (2000). Technology support: Its depth, breadth and impact in America's schools. http://www.crito.uci.edu/tlc/findings/technology-support.

Rummelhart, D. E., & Norman, D. A. (1978). Accretion, tuning, and restructuring: Three modes of learning. In J. W. Cotton & R. L. Klatzky (Eds.), *Semantic factors in cognition*. Hillsdale, NJ: Erlbaum.

Savery, J. R., & Duffy, T. M. (1995). Problem-based learning: An instructional model and its constructivist framework. *Educational Technology, 35*, 31–38.

Schwartz, D. L., Brophy, S., Lin, X., & Bransford, J. D. (1999). Software for managing complex learning: Examples from an educational psychology course. *Educational Technology Research and Development, 47*, 38–59.

Sharan, S., & Kussell, P. (1984). *Cooperative learning in the classroom: Research in desegregated schools*. Hillsdale, NJ: Erlbaum.

Slavin, R. E. (1983). *Cooperative learning*. New York: Longman.

Tan, O. S. (2002). Lifelong learning through a problem-based learning approach. In A. S. C. Chang & C. C. M. Goh (Eds.), *Teachers' handbook on teaching generic thinking skills* (pp. 22–36). Singapore: Prentice Hall.

Tan, O. S., Parsons, R. D., Hinson, S. L., & Sardo-Brown, D. (2003). *Educational psychology: A practitioner–researcher approach (An Asian edition)*. Singapore: Thomson Learning.

West, S. A. (1992). Problem-based learning: A viable addition for secondary school science. *School Science Review, 73*, 47–55.

CHAPTER *11*

Integrating Problem-based Learning and Technology in Education

George Watson

Motivation for Our Efforts

When business and industry leaders identify desirable attributes in prospective employees—our current students—the list generally includes the following elements (Wingspread Conference, 1994):

- High level of communication skills
- Ability to define problems, gather and evaluate information, and develop solutions
- Team skills, that is, ability to work with others
- Ability to use all of the above to address problems in a complex real-world setting

How can we help our students achieve these goals? Studies have shown that collaborative learning—learning centered on student groups—is a superior approach for developing the enhanced set of skills students need after they leave formal education. Research shows that collaborative learning results in both academic success (i.e., higher achievement, including knowledge acquisition, accuracy, creativity in problem solving, and higher reasoning level) and positive attitude effects (persistence toward goals, intrinsic motivation, transfer of learning to other situations, and staying longer on tasks) (Johnson, Johnson, & Smith, 1998). In short, keeping the learning focused on students via collaborative learning helps us achieve the desired goals listed above.

Many of us have commented along this line: "I really learned my discipline when I taught the material." When instructors prepare traditional courses for the first time, they engage with the course material as they hope their students do. Unfortunately, in traditional classrooms, the individuals learning the most are often the new instructors. Huba and Freed (2000) pointed out that instructors preparing for traditional course delivery "have reserved for themselves the very conditions that promote learning," which include:

- actively seeking new information
- integrating it with what is known
- organizing it in a meaningful way
- having a chance to explain it to others

In a problem-based learning classroom, we seek to provide our students with these same opportunities for learning.

Integrating Information Technology and Problem-based Learning

Problem-based learning (PBL) is an instructional method that challenges students to learn to learn through working cooperatively in groups to seek solutions to real-world problems (Duch, Groh, & Allen, 2001). These problems are used to engage students' curiosity and to initiate learning of the subject matter. At its most fundamental level, PBL is characterized by the use of real-world problems as a context for students to learn critical thinking and problem-solving skills and to acquire knowledge of the essential concepts of the course. Using PBL, students acquire lifelong learning skills, which include the ability to find and use appropriate learning resources, certainly important in the ever-changing world increasingly based on information technology.

Can information technology promote success in PBL courses? Or rather, should we consider the question if PBL can promote success in mastering technology objectives? Increasing numbers of instructors in higher education are beginning to look beyond content objectives for their courses. At the University of Delaware, the Institute for Transforming Undergraduate Education (ITUE) encourages faculty to embrace the process objectives, or active learning (AL) objectives, listed in Table 1, regardless of the content objectives of their courses. PBL has been identified as an approach that helps faculty guide students toward these objectives.

In addition, universities and colleges are beginning to articulate goals for their students in the area of information technology. An excellent example of instructional technology (IT) objectives comes from George Mason University in its Technology Across the Curriculum program (Table 2), where technology is promoted to enhance learning so that all students will be able to achieve common objectives.

Coupled with the content objectives for a course, the two sets of objectives above pose an intimidating and overwhelming task for the typical

TABLE 1 Active learning (AL) objectives

Undergraduate courses should:	
AL1	be student-centered and encourage students to learn to learn
AL2	provide opportunities to think critically and to analyze and solve problems
AL3	assist students in developing skills in gathering and evaluating information
AL4	provide experience of working cooperatively in teams and small groups
AL5	help students acquire versatile and effective communication skills
AL6	offer a variety of learning experiences
AL7	apply technology effectively so that it will enhance learning

TABLE 2 Instructional technology (IT) objectives

Courses should:	
IT1	engage in electronic collaboration
IT2	use and create structured electronic documents
IT3	make use of technology-enhanced presentations
IT4	use appropriate electronic tools for research and evaluation
IT5	use spreadsheets and databases to manage information
IT6	use electronic tools for analyzing quantitative and qualitative data
IT7	identify major legal, ethical, and security issues in information technology
IT8	provide a working knowledge of instructional technology platforms

Source: Modified slightly from the ten goals articulated by George Mason University in its Technology Across the Curriculum program.

instructor. Fortunately, the AL objectives and the IT objectives project well onto each other, as shown in Figure 1 for the first six objectives in each list. As an example of overlapping objectives, consider that the active learning objective of critical thinking and problem solving (AL2) is supported by the technology objectives of analyzing data (IT6), research and evaluation (IT4), and managing information (IT5). Similarly, the technology objective of electronic collaboration (IT1) is well served by the active learning objectives of gathering and evaluating information (AL3), student-centeredness and learning to learn (AL1), communication skills (AL5), and group cooperation (AL4).

Clearly, the marriage of PBL and instructional technology is important for student learning. How can technology aid student learning in a PBL course? How can PBL aid students in using technology to learn? The answers to these questions expand each semester as technology advances and our ideas for integrating it with PBL evolve.

Many instructors have adopted course web sites and web pages to organize their courses and to deliver course materials to their students. Web-

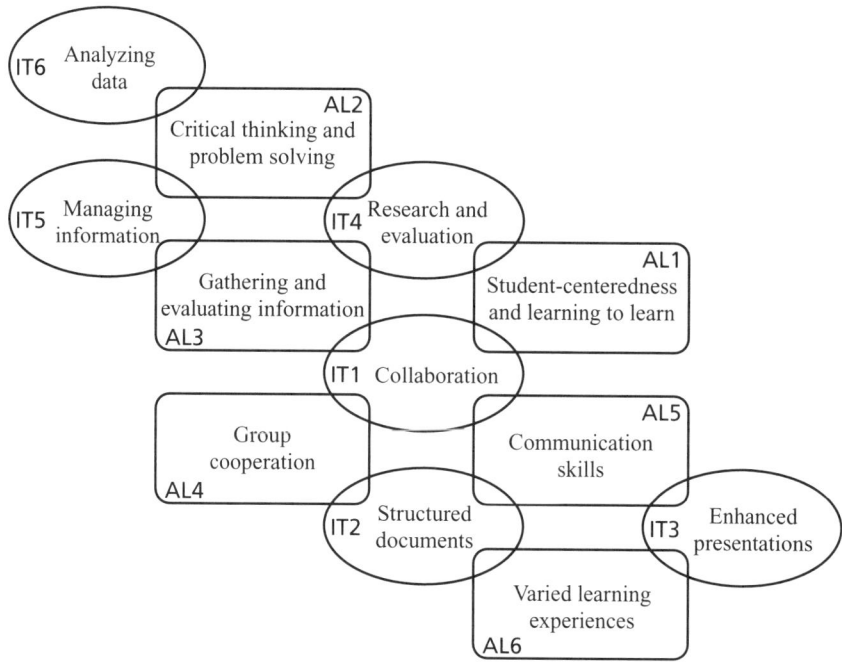

FIGURE 1 Overlap of active learning (AL) objectives (boxes) and instructional technology (IT) objectives (ovals)

authoring tools have become easier to use, and growing numbers of technology support staff and centers on campuses have facilitated the publication of materials on the Web. The use of the Web in PBL courses plays a critical role in their success in two major areas: (1) organizing the PBL course and (2) the use of online resources to support the PBL course.

Using Course Web Sites to Organize PBL Courses

As shown in Figure 2, a course web site helps organize a PBL course in several areas: (1) organizing the syllabus, (2) organizing groups, and (3) organizing student projects and reports. Many ideas for using a web site to organize a PBL course can be found by examining online syllabi for other courses. An advantage of the availability of course materials on the Web is the opportunity to adapt and incorporate suitable materials into one's own web site, with appropriate recognition and credit to the authors and instructors who created the materials. An example of an online syllabus for an introductory PBL science course is SCEN103 "Silicon, Circuits, and

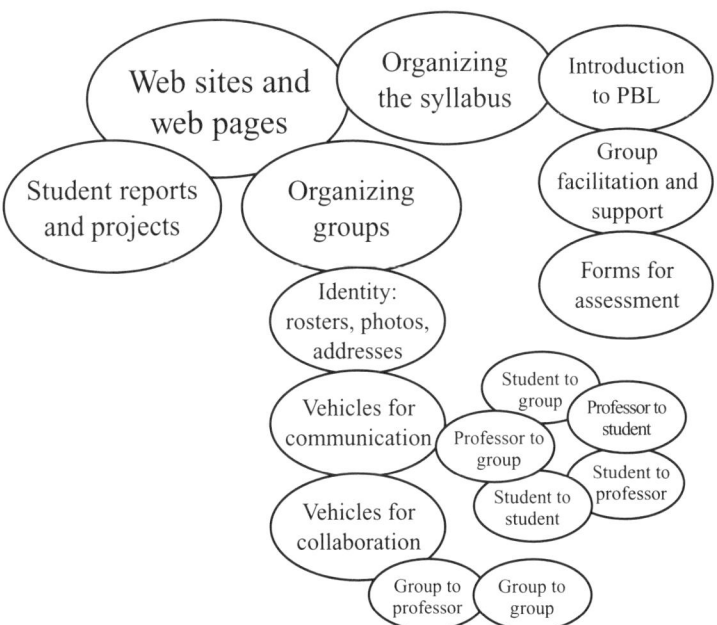

FIGURE **2**   Using a course web site to organize a problem-based learning (PBL) course

the Digital Revolution" at *www.physics.udel.edu/~watson/scen103/colloq2000*.

Instructors experienced in teaching PBL courses recognize that a critical element of success is achieving students' identification and bonding with the process. A significant amount of time should be spent explaining the process of PBL, why it is important for learning in the course, and the support structures that are available to help students achieve success. Actually, there is often more material available than can be comfortably reviewed in a given class devoted to introducing PBL. A web site makes it expedient to provide as much supporting material to students as one wishes, without burdening them with additional discussion or superfluous paper during class time. In addition to schedule and contact information traditionally included in a syllabus, many informative pages can be linked from the syllabus web page, as listed in Table 3.

Organizing communication with the class, particularly with groups, can be readily facilitated electronically. Efficient communication between the group (rather than just one member) and the professor and with each other has been evolving with the development of increasingly powerful technology solutions. A decade ago, the available alternatives were limited to electronic bulletin boards and newsgroups. These tools were limited in their effectiveness, often because of poor usability. The first breakthrough in managing groups online came from ventures such as *eGroups.com* (now available as *groups.yahoo.com*), which provided relatively easy-to-use interfaces for organizing small groups, chat rooms, file sharing, and

TABLE **3** Examples of supporting information that can be linked from an online syllabus for a problem-based learning (PBL) course

- Instructor's teaching philosophy
- Detailed course objectives (both content and process)
- General education goals
- Motivation and description of PBL
- Problem-solving process and strategies
- Roles and responsibilities of students, peer tutors, and instructor
- List of frequently asked questions about PBL and working in groups
- Forms for assessment of individual performance in groups
- Some thoughts on grading
- Anonymous suggestion box and responses to suggestions
- Academic services center
- Policies on academic dishonesty and responsible computing

scheduling meetings. Course management systems (CMS), designed primarily for distance learning, now provide superior packages for organizing and communicating with groups. These packages include controlled discussion forums, collaborative space, and whiteboarding capabilities. An additional attractive feature of a typical CMS is the ability to control the release of a document based on a previous action of a student or group—perfect for staging a PBL problem in a distance learning environment.

Clearly, organizing electronic communication for student groups and providing communication tools via a CMS empower students to engage in electronic collaboration (IT1), an important technology objective. Since cooperative learning is fundamental to PBL and instructors are responsible for ensuring that appropriate channels of communication are available for group collaboration, satisfying this objective helps bring success to the PBL classroom. Indeed, a PBL course makes an excellent context for students to develop skills in mastering tools for electronic collaboration.

At the conclusion of a problem, groups are typically required to report their findings to the class or prepare a written product for the instructor's review. In a PBL-intensive course, the weekly cycle of problem/work/report can take a toll on student enthusiasm and energy. Relying on a variety of reporting mechanisms, an instructor can alleviate this difficulty, while at the same time satisfying several additional technology objectives. Students can be encouraged or required to use presentation software to report their findings in class, thus satisfying objective IT3. Alternatively, groups may prepare a collaborative web site with multiple, interlinked web pages, thus exercising objective IT2. Unquestionably, a well-organized course web site presenting a wealth of hyperlinked material will provide students with an excellent model of structure and ease of navigation to emulate. A quantitative requirement within the final product, such as a graph or table, will offer students an opportunity to use graphing or spreadsheet programs, exercising objective IT5. Additional requirements of multimedia elements in their presentations will lead students to create images and use editing software.

Using Online Resources to Support PBL Courses

As shown in Figure 3, online resources can support a PBL course in several ways: by providing (1) ingredients for writing problems, (2) inspiration for problem design, and (3) information for solving problems.

The availability of engaging, relevant real-world problems is a critical element in the success of a PBL course. In the absence of suitable problems, an instructor is compelled to write his or her own problems, often needing inspiration and raw ingredients—here the Web abounds with support! Inspiration for a problem can come from international newspapers, often more readily available online than as newsprint in the campus library. Online newspapers from the region of a breaking story offer a local flavor and additional human interest that are hard to create otherwise. The variety of global views and regional perspectives can elevate the different stakeholders in a given situation or scenario, making them more interesting and more "real." If extreme positions are sought, the Web is replete with fanatic and quack sites, which should provide ample raw materials to fuel a good problem statement. Scripts and character materials are available from a large number of film and television web sites. Basing a problem on a popular media character or situation familiar to students may transform a good idea into a more engaging scenario for their consideration.

Ingredients for the problem design and statement can originate from a variety of sources. Background facts to support a problem can be effortlessly

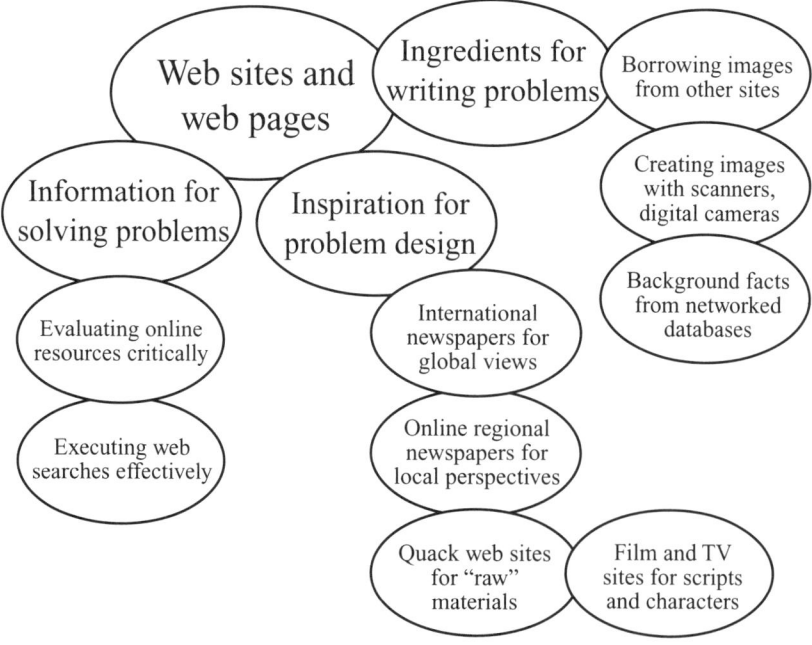

FIGURE 3   Using online resources to support a problem-based learning course

obtained from networked databases made available by university and other libraries. Online encyclopedias and almanacs provide additional biographical and geographical information needed to portray the scenario as accurately as possible. Scholarly journals have also become more readily available online, making access to the latest results in a discipline just a few keystrokes away.

Of course, students naturally turn to the Web in pursuit of information to solve the problems in a PBL course. Objective IT4 on using appropriate tools for research and evaluation is naturally fulfilled in an intensive PBL course. The old thinking that the Web is full of misinformation and biased representation that students should avoid in serious research must be put aside. The new thinking should be that the Web is an excellent proving ground for engaging and developing critical thinking skills. Evaluating online resources critically and executing web searches effectively are important lessons to learn for students being prepared to be lifelong learners.

Faculty Development in PBL and Partnerships for Integrating Technology

Despite the advantages that PBL offers in improving the learning experience, its adoption as a mode of instruction is a change not to be undertaken lightly. Giving up the safety and authority of the lecture can be unsettling for instructors accustomed only to a traditional lecture format. In addition, a lack of suitable material and problems designed for use in a problem-based format serves as a barrier to instructors who are ready to take up the challenge of PBL. The importance of faculty training in PBL and development of an appropriate curriculum cannot be overstated.

In PBL training workshops provided by ITUE, we model what we promote by presenting PBL methodology using appropriate technology and web resources. Our workshops introduce PBL concepts using the same active-learning and student-centered approaches that we advocate. We start each week-long session with an opportunity for faculty participants to work in small groups for a day, solving an engaging PBL problem and working through the process, much like students in a typical PBL course. By applying elements of our own philosophy, such as active engagement and appropriate use of technology, to the creation and implementation of our workshops, we have engaged faculty and modeled techniques that promise to transform higher education.

Our faculty participants appreciate exploring active learning techniques through an experiential approach, a hallmark of the successful ITUE experience. We do not simply lecture about the techniques, laying out their underlying educational theory and benefits, but rather participants experience the power of PBL and other teaching strategies directly. Using active learning strategies in faculty development programs as often as feasible is beneficial, even essential. They not only benefit participants' learning but model new approaches for participants who may not have yet encountered them. Having experienced these techniques firsthand, faculty are better able to incorporate them into their own teaching. By interacting intensely in small groups with their peers, they form relationships that go beyond departmental barriers and provide a conducive environment for discussing curriculum change.

In general, two types of instructors have been attracted to participate in ITUE workshops: those interested in PBL and those interested in using the Web and other technologies in their teaching. Their transformation during the week-long session has often been striking. Those coming primarily for the technology portion (and for supplemental funding to facilitate their acquisition of more technology) had their eyes opened to the possibility of PBL and other student-centered strategies. Those coming primarily for PBL saw how online resources can be used to facilitate student learning in their courses and were empowered both to design problems using rich online resources and to publish course materials on the Web for their students. ITUE has continued with this two-pronged approach to faculty development, which has, in our opinion, been an essential element in its success.

PRESENT (Practical Resources for Educators Seeking Effective New Technologies) is the teaching, learning, and technology center at the University of Delaware. It resembles a collaborative classroom and includes workstations and equipment for exploring uses of technology in teaching. The underlying philosophy of PRESENT is that identification of learning goals should always precede application of technology. Although PRESENT is where faculty initially come for technical assistance, they receive educational expertise as well. In developing an active learning course, for example, it becomes important to think creatively about the variety of ways—often effectively facilitated through technology—in which students can engage in interactions with the instructor, fellow students, and the course content.

Collaboration between ITUE and PRESENT began naturally as ITUE leaders enlisted the expertise of PRESENT staff to assist with the technology portion of the training. When ITUE training sessions end, PRESENT staff members continue to be available to consult and to provide ongoing reinforcement not only of technology but also of active learning strategies. PRESENT offers seminars all year round, demonstrating examples of applying technology to PBL when appropriate. Instructional technology training includes active learning components so that faculty participate as students would in an actual class and make suggestions for how the tools should be used to achieve the desired learning goals.

As a specific example demonstrating the partnership between ITUE and PRESENT, PRESENT staff members and ITUE leaders have taught side by side in our WebCT/Active Learning Institute. ITUE contributors illustrated how they used specific tools in their classes and, together with PRESENT staff, led participants through exercises designed to connect those tools to their own courses. In a class on WebCT Communication tools, Valerie Hans, a faculty member in sociology and criminal justice, presented a problem on justice for suspected terrorist detainees. Participants, divided into groups, used the online discussion group within a WebCT course to consider the various options available for justice. In another exercise, they used the discussion group to come up with questions for an expert in international terrorism. Subsequently, these questions were posed to a local expert on terrorism in a WebCT chat room.

Partnerships such as this one are essential in implementing technology-enhanced curricular reform. This partnership continues to flourish through sharing of the same vision, promoting and participating in each other's activities, and recognizing the efforts of each other. Administrators, librarians, faculty, and anyone charged with using technology to support learning should identify potential partners on their own campus and nurture a synergistic relationship that benefits the entire campus.

Recent Work on PBL at University of Delaware

Funding from external sources—the National Science Foundation, the Fund for Improvement of Post-Secondary Education, and the Pew Charitable Trusts—combined with local matching commitments have made possible many of the developments in PBL at the University of Delaware. Of course, external funding is not a requirement for implementing PBL on any campus; however, it did provide us with the means for infusing the concept at our institution more rapidly, for quickly creating and sustaining an effective faculty development effort, and for reaching the global community interested in PBL.

In addition to continued sponsorship of PBL conferences and faculty development workshops, university and external funding continues to drive development of PBL at our campus. Two of our current activities are highlighted in the following.

PBL Clearinghouse

One major barrier we encountered in the adoption of PBL by educators was the dearth of available problems suitable for use. With local programming support, we embarked on an electronic database of PBL problems and materials known as the PBL Clearinghouse. The problems and articles are peer-reviewed by PBL experts in the relevant disciplinary content areas. Teaching notes and supplemental materials accompany each problem, providing insights and strategies that are innovative and classroom-tested. Access to the PBL Clearinghouse collection is limited to educators who register via an online application, but it is free and carries no obligation. More than 5,000 users from all regions of the world have registered to use the PBL Clearinghouse, which now makes available more than 50 problems and continues to grow at several problems per month. Currently, the majority of problems focus on biology, physics, and chemistry, but the database has expanded into the humanities and social sciences. The PBL Clearinghouse is open to any educators who are looking for a suitable venue to publish the PBL material they have developed.

Wireless Computing in PBL Classrooms

We are fortunate to have classrooms specially designed for PBL, with reconfigurable trapezoidal tables and comfortable rolling chairs. These classrooms range in size from 36 to 72 seats. Given the constraints of movable furniture and the diverse use of the rooms, it had not been feasible to have access to the Internet for doing research during class in these classrooms. Thus, the need for research was often synonymous with early adjournment of groups from class. To alleviate this problem, two PBL classrooms were equipped with 16 laptops each, with wireless connectivity to the Internet. The wireless laptops are made available to facilitate collaborative learning, so access to only one or two laptops per group is not a problem, but rather a virtue (and saves costs too!).

One professor reported her use of the wireless laptops for online research, data analysis, and access to a CMS as follows:

> The laptops proved to be very valuable throughout this group work. Most importantly, from my perspective, it allowed some of the critical phases to be done in class with all group members present and with me available to give advice and direction.
>
> ... When my groups began their projects, they were able to do the initial work in class, searching [University of Delaware] library resources, online databases, and the Web for relevant articles and other material. I believe this equalized the input of group members during the initial research. So often, in group work, a particular person will be assigned to do the research independently and bring it back to the group. The group work can stall until that happens, but with the laptops allowing immediate in-class searching, the group work was facilitated.
>
> Having the laptops in class also allowed all group members to participate in the development of the scenario and questions, while one or more people in the group typed into a file, which was then placed using WebCT into a group discussions folder, making it available for further editing and use by all group members.
>
> When students came to class with their data, we used ... data analysis [software] ... to compare and contrast the responses to their experimental and control scenarios. Again, that was done in class (as opposed to one or more people assuming this responsibility outside of class, or arranging for an out-of-class meeting) and I was able to go around the room to the groups and work with them on their analyses.
>
> Finally, students put together PowerPoint presentations, which included figures and graphs, using the laptops, and posted them to the class using the WebCT Discussions tool.

Funding for this project was made available by the University of Delaware through its grant program Advanced and Emerging Technologies in Instructional Contexts, administered by the Center for Teaching Effectiveness.

Conclusion

PBL at the University of Delaware was advanced with the creation of ITUE to promote reform of undergraduate education through faculty development and course design. ITUE leaders drive the development of other educators by sharing ideas for transforming courses through incorporating effective techniques for the promotion of active learning and the use of technology in the classroom. If you are not already underway in a strong partnership for faculty development, we encourage you to likewise add a strong faculty development component to your efforts to help promote the growth and adoption of PBL as an instructional approach, underpinned by appropriate use of technology.

The rapid and relentless pace of technological development certainly makes it difficult to stay abreast of the latest applications of instructional technology. Nevertheless, it is critical that we lay a strong foundation in our education programs on which to build the latest developments in technology. PBL offers a secure foundation on the shores of pedagogy from which to build our education reform initiatives. Without that strong anchor, our reform efforts risk collapse on the shifting sand of technology.

> . . . like a wise man who built his house on a rock. The rain fell, the floods came, and the winds blew and beat against that house, but it did not collapse because its foundation was on the rock.
> . . . like a foolish man who built his house on sand. The rain fell, the floods came, and the winds blew and battered that house, and it collapsed, and its collapse was devastating.
>
> (Parable of the two builders, Matthew 7:24–27,
> International Standard Version)

Acknowledgments

With grateful acknowledgments to Deborah Allen, Janet de Vry, Barbara Duch, Susan Groh, Valerie Hans, and Harold White.

References

Duch, B. J., Groh, S. E., & Allen, D. E. (2001). *The power of problem-based learning.* Sterling, VA: Stylus.
George Mason University College of Arts and Sciences (2003). *Technology across the curriculum.* http://cas.gmu.edu/tac.
Huba, M. E., & Freed, J. E. (2000). *Learner-centered assessment on college campuses: Shifting the focus from teaching to learning.* Boston: Allyn and Bacon.
Institute for Transforming Undergraduate Education. http://www.udel.edu/inst.
Johnson, D. W., Johnson, R. T., & Smith, K. A. (1998). Cooperative learning returns to college: What evidence is there that it works? *Change, 30,* 26–35.
PBL Clearinghouse. http://www.udel.edu/pblc.

PRESENT at University of Delaware. http://www.udel.edu/present.

Problem-based Learning at University of Delaware. http://www.udel.edu/pbl.

Wingspread Conference (1994). *Quality assurance in undergraduate education: What the public expects*. Denver, CO: Education Commission of the States.

·

Looking Ahead: The Best Way Forward for Problem-based Learning Approaches

Oon-Seng Tan

Problem-based Learning and Practical Challenges

Problem-based learning (PBL) has been one of the most popular curricular innovations in education (Marincovich, 2000). Many education reform movements have embraced PBL owing to (1) its emphasis on enhancing flexible and multiple ways of thinking, (2) its paradigm of cross-disciplinary and multidisciplinary learning, and (3) its problem-solving contexts that enable integration of content knowledge with real-world applications along with the development of problem-solving acumen (Tan, Little, Hee, & Conway, 2000).

The PBL architecture typically involves a shift in three loci of educational preoccupation: (1) from content coverage to problem engagement, (2) from lecturers to coaches in the role of teachers, and (3) from passive learners to active problem solvers in the role of students (Tan, 2000). The active, self-regulated, and collaborative approach in PBL requires shifts in mental models, patterns of thoughts and behaviors, and the learning method. In theory, it is easy to tell students that they need to take the role of active problem solvers rather than passive learners waiting to be spoon-fed.

It is also easy to tell teachers that they should take the role of coaches rather than disseminators of knowledge. While many educators accept the rationale for PBL and recognize the potential value of such a learning paradigm, they are often disappointed with a number of practical realities (Tan, 2001). There is a need to deliberate on why the shift in academic architecture is not as simple as commonly assumed by champions of PBL.

In PBL implementation, it is recognized that staff development and student preparation are essential for mindset change. At the curriculum implementation level, there are often problems caused by confusion relating to the goals of implementing PBL, the content, the role of teacher, and the role of the learner. PBL is not a "one size fits all" methodology, but more a philosophy and approach that emphasizes the effective use of problems through an integrated approach of active and multidisciplinary learning. To effectively introduce a PBL curriculum, it is essential to review the desired graduate profile of the program, the nature of the disciplines, disciplinary goals, assessment criteria, current resources, and the profile of students. With good planning, management support, resource allocation, and staff development, PBL can become a predominant mode of learning supplemented by a range of good instructional methodologies. Many medical schools have successfully adopted PBL in their curricula (Berkson, 1993; Norman & Schmidt, 2000). Although the benefits of PBL may be apparent, the practical conversion from a traditional curriculum to a PBL curriculum can be a daunting task owing to administrative and logistic considerations as well as the lack of resources (Tan, 2002). To make the switch more manageable, PBL can be incorporated at the micro level, in project work or in certain subjects. However, we do not want too much of the same thing, such as repeating the same emphasis of the PBL cycle in all courses. It may suffice to have a few courses or modules where generic problem solving, collaborative learning, and communication are emphasized through the use of PBL approaches (Armstrong, 1991). The secret to using the PBL approach effectively to enhance thinking is (1) to use PBL strategically and align it with desired educational outcomes; (2) to understand the psychological and dialogical advantages of using PBL; and (3) to employ psychological, pedagogical, and technology tools as illustrated in the chapters of this book.

I would next like to raise several specific issues and misconceptions. For convenience, I would use the three foci described earlier (content vs. problem, teacher vs. coach, learner vs. problem solver) to point out some common misconceptions that arise in PBL transition and implementation.

In the name of changing student mindsets, some PBL curricula are advocating inquiry in a vacuum where students do not have the prerequisite foundation and the basic tools of learning. Here I think there is a chasm between advocates of so-called "pure" or "authentic" PBL and the reality of students' experience. There are those who claim that PBL need not activate prior knowledge and we could start with a problem from the outset in a domain totally unfamiliar to students. In practice, there are many instances where such an assumption is questionable. There are disciplines and subjects where foundation knowledge is best disseminated first, and effective PBL entails the activation of prior knowledge. Examples of such prior knowledge would be foundation principles of physics and basic mathematical tools. The axioms, language, and tools of certain domains are examples of essential prior knowledge. Apart from foundation knowledge, it is important to ask to what extent the problem scenarios should build on and activate prior knowledge. There is thus the need to understand psychological tools and the construction of knowledge in the use of PBL.

Another misconception is that PBL facilitators do not need to have disciplinary or "expertise" knowledge. While PBL has often been advocated for the teaching of what I call lifewide skills (e.g., collaborative learning), it should be noted that disciplinary knowledge should never be compromised. The "just-in-case" syndrome in traditional examination-based curricula tends to lead to too much coverage for the sake of comprehensiveness, just in case the material may be required by examinations or a particular professional or accreditation body. In PBL, instead of comprehensive coverage, learners are empowered with learning-to-learn skills. Nevertheless, there is often a core body of disciplinary knowledge that should be defined. The purpose of PBL is to enable students to appreciate the depth of the inquiry often unique to the discipline. It is thus unfortunate that some PBL advocates are saying that there is no need for content expertise. Some even claim that PBL can be facilitated by noncontent experts so long as they are trained in PBL facilitation skills. I would argue that such assumptions are the surest way to prepare a generation of superficial learners. The acquisition of problem-solving skills, depth of disciplinary inquiry, and discipline-related reasoning skills is of utmost importance for the challenges of the knowledge-based era. Enhancing thinking in PBL involves developing a repertoire of inquiry skills and deep disciplinary competencies that can only come about through dialogue with and critique from disciplinary experts. What is needed is for disciplinary experts to be equipped with cognitive coaching skills. In short, the teacher as a coach requires process skills for making students' thinking visible and disciplinary expertise for engaging in deep dialogue.

Another point of contention pertains to the sense of empowerment or helplessness for the learner as active problem solver. Firstly, problems should be well designed to provide context and meaningfulness, taking into consideration the background, needs, and prior knowledge of students. The purpose is to motivate and engage students with problems. Too often the problems presented are truly "ill-structured" with only a paragraph of scenario. Problems need to be well written—it is the issues that are unstructured. The use of technology to enhance the richness and authenticity of problems and to provide a network of databases, information, and other resources represents an innovation in problem design and presentation that is important for motivating and scaffolding learning in PBL.

Secondly, the PBL tutor's role is that of an active facilitator of process. As a cognitive coach, the tutor poses questions and probes students' thinking to develop their acumen in problem solving and critical thinking in that knowledge field. The tutor needs to scaffold learning through a protocol of questions. In PBL, self-directed learning is often taken for granted. Independent and self-regulated learning is a desirable outcome of education. In many PBL curricula, the self-directed learning needed is tantamount to students taking on the role of the teacher: the students determine the learning objectives, decide on probable resources, mine for information, plan the learning task and decide on the depth of inquiry, monitor their own thinking and progress, peer-teach, and so forth. Many times students are unsure if the learning objectives or issues they have identified are appropriate and relevant, about where to start in terms of learning resources, about the scope of the topic in the particular discipline, about the keywords to use, how to plan the learning task, and how much to study. They often have limited time to read, reflect, and get to the depths of learning. Research in educational psychology tells us that feelings of competence, motivation, and self-efficacy are often attained through appropriate scaffolding (Tan, Parsons, Hinson, & Sardo-Brown, 2003). In many PBL curricula, students are plunged into self-directed and self-regulated learning without appropriate mediation. This often results in unproductive use of time, unnecessary anxiety, loss of interest, feeling of helplessness, and superficial learning. Students also end up producing mediocre work in their presentations. The lack of mediation and modeling of learning and inquiry may result in producing novice learners, which defeats the goals of PBL.

The above observations point to the need for PBL approaches to be underpinned by sound educational and cognitive psychology. One major reason for the PBL confusion is a failure to understand the psychological basis of learning when infusing PBL approaches into the curriculum. The chapters in this book have attempted to address some of the problems raised.

PBL, Pedagogy, Psychology, and Technology

PBL provides excellent opportunities for the application of psychology to education. In Chapter 1, we mentioned that over the last few decades the challenge of pedagogy progressively changed from making content knowledge visible to learners by enhancing clarity of explanations and elucidating difficult terrains of knowledge, to making teachers' thinking visible through pedagogy that supports and models process skills, problem-solving skills, and thinking skills, and then to making students' thinking visible through design of learning environments and processes that enable students' ways of thinking and knowing to be manifested in active, collaborative, and self-regulated learning.

As noted by the National Research Council (1999) of the U.S. National Academy of Sciences: "The quest to understand human learning has, in the past four decades, undergone dramatic change. Once a matter for philosophical argument, the workings of the mind and brain are now subject to powerful research tools. From that research, a science of learning is emerging" (p. 5). Advances in neuroscience and the advent of brain imaging technologies have contributed to our understanding of the brain and learning, while recent developments in psychology have led to better understanding of the psychological processes of learning, memory, and intelligence. A broadened conceptualization of intelligence and an emphasis on practical intelligence, problem solving, and insightful thinking create opportunities for PBL models to be linked to some of these theoretical frameworks as well as applications. PBL provides possibilities of new ways of engaging the individual that can take into account "plasticity of development," individual differences, as well as problem solving in cultural, community, and social environmental contexts.

The desired outcomes of education worldwide often include two indispensable qualities: (1) the ability to be an independent, autonomous lifelong learner and (2) the exercise and harnessing of higher-order thinking. Two decades or so of research on teaching thinking points to a confluence of greater understanding of the individual as thinker and the importance of thinking about thinking (i.e., metacognition). There are excellent opportunities for research findings on the incorporation of self-regulated learning and metacognition in pedagogy and learning to be applied in PBL environments.

Progress in cognitive science has given new support for the use of problems in learning. We have mentioned in this book that seeing configurations (the whole is more than the sum of its parts), understanding perceptions, cognitive dissonance, problem solving, and insightful learning are important aspects of learning. It can perhaps never be overemphasized that insightful, flexible, inventive, and breakthrough thinking develops best when people are immersed in solving a problem over an extended period of time. The pedagogy of PBL helps make visible or explicit the thinking as well as the richness of the cognitive structuring and processes involved. PBL can benefit from many recent studies in psychology, such as human tutoring (e.g., Chi et al., 2001), how people evaluate information (e.g., Chin & Brewer, 2001), making hypotheses (e.g., Evans, Venn, & Feeney, 2002), reasoning (e.g., Manktelow, 1999), and insightful thinking (Sternberg, 1990; Sternberg & Davidson, 1995).

The psychological perspective is probably the best way forward for PBL practices. PBL models should be developed and rooted in research on understanding of cognitive functions, metacognition, cognitive coaching, and problem solving (Gijselaers, 1996; Tan, 2003). The other related area is understanding of the roles of emotion and interpersonal intelligence that underpin self-regulated learning and collaborative learning. Neuroscience and related research has provided new insights into the functioning of the "emotional" brain and the importance of emotion, such as learned optimism and resilience, in problem solving. PBL can incorporate emphasis of these specific developments, apart from general aspects of self-directed and collaborative learning.

Lastly, Internet technologies have opened up a myriad of new possibilities in the landscape of learning for a new generation of learners. The power of these technologies in advancing PBL remains largely untapped (Chen & Tan, 2002). There are abundant avenues for research and experimentation on instructional design in e-learning with PBL approaches. We need more projects such as those by Grabowski and her colleagues (see Chapter 10), as well as more insights into the creative combination of face-to-face mediation, technological mediation, and e-learning.

So long as there are problems and learning to be done, PBL will likely continue to be an important conceptualization abounding with applied research and practice. Not unlike areas such as problem solving, PBL from the psychological and technological perspectives will always have currency and relevance. The challenge, however, is the creative use of PBL to enhance thinking and intelligence in individuals, groups, organizations, and systems.

References

Armstrong, E. G. (1991). A hybrid model of PBL. In D. Boud & G. Feletti (Eds.), *The challenge of problem-based learning*. London: Kogan Page.

Berkson, L. (1993). PBL: Have the expectations been met? *Academic Medicine*, *68*, 79–88.

Chen, A. Y., & Tan, O. S. (2002). Towards a blended design for e-learning. *Centre for Development of Teaching and Learning Brief*, *5*, 6–8.

Chi, M. T. H., Siler, S. A., Jeong, H., Yamauchi, T., & Hausmann, R. (2001). Learning from human tutoring. *Cognitive Science*, *25*, 471–533.

Chin, C. A., & Brewer, W. F. (2001). Models of data: A theory of how people evaluate data. *Cognition and Instruction*, *19*, 323–51.

Evans, J. B. T., Venn, S., & Feeney, A. (2002). Implicit and explicit processes in a hypothesis testing task. *British Journal of Psychology*, *93*, 31–46.

Gijselaers, W. H. (1996). Connecting problem-based practices with educational theory. In L. Wilkerson & W. H. Gijselaers (Eds.), *Bringing problem-based learning to higher education: Theory and practice* (pp. 13–21). New directions for teaching and learning, No. 68. San Francisco: Jossey-Bass.

Manktelow, K. I. (1999). *Reasoning and thinking*. Hove, East Sussex: Psychology Press.

Marincovich, M. (2000). Problems and promises in problem-based learning. In O. S. Tan, P. Little, S. Y. Hee, & J. Conway (Eds.), *Problem-based learning: Educational innovation across disciplines* (pp. 3–11). Singapore: Temasek Centre for Problem-Based Learning.

National Research Council (1999). *How people learn: Bridging research and practice*. Washington, DC: National Academy Press.

Norman, G. R., & Schmidt, H. G. (2000). Effectiveness of problem-based learning curricula. *Medical Education*, *34*, 721–28.

Sternberg, R. J. (1990). *Metaphors of mind: Conceptions of the nature of intelligence*. New York: Cambridge University Press.

Sternberg, R. J., & Davidson, J. E. (Eds.) (1995). *The nature of insight*. Cambridge, MA: MIT Press.

Tan, O. S. (2000). Reflecting on innovating the academic architecture for the 21st century. *Educational Developments*, *1*, 8–11.

Tan, O. S. (2001). PBL innovation: An institution-wide implementation and students' experiences. In P. Little, O. S. Tan, P. Kandlbinder, A. Williams, K. Cleary, & J. Conway (Eds.), *On problem based learning: Experience, empowerment and evidence*. Proceedings of the Third Asia Pacific Conference on Problem Based Learning (pp. 318–33). Newcastle: Australian Problem Based Learning Network.

Tan, O. S. (2002). Project management in educational development: A Singapore experience. In M. Yorke, P. Martin, & C. Baume (Eds.), *Managing educational development projects: Maximising impact* (pp. 153–70). London: Kogan Page.

Tan, O. S. (2003). *Problem-based learning innovation: Using problems to power learning in the 21st century*. Singapore: Thomson Learning.

Tan, O. S., Little, P., Hee, S. Y., & Conway, J. (Eds.) (2000). *Problem-based learning: Educational innovation across disciplines*. Singapore: Temasek Centre for Problem-Based Learning.

Tan, O. S., Parsons, R. D., Hinson, S. L., & Sardo-Brown, D. (2003). *Educational psychology: A practitioner–researcher approach (An Asian edition)*. Singapore: Thomson Learning.